DISCARDED BY VERMILLION PUBLIC LIBRARY

EDITH B. SIEGRIST
VERMILLION
PUBLIC LIBRARY
VERMILLION SD

D0283758

# A Collection of Cowboy Logic

## A Look at the Lighter Side of Going Broke, Raising Cattle and Living on the Prairie

Ryan M. Taylor

*Sandhill Communications*

I

Copyright 1998 by Ryan M. Taylor

All rights reserved. Printed in the United States of America. This book, or parts thereof, may not be reproduced in any form or by electronic or mechanical means including information storage and retrieval systems without permission in writing from the publisher.

The Publisher:
Sandhill Communications
1363 54$^{th}$ St. N.E.
Towner, N.D. 58788

Illustrations by Steve Stark
Edited by Kim Deats
Layout and cover design by Hennessy Graphics
Printed and bound in the United States of America by
    Knights Printing, Fargo, N.D.
First Printing, 1998
Library of Congress Catalog Card Number: 98-96646
ISBN 0-9667756-0-0

For every farmer or rancher who was ever
struck by a peculiar thought while
they were mending fence, baling hay
or moving cows around.

# Contents

# Introduction

Life definitely takes some interesting turns. A long time ago, when I was about 3 feet tall and riding my pony, I decided that I wanted to be a rancher like my father. Somewhere along the way I became a writer, like my mother, and a prairie philosopher with a healthy sense of humor like both of them.

Cowboy Logic was born in *Agweek* magazine on July 18, 1994. My association with *Agweek* had a pretty fortuitous start.

On the eve of the deadline to submit essays for the American Quarter Horse Association's "I'll always remember the ride" writing contest, I penned a few paragraphs about the life of Dude, my faithful ranch gelding, and put it in the mailbox on the very day of the deadline. The AQHA received more than a 1,000 entries from around the world, but they put mine in the top 10. Ann Bailey, a reporter for *Agweek* and the *Grand Forks Herald*, thought it would be interesting to do a story on this rancher from Towner, N.D., who was as handy at the keyboard as he was in the saddle.

The rest is history, as they say. She found out that I was doing some free-lance writing to support my ranching habit, and a few months later, Julie Copeland hired me to be a roving correspondent and soon-to-be columnist for *Agweek*.

After a year or two of writing Cowboy Logic for *Agweek*, it spread out to Canada's *Western Producer*, the *N.D. Horizons* and the *Nebraska Fencepost*. On occasion, it's run in *RANGE* magazine and *Canadian Cowboy Country*. The reception has been mighty kind.

An English teacher I had in college told our class that our best essays would be the ones we wrote about ourselves, our own thoughts, our own true stories. We are truly experts on just one subject — ourselves. One of the nice things about writing a personal column is that you don't have to do any research. Just peer inside your own brain and see what you can pull out.

I kind of hate to admit it, but all the columns in this book are true stories. Life on the ranch flirts with that much talked about fine line between tragedy and humor. Ranchers laugh at a lot of things that normal people would cry about. Humor is our therapy for physical abuse and financial distress. It's not unheard of to find us trampled beneath the hooves of some ornery animal. After your so-called cattle workin' buddies check for a heartbeat, they'll quickly bust a gut laughing about the look on your face as you were being tenderized beneath the hooves of the critter. That's humor. But hit your thumb with a hammer and you'll probably get lots of sympathy. That's tragedy. Lose $10,000 or $20,000 feeding cattle or grazing yearlings, and you have to  find some way to make a joke of your misfortune. That's humor. But lose 50 cents in a pop machine and there'll  be hell to pay. That's tragedy.

Most of the stories in this book have that subtle connection between tragedy and humor. They cover a period of time from 1994 to 1998, an era long on tragedy in the cattle business and desperately needing a humorous angle. Like one rancher told me, "I like to read your column first. It cheers me up before I have to turn to the markets."

I have a few people I'd like to thank, so here goes: my father for teaching me what it means to be a real cowboy of integrity and true grit; my mother for instilling in me a love for reading, writing, and the magic of words, written, spoken or sung to a tune; my neighbors for being there when I needed them and providing a good share of the tales in this book; my friends and family who've made life pretty enjoyable; and to anyone who's ever written me an off-ranch paycheck, thanks for keeping me afloat in the rough seas of the modern cattle business. Also, a special thanks to Steve, Kim and Julie for their tireless work and creative contributions in illustrating, editing and laying out of this book.

So here goes. A nearly complete collection of columns gathered up and offered to the literary world so that all will know what it's like to be a young rancher in an aging occupation, deep in debt and in love with a way of life that is simultaneously frustrating, entertaining and gratifying.

Ryan M. Taylor
Taylor Ranch

# Git along little dogies

# Til the cows come home
## Procrastination on the prairie

Some folks have things they say they'll do "til the cows come home." Myself, I've got things I don't do "til the cows come home." Fencing is something that easily can be put off til the cows come home.

But if your cows are coming home, there's probably some fence that needs propping up somewhere. It's really not such a bad system. You get up in the morning, survey the yard and the hay fields, and if the cows are there to greet you with a green slobbery good morning, your plans have been made for you.

It's time to forget about the things you'd like to get done and time to get after what needs to be done. It's a Code Red situation, throw some posts and wire in the pickup and go scout the perimeter.

**Functioning by crisis**

A couple of days ago, I thought I was really going to hit the hay hauling project hard and make a recognizable dent in one looming fall task.

Everything was set for a day of successful ranching. I checked the fuel, filled the oil, aired up the tires and welded up the loader. It was all too good to be true.

Heading down the road, I spotted about a dozen small dots coming right at me followed by a small cloud of dust. I rolled to a halt as the blur of hooves and hair sped by me.

I was able to spot our brand on them, recognized my handwriting on their ear tags and made a personal identification on a few of the mobilized moo cows. Wherever they were headed, they were in a hurry.

It kind of looked like they were out for a morning jog. You know, a couple laps around the ol' ranch to tone the thighs and firm up the hindquarters. Too much time in the creep feeder or too many grassy snacks between meals had them feeling guilty.

The calves probably had been watching the cattle market head south and figured they'd run off a few of those excess pounds since they wouldn't be worth anything this fall anyway.

Anyway, it was clear to see the hay moving would be put on hold as I went out to fix the spot in the fence that had been down all summer. Fences are like optical illusions for cows in the summer. They see the posts and at least one slack wire stretched between them and they stay in. Come fall, they realize they've been fooled and they walk right through the illusion.

We all do our best, of course, to keep more than one rusty wire and a few spindly posts on our fences, but there never is enough time in a rancher's year to get all the fences in tiptop shape. When schedules get tight, we do a lot of drive-by or ride-by fencing where we simply check the status of the illusion.

Sometimes, we can count on our neighbors to do a better job of fencing than ourselves. This works in a pinch, but let your fences slide for too many years and you'll have a neighbor who won't even wave to you as you drive down the road, much less help you work your calves or do your chores when you're gone.

In my country, poor soil allows us to keep some poor fences. We're lucky enough to live on land that's just about worthless.

If your cattle do get out, there's not much that they really can harm. No bumper crops of durum or 8 foot-tall corn for them to ruin if they stray. Just more of the same — grass, hay and sand. The economics just isn't there for people to call you up and chew you out if your cattle leave your pasture and get into theirs.

Hay bales are another story, but, really, who needs those outside wraps of twine anyway? Our cows are starting to prefer grazing on the hay meadow to grazing in the pasture. I could either fix the fence or move the bales off before they ruin them. I better get going, I've got hay to haul.

# Who's who in the cowherd
## New and improved identification?

Entrepreneurial inventors say the key to success is to build a better mousetrap. Maybe, but I'll put my bets on the creative cattlemen who can come up with a better eartag.

Livestock identification has challenged us for decades.

But it wasn't always so. My family remembers when the first plastic eartags hit the drugstore in downtown Towner. Dad and the other local ranchers got quite a kick out of it.

Ear identification? "It's a pretty poor cow who can't recognize her own calf," they said. "What good's a numbered eartag? Everyone knows cows can't read."

While Dad and the boys had a good laugh over the new fangled calf earrings, their comments likely will go down in history with the wise guys who said the automobile never would replace the bicycle, the airplane never would be used for passenger service, and the computer never would find its way inside the home.

We've been piercing calf ears ever since, regardless of whether or not the cow could find her calf on her own.

## A better way

And we've been tweaking and tuning the eartag concept ever since.

Most ranchers I know have a box full of eartag paraphernalia to document its evolution. An assortment of punchers, pokers, crimpers and clampers decorate their calving bags.

To protect the innocent, I won't cite brand names, but a number of companies have successfully failed at building a better eartag.

Arrowheads date back to Paleolithic times, and just as Native Americans experimented with a host of materials and designs for the tips of their arrows, eartag inventors have tried it all for the arrowheaded tips of their eartags.

Curved, straight, one-piece plastic and two-piece rubbery. Some follow the arrowhead concept but don't even resemble arrowheads. They look more like a "z," or a "zed" as they say in Canada.

Others go with the button method of eartagging. I know guys who can't even button their shirt straight who'll swear by the buttons on their eartags. Button materials range from rock-hard plastic to the rubbery kind, depending on the level of infection you want in the calf's ear.

The button boys have to pack around a bulky tagging tool about the size of a fencing plier, and some tell me the two tools are interchangeable if you're in a bind.

## Readability

Numbering systems vary as much as the eartags themselves. Some even come pre-numbered. That's about as creative as having your children born pre-named.

For those preferring personalization, ink comes in bottles and pens and a variety of qualities, depending on whether or not you want to be able to read them after the first spring rain.

Me, I'm an engraver. Tired of fading ink, I bought a little grinding tool and started engraving my numbers onto the multicolored tags.

The cattle still lose their tags on a regular basis, but I can read them for years to come as they surface next to the bale feeders, brush and barbed-wire fences.

# Lookin' for trouble
## Wishing we wouldn't find what we'd hoped we wouldn't

Checking. The word either conjures up the image of some bank account that's usually overdrawn or the picture of a nonproductive task performed by virtually everyone in our society on a daily basis.

Entire careers are built around the idea of some people checking up on other people. They walk around checking progress, checking deadlines and sometimes even checking people's well-being.

"How's it coming? Are you done yet? Do you feel okay?" Regardless of how we answer, checkers receive their paycheck to respond with a heartfelt, "oh, just checking."

I do a fair bit of checking myself. During this time of year, I'm out about every three hours or so checking calving cows and heifers.

### Lookin' for nothin'

The really odd thing about the business of checking is you're usually looking for something you hope you don't find.

The other night at 2 a.m., I was out in the corral hoping I wouldn't find any cows with calving trouble. But there was. I was hoping she wouldn't be one of those mean, ornery sonofaguns who'd just as soon put you over the fence as look at you. But she was. Finally, I was hoping she wouldn't be one of those cows that would take an hour to get into the barn. But she was.

I'd checked for trouble, temperament and herding ease. In each case, the things I'd checked for and hoped wouldn't be were. "Success" in the checking profession is hard to feel good about.

My definition of a successful check of the cowherd is one where I can get up, stumble around with a flashlight for a bit and be back in bed between the sheets before I really realize I was even awake. Eight minutes tops.

Of course, the trouble with those kind of successful checks is you wonder why you even bothered disturbing your slumber to do the job.

It kind of leads to the old theory about, "If a tree falls in the forest and no one's there to hear it, does it make any noise?" Or, put in rancher lingo, "If a cow calves in the corral and no one's there to check on it, will the calf likely live anyway?"

Probably not. An unwritten law of ranching says quit checking and you're sure to wake up in the morning to breech births, troublesome twins and big dead calves.

Calving isn't the only time of year that we do a lot of checking.

We check fences and hope there's no holes. We check pastures and hope there's no leafy spurge. We check the oil, the antifreeze and the tires and hope they're all there. We check our bank accounts for money and hope something's there, too.

I could go on, but I need to run the spell check and get this sent off. I hope I didn't misspell any words.

# Calf workin' crisis

## New census doesn't offer much hope to ranchers in need of a hand

The old neighborhood is starting to feel even older this spring.

Springtime is calf workin' time, and in our part of the world, that means rounding up not only your cattle but your high school aged neighbors as well. The local youth fill a vital role as calf throwers at our calf workin' bees.

Maybe "throwing" is a bad choice of words. Those poorly versed in cow speak may envision innocent young calves being hurtled through the air like the shot - put, or being tossed back and forth like a medicine ball.

Calf constrainment specialists might be a safer term.

At any rate, "calf throwers" of prime calf throwing age are getting pretty scarce south of Towner.

The prime age of calf throwers is somewhere between 12 and 18 years old. Much younger and they don't have the physique to wrestle a couple hundred pounds of beef to the ground. Much older and they've figured out that the other jobs — vaccinating, branding, castrating, implanting — are a whole lot easier and not nearly as damaging to the aging body.

Aging is the problem. Our local ranching community isn't getting any younger. And, worse yet, they're not getting any more prolific, and many aren't even partnering up so that they could possibly be more prolific!

### Not alone

Our little community isn't the only one fighting this geriatric phenomenon. The entire country is in the same fix.

According to the U.S. Census Bureau, the fastest-growing age group in America today is people in their 50s, and most of them don't have kids.

Ever seen a bunch of 50-year-olds wrestle a hundred calves to the ground? Forget the cooler full of beer, just make sure you've got plenty of liniment to pass around afterward.

We've got a few pretty good hands in that 16 to 18-year-old range, but after that it'll be time to draw straws for calf throwing and see who gets to buy their chiropractor that Hawaiian vacation.

And it doesn't appear to be improving. The Census folks tell us that in the year 2010, nearly three in five American families won't have any children under 18 living at home. And they say fewer people will be getting married, too.

So much for romancing our way out of the labor shortage. It looks like ranchers in my area will have to come up with some new strategies for the annual calf workin' bee.

**Baby boom bust**

The baby boom is about to go bust, according to those who deal in demographics. The baby boomers are growing up, and as a result, the entire American population is aging.

In the past, we've been able to work our calves quickly with the abundant labor of baby boomer's babies. No longer will that be an option.

Looks like we might have to pool together and buy a mechanical calf-working table. But it might be cheaper to just pool together and get the volume discount on that muscle-soothing liniment.

# Dealing with all the bull(s)
## Pondering new strategies

Several weeks ago, we pulled our bulls out of the cow herds and put them in their own separate fall pasture. Nothing really extraordinary about that, except for the fact that the bulls are still in that pasture. They haven't broke any wires, bent over any posts or severely mangled any part of the fence in their quest for continued romance.

Bulls, almost regardless of breed, age or temperament, have a mind of their own when you try to confine them and isolate them from their female counterparts. This is where bulls and ranchers go toe to toe, and the bull, on account of obvious advantages, usually wins the meeting.

Ranchers, being of superior intelligence, spend countless hours thinking of new strategies to change the outcome of their inevitable bull encounters. Even I have come up with a few ideas for controlling these beef-bound beasts.

## Cruel and unusual isolation

Banishment to far-away places is probably the most popular bull control strategy used by ranchers. They'll try to find pastures surrounded by farmland, roads, empty pastures or ugly cows with bad breath. Taking away the options will convince most bulls that standing around with the boys and eating grass isn't such a bad deal.

Sometimes mild isolation doesn't always work. Then we call our cousins, uncles, in-laws and outlaws and try to pawn our bull battery off on them, thinking the more miles away the better. The further from the temptation, the better the behavior.

Personally, I've been toying with the idea of cash renting some grass out in California during the breeding off season. I heard that Alcatraz Island is going unused in the human penal system and I'm thinking there might be some good grazing out there in that warm climate.

I'm not sure how many acres are available on Alcatraz, but if we could get it rented right, I'm sure I could throw together with a few of my neighbors and put together a semi pot load of unemployed breeders to go out west.

## A whole new strategy

Some days, when the bulls have really got me cookin' mad, I revert to the "if you can't beat 'em, join 'em" philosophy. Why do we need to take the bulls away from the cows anyway?

Sure, that 60-day breeding season will shorten your calving time, lower your stress level and give you that uniform set of calves that the buyers will all be scrambling for in the fall. But is it really worth it?

You don't see buffalo ranchers out there pulling bulls, PG'ing their cows and trying to get them all bred in the first 21 days. Maybe beef ranchers could go with the buffalo management method and let nature take its course.

We could let the bulls breed the whole year through, calve all year long and be grumpy, tired and overworked from January to December.

Pretty soon, we'd have our cow herd so messed up that we could begin marketing our calves like some hog producer market pigs, every month, all year long. That'd give us some steady cash flow and allow us to take advantage of each month's market instead of waiting for things to bottom out in the fall before we sold them.

We could be on the cutting edge of marketing. Not only could we have a spring calving herd and a fall calving herd like some are experimenting with, we could have spring, summer, fall and winter calving herds and get the moisture and scours, heat and flies, surprise snows, cold and pneumonia that each season has to offer.

Maybe the best idea anyone had to deal with bulls is just to sell all the ornery bums in the fall and buy a whole new set the following year. May be a little troublesome on the balance sheet and throw any consistency in the program right out the window, but the peace of mind may be worth it.

Me, I'm going to start building up my left arm for a breeding season completely done by artificial insemination.

# Cattle rancher's midwife corps
## Childbirth and calving comparisons

I became an uncle for the first time several weeks ago. Childbirth is truly one of life's greatest miracles, and I was thoroughly amazed that anyone I knew, especially my sister, could perform such a feat.

That feeling of amazement is similar to the feeling I get during calving season.

There, I did it again. I just mentioned childbirth and calving in the same paragraph. If there's one thing I've learned throughout my sister's pregnancy and my nephew's birth, it's that women don't like to be compared to cows.

This all came as quite a surprise to me. You see, I like cattle, and I like women. It seemed pretty harmless to me to make comparisons about two things in my life that I like so well.

The fact that females can give birth and bring life into this world is a wonderful thing. I didn't mean anything personal when I made comparisons between childbirth and calving, when I made correlations between a breast-feeding mother and a freshening cow or when I mentioned dirty diapers and scouring calves in the same breath.

It's amazing the dirty looks you can get when you strike up a little chit chat with a pregnant woman about O.B. chains and calf pullers. If you really want to get cuffed up alongside the head, just try and relate calving stories about Caesarean sections or prolapses!

Ranchers don't mean any harm. We're just trying to put things in our own terms and share some of our knowledge with the women in our lives. We really shouldn't be slapped or snarled at. I think a little appreciation of our experiences would be in order.

### An untapped midwife corps

With our health-care system under such scrutiny these days, I've put my mind to work to try to come up with ways to make the system more efficient and affordable, especially for rural America.

We've got a great resource going untapped out here. Ranchers have spent countless hours interning in barns and calving pastures every spring. Why not recruit these birthing experts and form a ranchers midwife corps that could help counsel the pregnant portion of our population and help deliver new ranchers into the world?

Small, rural hospitals strapped for cash could save countless dollars by not having to hire so many expensive big city physicians. It really could lighten up the load on the doctors whose valuable time could be saved, making our health-care system much more efficient and streamlined.

### Ranchers-only Lamaze

Ranchers interested in joining the corps would, of course, be required to take some coursework in human childbirth. But think of all the time the instructors could save by not having to go over all the basic stuff that ranchers already know.

I'm sure ranchers have attended Lamaze classes with their wives, only to find out how much more they know than their urban classmates.

In general, ranchers are a kind-hearted lot who believe a gentle hand and a soothing voice will get them the furthest in their dealings with laboring females. Our patience with baby animals is an asset we surely could put to use as fathers, grandfathers or uncles.

We've doctored enough scouring calves and nursed along enough sick ones late into the night to easily change a few diapers and stay up with a baby to nurse them through an ear infection. So, ladies, if we look at your child and compare his vigor and health to that of a good little calf we once knew, don't take it the wrong way, it's really a compliment.

### Auxiliary uses

The ranchers midwife corps probably could expand into a more broad-based corps of medical technicians to provide more accessible health care to rural America.

We probably could take over the immunization programs since most of us have either vaccinated ourselves or others when we've crawled over a fence with a loaded syringe in our pocket or handed a vaccinating gun needle first to the guy on the other side of the chute.

We're pretty good at putting in or taking out stitches, and we're pretty handy at setting broken bones with a piece of PVC pipe and a roll of duct tape. Good ranch med techs could administer a variety of different antibiotics, take care of unsightly warts and lance any boils you might have.

One word of caution though, if you break your leg really bad: We might have to shoot ya.

*Author's note: Writing columns that mention childbirth and calving do have the potential to offend a few females who don't understand the way ranchers think. This column gave birth to a disclaimer that has followed my column in Agweek to this day. However, I did meet a rancher and his wife at a banquet in Steele, N.D., who saw no need for anyone to take offense to this column. He had made a miniature calf puller, complete with a little crank, a string and a suction cup that he presented to his wife's doctor as they began their family. The doctor, a female as well, got a real kick out of it.*

# Rancher Olympics
## Cowboys forced to run farther, jump higher

The cattle workin' pens and sortin' alleys across the region have been bubbling with activity lately. 'Tis the season for PG'ing cows and selling calves, as well as vaccinating, weighing, pouring and performing a host of other management chores that force cowboys to meet their namesake eye to eye.

Imagine the match-up taking place in the pens. Picture your typical skinny cowboy armed with a 4 foot sliver of plastic and fiberglass. Pit him against a supposedly domesticated animal weighing from 500 to 1,500 pounds and armed with four sharp hooves and back legs that can practically come out of their sockets, enabling them to reach out and kick you no matter how far back you are.

Cattle come complete with a leather suit of armor and one of the highest thresholds of pain in the business. Cowboys are tough enough in their own right, but their hides are considerably more tender than a cow's. Not so much as a protective hair coat on our bodies, aside from the few strands that abandon our craniums on a daily basis.

We make up for this shortcoming by armoring ourselves with long johns, denim jeans and insulated bibs. A pair of mud-caked four bucklers serve the dual purpose of protecting our feet while weighing us down so we can't run from our four-legged pursuers. Imagine yourself in front of an extremely cross crossbred with a pair of concrete blocks strapped to your feet.

### Ranch gymnastics

What cowboys lack in strength and sheer size in the sortin' pens, they make up for in agility and elasticity, much like a gymnast or an ice skater. We can scale tall fences, dodge super ballistic swinging gates and bounce off of corral boards with gymnastic flair.

Heave yourself over the top corral board and you've got a routine that could make you a contender on the pommel horse at the Olympics. The walk plank along the working chute is good practice for the balance beam, pulling ourselves up on the corral crossbeam could build us up for the rings.

A couple weeks ago, I was weighing calves with a friend of mine, recording some of that valuable performance data that'll help bring the ranch into the 21st century. I was crouched down in the working chute, writing down weights while holding back the calves that were next up on the scale.

I was sitting there registering records when one of my six weight feeders decided to challenge my body barrier and make his way toward freedom. I tried the moving block, but before you know it, he had me pushed out of the chute and I found myself admiring his underside while he ran me over.

I gathered my senses, wiped off the Nancy Kerrigan frown and replaced it with a Mary Lou Retton grin. I finished the black baldy hit-and-run incident with a dazzling forward somersault, and with an unfailing concern for statistics, I hit the ground running to identify the number of the culprit so I could get him back in the corral and across the scale. You can't let one bad apple spoil your most probable producing averages.

**Pick your teams**

Fall ranch gymnastics could provide us with our own rural Olympic competition. We could stagger it between the summer and winter Olympics in case the major television networks want to bid on the broadcast rights.

Teams could be from different states, different ranches or different livestock occupations. The toughest team on the field likely would be the large animal veterinarians. They'd more than likely prep for the games by PG'ing a few thousand cows. Provided they didn't break any bones during their warm-up period, they would be very stiff competition.

I envision a round robin tournament with rotating breeds of cattle to challenge the competitors. The lowest level of competition would start with a herd of docile Herefords and get progressively tougher with varying crossbreds and continental exotic breeds to test the team's skills.

The championship round would bring in the big boys, a bunch of Brahmans that could force the teams to run faster, jump higher and vault themselves farther. If the competition gets a little too dangerous though, we may have to go with a double layer of insulated bibs.

# Ahead of schedule for once
## Heifers forgot to look at the calendar

I'm never early for anything — just ask my editor.

My heifers, on the other hand, should win an award for their promptness.

The only thing ahead of schedule in my schedule these days is calving. I still don't have all the hay in, this column is past due and my pickup is in dire need of an oil change. I'm two weeks ahead of the game, though, when it comes to calving.

14

## The calendar lies

The trusty 285-day gestation table says cattle bred May 29 should calve March 10. OK, throw in a few minor adjustments for the color of their hide and fertility of their ancestors. I still come up with a calving date of March 5.

No. 305 apparently forgot to check her calendar because she jumped the gun with an extremely prompt parturition date of Feb. 25.

The weather performed about like you'd expect. There's nothing like a few laboring heifers to bring on a spell of below-zero temperatures. I think I could be calving heifers in July and a blue norther' would swoop in and drop the mercury to 20 below zero on the Fourth of July.

Ears and tails on calves are kind of a frivolous option anyway. If a guy calved out his whole herd in below-zero weather, he wouldn't need to brand, he could just spot them by their short, frozen ears.

## Wild cow milkin'

If you've ever seen a wild cow milking contest at a rodeo, you've seen a pretty realistic rodeo event. My yearly duties on the ranch don't require me to ride many bulls, tie any goats or race any barrels, but I do find myself with a 2 quart jug trying to coax some lacto out of ol' Bossy every spring if a calf isn't nursing for some reason or another.

I had a heifer calve last week that wouldn't get up after she'd given birth to a nice baldy bull calf. She was pretty pooped and down for the count. I carried the calf in the barn and figured I'd better run get him some breakfast.

Far from a wild cow milking contest, this was more of a sedate cow milking contest. She laid there while I did my best to milk out her west side, then I rolled her over and milked out her east side.

Pretty easy going aside from one of our no-name cats who kept getting in the way and an old pet calf from last year that came over to chew on my cap. The cat got punted about 50 yards (landing on her feet of course) and the calf got an NBA style elbow right in the snoot (which slowed him down for about five seconds).

Getting much milk out of a heifer is like squeezing blood from a turnip. There's just not much in them. But I was mighty proud to have coaxed a quart from Miss 305. The calf got to eat, the heifer got up and the cat got a name but it's not fit for publication.

## Late nights ahead

Despite the challenges, I really like calving. It's my favorite time of year and I look forward to each new calf.

I forget my fondness for the activity sometimes at 3 a.m. when I'm stumbling through the herd with sleep in my eyes and a flashlight in my hand, but even the 3 a.m. check has its high points.

If you were asleep last night at 3 a.m., you missed a spectacular show of northern lights. But if you'd like to see them tonight, come on over, I'll set a flashlight by the corral gate and I'll concentrate on getting a little extra sleep.

# Expanding the beetle herd
## A cowboy's guide to beetle ranchin'

To heck with Angus, Hereford and Charolais. From now on, I'm centering our breeding program around Aphthona Nigriscutis.

It's not that our baldy cows and smoky calves aren't doing a good enough job of converting grass into beef, but a bumper crop of leafy spurge has convinced me that I need to diversify and add some flea beetles to our beef cattle enterprise.

The spurge crop was kind of touch and go this cool, wet, cloudy spring. Some ranchers in McHenry County were afraid they weren't going to get a good catch of leafy spurge this year.

But sunshine, sand and a super-high water table have gifted us with a real nice stand of spurge again this year. We often water our spurge crop with herbicides, but low budgets and low-budget spraying machines make control financially, physically and environmentally challenging on sandy pastures of hills and trees with high water tables and a rental worth of about $7 an acre.

Spurge-eating flea beetles are looking better and better as the hills turn yellower and yellower.

### Beetle roundups

Last summer, I got into the beetle ranchin' business and turned out 500 head in an especially nice patch of spurge. The grazing looked good for my start-up herd of Nigriscutis as my new livestock bolted out of the corral, in this case a brown paper bag, and headed for yellow pastures.

Beetle ranchin' is a low management business. No fences to build, no winter feed to lay in and no timely health, breeding or marketing decisions to fret over.

There is, however, the annual beetle roundup in the summer. But no horses, corrals or hired hands are needed. A sweep net, a quarter meter square and a measuring stick are all you need to get a good head count on your Nigriscutis.

16

The other day, I went to rounding up my beetles with gusto. I yelled a couple of "head up, giddyup now, hy-ooo" to get the true round up feeling and started sweeping. A few of the snakes in the herd slipped through the gate on me, but all in all, the count was good.

I then began to monitor my spurge crop. I counted stems, measured heights and calculated flowering to non-flowering plant ratios. Good leafy spurge management is an intricate process.

## Expansion phase

Impressed with the low management and high reproduction possibilities of the beetles, I decided to triple my herd size this year.

Getting bigger seems to be the key to survival in farming and ranching. Having turned out another 1,000 head of flea beetles last week, I would consider myself a pretty big operator. Kind of a bonanza-sized beetle farm.

Increasing spurge acres are signaling even greater herd expansions in the future. I think a Nigriscutis herd of 10,000 head or more is entirely possible for a ranch of our size and hills of our color.

I'm especially looking forward to the bragging rights that come with being a big operator. Out west where cattle herds number in the thousands, I can imagine myself leaning up against the bar with a couple of ranching giants and talking herd size.

"How many head do you run, son?" my cattlemen cronies would ask. "Oh, just a little over 10,000 head," I'd say loud enough for all to hear, but concluding under my breath, "counting the flea beetles that is."

# Thanking the bulls
## A little appreciation for our bovine males

As a writer, I have a lot to thank the mighty beef bull for. Great words and terms like bullheaded, bull's-eye and bull shipping have their origin with the humble herd sire. Nonwriters should take a moment to thank him as well.

Where would Teddy Roosevelt's place in history be without his "bully" trademark? Baseball players owe him for the bullpen, road builders can thank him for the bulldozer and the folks pinning up auction sale bills can be grateful for the bulletin board.

Great words and great contributions from that intact bovine male roaming free on the range in cattle country.

And as a rancher, I have even more things to thank that frisky friend of mine for.

Big sandy holes in the pasture, long stretches of tore-up fence and massive piles of broken boards and twisted corral panels can be traced back to the tyrannical temperament of the fellas I need to produce these 70-cent calves.

But I'd forgive him all his bad points if he could just find something bullish in this year's cattle market.

## Bully neighbors

Bulls probably can be credited for one of the truly great achievements in modern beef production. We have to hand it to him for the revolutionary concept of crossbreeding.

Yes, it was that fence-jumping bull who gave us the black baldy heifer, the smoky-colored steer and the horned "Angus." Quite modest about their achievement, bulls take very little credit for the hybrid heterosis in our world today.

But back when those pioneer bull geneticists were conducting their initial experiments, they were highly disregarded and often scorned by the rancher whose cows he had chosen to be his test herd.

I recently read about a state law in South Dakota that allows citizens to castrate free roaming bulls. It probably was enacted by people whose neighbors had poorer bulls than they did.

My neighbors, however, are pretty good about buying high-quality herd sires, so castrating is the last thing crossing my mind if they get in our pasture. More than likely, I might wait a day or two before I call them up, hoping to improve the weaning weights on my next calf crop.

In South Dakota, a couple of ranchers weren't quite as tolerable of each other. I guess one rancher locked a gate across a road that his neighbor used to get to his pastures. So the roadless rancher cut one of the padlocker's bulls to get even.

Looks like its headed to court and the bull's probably headed to the sales ring, and a little lighter at that.

## Here to stay

Our bulls haven't caused any feuds between the neighbors and me, but they've been the root of plenty of other problems.

They've bent some posts, stretched some wires, dug some holes and broke some boards. They've even thrown a couple of hard-pulling 110-pound calves and produced a couple of replacement heifers that weren't worth a hoot, but I think I'll keep them.

It's not that I have any emotional attachment to them, I just need a lot more than 38 cents a pound to meet the salvage value on my 1992 depreciation schedule.

# Rounding up the roamers
## Tough to maintain the fall inventory

Our ranch is starting to remind me of the kitchen stove sitting next to the highway north of Bowman, N.D. The stove sits in a pasture along the highway with its door down and a sign next to it that says, "Open Range."

No catchy little props like that along our road, but my cows are convinced that this is "open range" country.

They pretty much roam where they please. Jumping fences with the greatest of ease, they can be seen grazing the road ditches and hay fields like they were born to be there.

They're easy to track. Just follow the out-of-place cow pies and the roughed-up round bales. It's kind of a bovine Hansel and Grettel bread crumb system.

Those fence-crawling cows relish in the pleasure of walking up to a perfectly round hay bale, pushing it around a bit, rubbing all the twine off and making it look like the baler operator was a rank amateur.

The bales weren't made to look at anyway, I guess. They were made to feed and those unruly cows just sped up the process a little.

### A widespread rebellion

We're not the only ranchers in our neighborhood out on the community grazing lands we call our hay fields.

One of my neighbors was out rounding up some of his cows that had gotten out on the open range when he saw some of ours in the same predicament. He swung in to tell me about it, and when I was out gathering my strays, I spotted a third neighbor's wandering cow herd.

So, if you've got fence-crawling cows in this neck of the woods, you don't have to feel like the Lone Ranger. For every roaming herd of our own that we're out to gather, we usually can find the nomadic segment of a neighbor's herd as well.

It gets to be kind of like a local chain letter or phone tree as we notify everyone of their free-ranging beeves.

### Open range options

The cows get pretty used to the chasing ritual after awhile and become trained like good ol' milk cows. Just drive out, honk the horn a couple times and they all begin to migrate toward their favorite hole in the fence.

But we're starting to get a little sick and tired of the daily cow chase no matter how easy it is.

The thing to do probably would be to sell those wire-stretching wanderers and be rid of them. Of course, the prospect of selling cows for $500 that I paid $900 for doesn't really excite my banker or me.

I've been experimenting with other more creative ways of keeping the cow herd a little closer to home, though. Using the theory tested by scores of mothers who bribe their children with candy so they stay put during church and such, I thought I'd load up the creep feeders for my fidgety calves.

I figured if I could keep the calves in the pasture eating their candy then the mothers would be inclined to stay as well. It's not working as well as I had hoped, though. It may be time to sweeten up the mothers as well. Any feed salesmen out there with a good deal on those molasses lick tubs?

# Questioning confidence
## Bold and assured turns into broke and embarrassed

Self confidence is nice trait to have in job interviews, but it can get you in trouble when you're on the job.

Last weekend, a young rancher I know was out sorting a pen of heifers to take in to the local feeder calf show. He didn't really have the time to take a pen of heifers into the show, but as president of the group putting on the calf show, he thought it was important for him to do what he had asked everybody else to do — bring in calves.

He had a couple of favorite black brockle-faced beauties in mind and he quickly peeled them off from the herd. A third match surfaced that looked just like the other two. Running late and in a hurry, he threw the likely volunteer in to complete the pen and slammed the gate.

To make the trip to town with the stock trailer worthwhile, he put together a pen of steers to further fortify his status as a leader willing to toe the mark and support his community calf show.

With a couple hundred calf show details on his mind, he jumped in the pickup and headed to town. He felt pretty good about his taking the time to chase his cows in early that morning so he could contribute a couple of entries to the show.

Wheeling into the calf show, his cronies unloaded his calves, but were a little perplexed with their leader's pen of three heifers. The three calves were color coordinated, uniformly sized and evenly matched, but the self-confident leader's pen of heifers included a steer.

There's certain things you can slip by the judge in a calf show, but male appendages in a female competition isn't one of them.

The young rancher took his share of guff and grief from his so-called friends at the calf show, but he didn't let the "steifer" incident shake his confidence.

The next day, he hoped to re-establish his reputation as a savvy ranch hand, with a progressive pre-vaccination program for the entire calf herd — heifers, steers and even the steifers.

The vaccine was pretty spendy, but he had confidence in his ability to keep losses to a minimum. No vaccinating the dirt or corral boards, and no immunization by annointment with this guy pulling the trigger on the $3 dosages.

He checked his accuracy. Precisely two milliliters. Just what the doctor ordered.

Vaccine seemed to be going quickly. He double checked the settings on the syringes, still set at two mills. It didn't seem like that many calves had gone through the chute and he'd already burnt up 100 doses.

He counted 71 calves when he finished the pen. The 71 calves should have gotten immunized for $214, but his precise management allowed him to needle 71 calves for a mere $300.

He confidently checked his syringes one more time. Oops, the numbers were supposed to line up on the side, not on the top. The calves were fully protected with three milliliters instead of a measly two.

I'm not allowed to release this guy's name, but I'm $86 poorer, one "steifer" wiser and from now on, my self confidence is tempered with a weekend's worth of learning.

# Synchronized ranching
## Twice as productive as a tandem back stroke and almost as pretty

I never used to see the beauty in Olympic synchronized swimming.

I always thought the idea of two rubber-capped goofballs swimming in time to the music of Bolero was pure nonsense. Even sillier was the advent of solo synchronized swimming. Call me crazy, but I'd think going solo would take a lot of the challenge out of the synchronizing part.

But I'm now convinced that those artistic, talented dog paddlers and breast strokers truly deserve a medal-winning competition in the summer games.

My mind was changed when I began working my three off-farm jobs and began getting involved in my own semi-artistic sport — synchronized ranching. The coordination required in synchronized ranching surely could make it worthy of a medal round in Atlanta this summer.

## Perfect harmony

The most scientific leg in the sport of synchronized ranching would have to be the synchronized heifer breeding. Looking at my schedule this spring, I realized my artificial insemination program likely would suffer because of the additional irons in my fire.

But I quickly spotted a spare weekend and, thanks to the wonders of modern ranching, I was able to rescue the continued genetic advancement of the cow herd.

A couple weeks of fancy feeding, one afternoon of needle and syringe sharpshooting, and I was entered up to get all the heifers bred in one mere weekend.

It's pure harmony to see all 32 of your heifers cycle at once. Well-timed estrous is a beautiful art form, admired by all overworked cattle ranchers who want to partake in a successful A.I. program. And ask anyone who's spent time on heifer heat detection patrol — it's definitely a spectator sport.

Not nearly as scientific, but every bit as awe inspiring is the synchronized cattle chasing division. Coordination is the key here. If you can put together three or four horses and riders with less than a dozen phone calls, you're well on your way to the semifinals.

The challenge is that all your cattle chasing friends are trying to earn a living during the week as well, and that makes everybody's weekends pretty crowded. It gets extremely competitive when the rest of the crew is trying to outmaneuver you to get weekend priority on their own projects.

## Everything in sync

When work keeps you away from the green, green grass of home, even the simplest of chores take on a new synchronized twist.

Putting a week's worth of fence mending into two days of weekend forces you to get in sync with Mother Nature as well as Father Time. You hate to have a weekend full of work all lined up and have it all spoiled by a steady drizzle.

That'll become especially important when I get into synchronized haying season. But who knows. Maybe with a little cloud seeding and some domed biosphere construction, science will allow us to really get the ranch in sync regardless of the weather handicap.

# Ranch reimbursement
## Looking for a little salvage value

You just can't win some days.

You try to do the right thing, and it blows right up in your face.

Take, for instance, doctoring calves. Doctoring is a good thing, right? Stimulate the healing process, give the immune system a little help, and practice a little good animal husbandry.

That's good in theory.

### Dr. Do Good

I was checking calves last weekend and noticed one of the little beefers was really lookin' tough. It looked like a case of pneumonia made worse by a mother that didn't milk.

He was healthy enough to outrun me on foot, but not to be outdone by a dogged little dogie, I went home to get a horse so I could do a proper job of restraining my new patient.

I saddled up my best ambulance, and my sister and brother-in-law followed along in the pickup for moral support. The calf was quickly captured and I got right to work saving her.

She was mighty gaunt and dehydrated, so I figured I'd start by tubing her with a bottle of electrolytes before giving her a few of my magic pills.

As always, I checked to make sure the tube on my bottle of electrolytes went down toward the stomach and not toward the lungs. I've heard horror stories about guys who weren't so thorough and drowned calves by accidentally drenching their lungs.

I was a seasoned pro, though, having tubed hundreds of calves without so much as a close call. But winning streaks seldom last forever.

Sure enough, my patient got a little impatient, started fighting the tube and somehow ended up with a quart of healing fluids on top of her lungs.

It was like one of those high drama episodes of "E.R." My calf was going into Code Red, but there were no paramedics I could call in to help. I didn't even have one of those electric defribulator deals that they use to jump start the guys on television. I thought about using a pair of jumper cables and the pickup battery, but decided it would take more than a weak 12 volt to bring this calf back to life.

My sister and brother-in-law were pretty helpless as they watched me tube it in, then try and pump it out. They saw me go through the stages of concern, panic, and remorse, just like Hawkeye trying to save a soldier on "M*A*S*H".

In a matter of seconds, I'd turned a sick calf into a dead calf. Like any young doctor, I'm still blaming myself. Financially, I'm trying to recoup my losses by writing this column, and I worked it into an after-dinner speech I gave at an annual meeting in Killdeer.

But emotionally, I'm still kicking myself. My brother-in-law hasn't been a heck of a lot of help. The only consolation he could come up with was a new nickname for me — just call me Dr. Kervorkian.

# Slivers and toothpicks
## Wooden reality and steel ambitions

There's no sound more disturbing at a fall cattle working than the snap of fence posts and the splintering crack of corral boards.

Last week, chasing the cattle in for the annual fall calf vaccination, I heard the unmistaken sound of cattle doing their best to ruin everything forever on the Taylor Ranch.

Things were going along pretty well as we trailed the cows into the home place. A little too well, actually. The cows were a bit frenzied, but I was optimistic that our corral would hold them in check.

Of course, I've heard it said that a pessimist is nothing more than a reformed optimist, and the cows were about to reform my optimism.

When I heard the herd crashing through my corral, I vaulted myself over the fence to stem the tide of exiting bovines before they all took off with their unimmunized calves at their side.

### A family loss

Although I was able to hold the loss to six cows and zero calves, I could see that Dad was visibly disturbed by the whole event.

You see, to him, it was more than just some blankety blank cows tearing down another piece of fence on the Taylor Ranch, it was the loss of a legacy built with boards.

"I built that corral when they were putting in Garrison Dam. They logged that lumber off the bottoms before they flooded it and we built these pens. Heck that was only 40 years ago. It should've been good for at least another 10 years," he lamented.

"It's not so much that the cows broke it down and got loose. They had to do it with such a lack of respect. They stepped on those boards like they didn't even care," he growled as the six cows pursued their escape route.

Some days we all realize that the worst thing about running a cattle ranch is the fact that you have to have cattle on it. If it weren't for those destructive cows bent on total demolition of everything you ever built, ranching would be kind of a nice occupation. Plus, it'd be a lot easier to keep the corrals intact.

### Admirable qualities

After I patched the hole with a portable (soon to be permanent) corral panel, I began to see some admirable cowboy logic qualities in the cows who had created that pile of slivers and toothpicks.

You had to hand it to them for their focused team effort. A single one of those cows never would have been able to topple that fence alone. But with a little cattle cooperation, they pushed it over with the greatest of ease.

Now, I sure wasn't shouting, "Way to go team," when I sprinted to the hole to halt the jailbreak, but in hindsight, those cows taught me a good lesson on teamwork and cooperation. I just wish I could have learned it without having to pick up all the broken pieces.

# On the hunt
## Meat's meat, either game or tame

Deer hunting is in full swing and I've got to say that I really admire folks so successful at living the good life that they've got time to go hunting and try living the rough life.

Unfortunately, I'm so busy living the rough life that I barely can find the time to concentrate on living the good life that would allow me to live the rough life at my leisure.

It's not that I don't get out to hunt once in awhile, I just don't call it hunting — I call it moving hay, chasing cows or chopping waterholes. It's too bad that other guys who drive around with their guns don't have something else they can do simultaneously to make their time count double.

Last Sunday, I threw the gun in the pickup and went to go break open a waterhole.

### Bait and switch

After busting the ice, I decided it might be best just to get the heifers a couple miles closer to hay and melted water. One-man roundups can be a tricky maneuver, so I opted to use the intellectual advantage I had over my four-legged friends.

Grabbing an empty mineral sack out of the back of the pickup, I commenced to calling "Come bossy, here boss," all the while rattling the air around in the sack.

25

Using an empty feed sack to call heifers is kind of a cruel trick, like catching a horse with two rocks and an empty 5-gallon pail.

I compare the empty sack trick to the sweepstakes offers you get in the mail or the casino ads you hear on the radio. By the time you mail in your sweepstakes magazine order or drop your month's paycheck into the slots, its too late to realize you've just been bamboozled with an empty bucket and some smooth talker saying "come cows, here boss."

But before you know it, I had the herd coming my way and we headed for the gate. Although I felt bad about the deception, I promised myself not to make a habit of it. Like they say, you can fool some of the heifers some of the time, but you can't fool all of the heifers all of the time.

## Bonus flock

Although the deer hunting didn't go worth a darn, I felt pretty good about getting the heifer herd home all by myself through the hills and trees. Heck, I even picked up a bonus flock as I cut through the sheep pasture and had 12 gregarious ewes decide to trail along for the ride.

The reception at the home place was less than ecstatic, though. The family figured I must have surely gotten a deer since I was gone so long.

There's just no pleasing some people — bring home 30,000 pounds of beef and 2,000 pounds of mutton and all they can do is complain about the 150 pounds of venison you left behind.

# Every third day
## New efficiencies in absentee ranching

New automated systems of feeding cows are sweeping across ranch country like unpaid bills and neglected mortgage payments.

The current economics of cattle ranching is turning resident ranchers into absentee ranchers who hope to someday become resident ranchers again.

The need to take a job off the ranch in the winter to support the ranching habit has turned many an overemployed young cowhand into time management specialists with a flair for the logistics of multiday feeding regiments.

Gone are the days when a fella can count on having the time to get out and feed cows every morning of every day. With jobs in town and new daily time constraints, a fella's lucky if he can spend a little quality time with his cowherd every second, third or fourth day.

## Elaborate schemes

I've seen it all, from feed salesman/ranchers who bought enough round bale feeders to keep 300 cows fed for three days at a crack, to teacher/ranchers who pull enough hay wagons into the corrals to keep the bovine bellies full for nearly a week.

I, however, decided to go with an elaborate 68 paddock barbed-wired corral system huddled around two semi-dependable water pumps. I only need to be home every 34th day to roll out the hay.

Well, maybe it's only six paddocks, and I only need to be home every second or third day, but it's still pretty elaborate.

With my work as communications director for Northern Plains Premium Beef taking me down to Bismarck/Mandan for three or four days every week, a sophisticated time management feeding scheme has become a necessity.

I've built enough pens out of barbed wire and high-tensile electric fence to let me get off the ranch without starving the cows. A family friend from town feeds for me quite a bit, but since he's got three or four jobs himself, he appreciates the every third day feeding strategy quite a bit as well.

By rolling out enough hay for two herds of cattle in six different pens and promoting my 64-year-old mother to the position of daily gate-opening boss, I can go do my work off the ranch which, of course, allows me to ranch.

Coupled with a few bale feeders and a propane stock tank heater, the place can pretty well be set on "auto-ranch" while I'm gone trying to make the new cattle cooperative a reality.

## Option No. 2

Although the elaborate six-pen feeding system has its merits, another option surfaced last week that probably would allow me to be away from the ranch indefinitely.

The gate on Pen No. 5 had succumbed to the pressure of 200 cows leaning against it, and all of a sudden, I had the herd out self feeding on all the hay the ranch had to offer.

I was pretty furious because the buggers were tearing twine, eating holes and rubbing against every once-perfect bale they could get their shoulder against.

But my easy-going father soothed my frustration with some classic fatherly reassurance. "It ain't so bad," he said, "they can only ruin the outside row."

# Final resting place
## Death loss on the Dakotas

We've been pretty lucky around Towner this winter.

Sure, the winter's been cold and miserable. And if you measured snow on a scale from "A" to "Z", we're up to "R" "S" in snow. But we're kinda prepared for it up here.

We just plan on having to feed cows six months out of every year. Sometime in November, we face the music and bring the cows home, bring the hay home and start rolling out hay until May.

A lot of ranchers on the prairie generally have it a little better. Fall and winter grazing with a little cow cake is the rule for folks a little south and west of the Taylor Ranch. But every rule has an exception, and the winter of 1997 was that exception.

We've all heard the horror stories about the big blizzards and death loss numbers that seem too high to be true. Unfortunately, they probably are true.

I'll be the first to lend some Cowboy Logic sympathy to my ranching counterparts caught in the worst of the weather with no way to get to their cows and no feed to get to them.

Times are tough enough in the cow business with live cows, much less dead ones.

Ranchers know the realities of life and death better than most. We learn to accept it, but we never get used to it.

But having cattle die from storms, disease or hard luck is only half the battle. Figuring out what to do with them once they've gone to the great beyond is a whole 'nother problem in itself.

### Loader accessible

I don't know if everybody's cows are as spiteful as mine when it comes to dying, but I've yet to see a cow die in any kind of spot that's even remotely handy.

The problem usually comes in my overzealous management. I've convinced myself that sick cattle oughta be put in the barn for intense therapy and close observation.

Of course, by the time I've made that call, it's too late for everybody but the undertaker. It usually turns out that I put cattle in the barn so they can die in a small place with low ceilings and narrow doors to be pushed, pulled or dragged out of.

I only lost one cow this winter and it wasn't necessarily weather related. She was only 17 years old; she should have lived longer than that. Anyway, I didn't put her in the barn. Instead, she found the tightest, fenced-in corner in the corral to go and expire.

I can see I'll be tearing down fence and waiting for a thaw before I get her drug out to the cow cemetery.

I'm still pretty young, but I'm already making plans for my inevitable demise. I want the people I leave behind to have it easier than I did with the cows I've known. As a matter of fact, if I can see the end coming, I'm going to drive myself right to the funeral home and lay down on the slab just to make it easier for everybody.

# Calf cologne
## After the birth, try a little aftershave

It's too bad cows have to be heifers before they can become cows. Getting calves pried out of first calf heifers and then keeping the right calves with the right heifers can be about as much fun as hauling jack rabbits on a flat bed.

Actually, the first calfers have been pretty good at the Taylor Ranch this year. So far, I'm batting a thousand (knock on wood), going 13 for 13. Only had to strap the o.b. chains on one big lugger so far, and only had to fight one heifer to get her to claim her newborn bundle of joy.

### Model of motherhood

There's nothing I hate more than a heifer who snubs her calf. Something about a cow that'll give birth and then walk off nonchalantly just ticks me off.

And my blood really boils when I get the aloof young mom into a pen and the damn dam won't let junior nurse.

If she starts kicking the little guy and commences to roughin' him up just because he's hungry, I really lose my cool. Now I'm not generally a violent person, but seeing a cow commit calf abuse is enough to make me locate a two by four and begin inflicting a little motherhood.

Usually though, after a couple days of close supervision and a few splinters, the mother/calf relationship is up and running.

### The smell of success

I hear tell, though, that there's an easier way to cement the bond between cow and calf. It's a little elixir called "Calf Claim." I've never tried the concoction, but some of my friends swear by it.

A little dash of this sweet-smelling calf cologne on the abandoned animal and it's love at first smell. Supposedly, when the mean mama gets a whiff of junior's new aftershave, she forgets all about her postpartum orneriness and gets right down to the business of calf rearing.

29

The key ingredient in this secret sauce is, of course, a secret. The label lists a host of generic ingredients and something called "natural flavorings," i.e. grandpa's special recipe.

I've been told that users should exercise some caution with the product. Spill a little on your coveralls and you'll have cows droolin' and following you all around the corral.

I believe a potion that powerful could have a lot of good uses away from the ranch.

Next Saturday night, I think I'll trade in my regular cologne for a little Calf Claim. It sounds perfect for the weekend bar scene — splash a little on and the females should come a runnin'.

If it works on females of one species, you'd think it'd work on others.

But I do have a few reservations. This new addition to my bag of tricks could backfire. It may just work on the more maternal types, and I could find myself at the bar mothered up to gray-haired grandmothers and time-stressed soccer moms.

Or, worse yet, I could be standing next to the dance floor surrounded by cows. Maybe I should just stick with a little Old Spice.

# Rummage sales for ranchers
## Kick the tires, socialize and buy your tools back

Auction sale season is upon us once again. It's the time of truth when sale bills list everything you ever owned for all to see. It's amazing how a lifetime of farming and ranching can be listed on a piece of paper 8.5 inches wide and 11 inches long.

The best compliment a career farmer or rancher can receive when they sell out is, "It was a good sale." Retirement auctions are good social events. If the retirees are ready and glad to be leaving the business, there's good feelings in the air. Kind of like a going away party for a good friend.

Gone broke sales are a whole different matter. There's not a lot of joy in these deals, especially if the folks worked hard, scraped by and just fell victim to the unforgiving nature of weather, markets, and the new farm economy.

The machinery is usually pretty well depreciated on these cost-conscious operations and your only wish is that you could bid a little more to help lighten their load. It's tough when you see good people forced into town to stand on concrete and punch a time clock.

However, some bankruptcy sales are kind of gratifying. These are the sales of folks who overspent, overextended and overshot their debt-to-equity ratios, all the while living like kings and queens.

Call me cruel and unforgiving, but I'm always mildly satisfied when the guy goes broke who drove by in his super-cushy air-conditioned tractor and made fun of my "A" John Deere.

These high rollers always have good sales — lots of new paint and nice equipment. Unfortunately, I can't afford these implements any more than when they were on the dealer's showroom floor.

## Swap time

Like all ranchers, I enjoy the chance to buy some good broken down equipment at the neighborhood auction sales. We're always on the lookout for a wore-out hay mower, some bent-up corral panels, or another Johnny Popper with good 38-inch tires.

Sometimes we go to the neighbor's auction just to buy back the tools they borrowed. It's easier than hounding them to return the fence stretchers, tow ropes and sockets they borrowed over the years. And it usually won't cost you too much if you tell the bidders who are standing around that the tools were yours anyway.

But borrowing works both ways and what comes around goes around.

I've been breeding my heifers by artificial insemination for several years, using my neighbor's nitrogen tank to keep the semen cool. I've had the tank for so long, I've begun to think it was mine.

Well the neighbor's got an auction next Monday and the nitrogen tank is listed on the bill so I better wrap up my A.I.'ing and take the tank along to the sale.

I'll have to show up early, though. It's going to take a little time to chase away any other interested buyers.

# Life in the not-so-wild Kingdom
## Darting the beast on the North American savanna

I remember watching those exciting episodes of the Mutual of Omaha's "Wild Kingdom" when I was an impressionable young lad.

It all seemed so exciting. Jim Fowler out eartagging full-grown gorillas, Marlin Perkins providing the commentary in Omaha; Jim out weaning elephant calves from their enraged mothers, Marlin jotting down the tally in Omaha; Jim out castrating crocodiles under water, Marlin backing him up... in Omaha. That was a great partnership.

Of course, once in a while, Marlin did get out in the Land Rover to help Jim out a bit. Whenever Jim and Marlin got out in the Land Rover, you could bet that one of them was carrying either a net or a dart gun.

Driving hell bent for election next to a leggy giraffe or a galloping wilde-beest, they'd craftily dodge the rocks and holes until the job was finished.

It's a good thing that there were never any speed limits posted out on the savanna. If there had been, lead foot Perkins surely would have been tossed in some Tanzanian hoosegow with no chance at bail.

## Doctoring pinkeye

Thoughts of the Wild Kingdom show came back to me last week when my kind hearted neighbor brought over his dart gun to help me doctor a 2-year-old bull with pinkeye.

The bull was a pretty good one-eyed breeder, but I didn't want to take any chances. And since the neighbor had made the investment in the new darting technology, the least I could do was make use of it.

Instead of a Land Rover we had to make do with an old red four-wheel-drive Dodge, but the bull didn't put up much of a chase anyway. The bull was pretty preoccupied with winning the love of young black baldy cow, so he was pretty easy to sneak up on.

Before the bull knew what hit him, Shane had sunk a dart in his rump with five mils of sleepy time loaded in its tip. This was where things usually got pretty hairy for Marlin and Jim.

It was a little disappointing for Shane and I, though. The bull just stood there and walked around a little. No pawing the dirt, no nostril flaring charges, not so much as a mild goring or even a swipe at the Dodge.

So we did what most brave adventurers do. We sat in the pickup and listened to the radio, waiting for the big guy to fall asleep.

When he did, I jumped out and needled him with some antibiotics, then glued a nice blue denim patch over the infected eye. But before the beast came back to his senses, we had one final task. We had to get a quick photograph.

With one foot perched atop the raging, but sleeping, animal, we immortalized the moment on film. It should make for good documentation as we tell our story and continue to defend our title as the Champion Cow Tippers of Smokey Lake Township.

# Dripping dollars
## Fall vaccination may call for more training time and gaskets

Needle-shy calves are getting pretty nervous again out in the pastures. They haven't had to fret over the thought of some cattle nurse hovering over them with a needle and syringe since birth.

At birth, they got their first dose of disease protection, and they were probably too young to remember the sting of an 18-gauge needle piercing the loose skin ahead of their shoulder.

Now, however, they're a full 5 to 6 months old — and about as fidgety as a 5 or 6-year-old kid in the doctor's office.

Admittedly, the bedside, or chuteside, manner of a rancher has something to be desired. We could be a bit more soothing, but time is short and there always are lots of calves in the back pens that need to be run through the inoculation gauntlet.

## Learning curve

Used to be there wasn't a lot of vaccinating going on at the ranch. The only vaccine a calf would see is a cheap dose of seven way at branding time. And at 20 cents a dose, guys could afford to make a few mistakes.

An amateur cowhand might have just as much vaccine on the ground as in the calf, but what the heck, it didn't cost much.

But, in today's era of proactive prevention, we have all kinds of wonderfully expensive vaccines at our disposal to keep the calves healthy and the cattle feeders happy.

It does cost less to prevent disease than it does to treat it, but it's a big jump for a rancher to put $3 or $4 worth of vaccine in a calf that used to get just 20 cents worth.

And nothing is more nerve-wracking for the cost-conscious cowboy than $2-a-dose vaccine and a leaky syringe.

## Dry run

My nerves definitely were wracked last week when I run through our first group of calves for pre-weaning vaccination. I had a good crew, adequate facilities and probably the worst set of syringes ever assembled.

We run in the first 10 head and used up enough vaccine to do 20 head. I dripped more vaccine on their backs than I got injected under their skin. It was more a process of religious annointment than scientific immunization.

"Bless you my calf," I chanted as I walked the plank and dripped high-dollar dosages on their back. "May the cattle god watch over you and keep you in his grace in the kingdom of Nebraska feedlots."

Very ceremonial, but questionable in terms of effectiveness. After 10 calves and $50 worth of vaccine, we got our guns tightened, repaired and sealed to the point where the number of doses used almost matched the number of doses actually needed.

Next time, though, I think I'll implement a test run. We'll put the first 10 head in the alley and inject them with nothing but water or saline solution. Then when we've got all our gaskets, needles and barrels replaced, we can start vaccinating with the real stuff.

I just hope we remember to give them the real shot before we turn them out.

# Knife for all purposes
## Jackknives ain't just for whittlin'

A funny thought struck me the other day while I was lancing a lump on a calf's jaw with my trusty jackknife. As the blood streaked, lumpy yellow ooze ran down along the blade I wondered: How long should a jackknife be hip pocket sterilized in lint before one should use it for eating an apple?

I didn't come up with a firm answer, but two days later, I was slicing into a cantaloupe with my lump lancing blade.

All the recent talk about food safety and proper kitchen habits really has me re-examining the way I handle my favorite eating utensil.

I'm not so worried about the grease and oil I pick up on my pocketknife while I'm using it for a screwdriver, sprocket scraper and hydraulic hose cutter. A couple swipes on your pant leg and those minor petroleum products disappear.

I'm not even that concerned with chemical residue. When I'm using my knife to cut open the foil seals on toxic pesticides, I triple up on my protection. Two swipes on the pant leg plus a quick plunge in the dirt and then another two sterilizing swipes.

What's really got me worried, though, is the animal activities I partake in with my pocketknife. Who knows what kind of bacteria I might be picking up by cleaning horse hooves, castrating calves and skinning small animals.

Chemicals and petroleum products are child's play next to those nasty little bacteria that live in living organisms.

### Try a fork

Maybe the knife and bacteria aren't the problem. The root of the problem could be my bad table manners.

I know you're supposed to use things like silverware and other eating utensils that are washed and sanitized on a regular basis, but digging into your pocket for the all-purpose knife/fork combination is so much handier.

It could be one of those quirky, self-sufficient farmer and rancher things.

I remember one time when I was sitting at a table with a few ranchers, a few urbanites and a big bowl of Washington red delicious. Without exception, every cowboy at the table grabbed an apple and then immediately dug into their pocket for the proper flatware.

Jackknives were slicing, dicing and spearing. It actually looked pretty tidy. The jackknife method was considerably neater than just biting into the fruit and letting the juice run down your chin.

And they were efficient, too. Not a core in sight. Nothing left but six seeds and a stem when they got done with those Washington reds. Everyone wrapped up the activity with some swipe sanitation before ramming their mini swords back into their pockets.

It's a tough call. Jackknives are the perfect tool both on the ranch and at the table.

The best solution might be to just start carrying two of them. One in the right pocket for slicing into animals and one in the left pocket for slicing into lunch.

Just don't get them confused.

*Author's note: One reader informed me of a couple other jack-knife uses that she personally had witnessed by the men in her ranch family. She said they use their knives to scrape off the bottom of their boots and pick their teeth — and in that order!*

# Good riddance
## Bull shipping a cause for celebration

We don't name many of our bulls here on the Taylor Ranch. Sure, they'll pick up a reference from where they were raised — the Effertz calf, the Medalen bull — but, occasionally, you have an animal on the place that really deserves a special name.

I just sold one of those special cattle. We called him S.O.B. (surly ornery bugger). I can't say that we shed a lot of tears over his departure.

In his defense, I'd have to say he had good bloodlines, was bullet-proof on his calving ease, and he was always in good shape.

Aside from that, he was a corral-busting, gate-bending, man-hunting, horse-rolling, snot-blowing, high-headed, surly, ornery bugger.

### Time to go

S.O.B. came home with his heifers last week. All the rest of our bulls get pulled from breeding duty after about 55 days of amorous courting, but not S.O.B.

You could try and get him out of the pasture, but he either would run straight at you and try and flip your horse over or head straight into the trees and stand there with that "make my day" look.

When we finally did get S.O.B. peeled away from the rest of the herd this fall, I pondered the thought of spending another winter with him. As I pondered, he went crashing over a gate and the marketing decision was made.

We tried loading him in our old standby chute. S.O.B. promptly laid down a chunk of the old standby.

So we backed the horse trailer up to the headgate on the working alley. Good idea, but two of the calves we chased in to bait old S.O.B. decided to go up the alley ahead of him.

S.O.B. thought it would be fun to push on them 500-pounders as hard he could to see if they would pop. As the two calves began to moan, I pulled the trailer ahead to see if we could sneak them out.

They snuck out and I slammed the pickup in reverse and rammed that headgate a good one before S.O.B. found his freedom. I was never so glad to shut the gate on an animal in my whole life.

I packed a few precautionary tools for S.O.B.'s final trip — a sorting stick, a rope, a high-power rifle and a butcher knife, just in case.

He rocked and banged the trailer all the way to the sale barn. I got him unloaded, but I didn't get to see him sell. I kind of hope he took a couple runs at those cattle buyers, maybe causing them to swallow their cigars and momentarily drop the telephones from their ears.

When it was all done, I collected my check and thought about celebrating.

I made some quick calculations — one day's trip to the packing plant, a day for the slaughter, a day for the grinding and a couple days for distribution. Yup, come next Wednesday, I'm going to celebrate at McDonald's with an S.O.B. hamburger.

Ah, the sweet taste of revenge.


# Sleep deprivation
## How to tell if you're a walking zombie

The research is in. We mortal humans need $8^1/2$ hours of uninterrupted sleep to fully function throughout the day.

Great idea! Now, if someone would just inform the heifer population, those of us who sleepwalk around the "first-calvers" every couple hours, every night, could begin to fully function.

The television reporter who was discussing America's sleep deprivation said there were some telltale signs you could use to identify the nocturnally challenged.

### Sleepless symptoms

They said that if you rely on an alarm clock to get up, you might not be getting enough sleep. In a perfect world, you're supposed to wake naturally and roll out of bed with a skip and a jump.

Another way to tell if you aren't getting enough sleep is to see how long it takes to nod off at night. The experts say it should take at least 10 or 15 minutes to enter dreamland. It's a bad sign if you go out like a light the minute your head hits the pillow.

If you find yourself dozing off during meetings, you probably could use a little more shut-eye, they say. Besides that, you might need a hanky to wipe up with if you're a drooling dozer, and, possibly, a neck brace if you're a violent head bobber. And, depending on the importance of the meeting you fell asleep at, you might need a good story to tell your boss when you're jarred awake, too.

## A cowboy's guide

I think there are more accurate ways to tell if you're suffering from sleep deprivation, especially if you're a rancher. Here's a few things to look for if you suspect that you or a neighbor of yours may be suffering from too little sleep.

First, check the thermometer, and then, the heifer pen. If the mercury reads anywhere from 5 to 25 below zero and the heifer pen reads anywhere from "about to pop" to "just waiting until 2 a.m.," the resident rancher could be a bit bleary-eyed and short of Z's.

Another good test is to eyeball the "heifer bull" that was used on the herd. Does he look more like Arnold Schwarzenegger or Jerry Seinfeld? If he's a big-shouldered, double-muscled freak of nature with a head like an oil drum and leg bones like tree trunks, there could be a sleep problem.

A good way to double check this sleep starving phenomena is to inspect the bill at the local vet clinic. If it shows a number of 3 a.m. clinic calls and a "buy 10 Caesarean sections get the 11th one free" deal, it doesn't signal a healthy sleep pattern.

It is tough to predict the kind of weather you'll have when you're calving heifers in March, and, I admit, it's hard to really know what kind of calves your new heifer bull will throw, but there is one sure-fire way to get the ideal $8^1/_2$ hours of sound, restful sleep.

Forget calving those heifers and just replace the cows you cull with some experienced 3-year-olds who kept someone else up at night the year before.

# Give 'em a squeeze
## The big push for calving convenience

When people think of the term "freshly squeezed," they generally think of orange juice. But after last week's cow working, I think of calves when I hear the words, "freshly squeezed."

It was that time of year when we round up the cows and give them their pre-calving scours shot, retag the anonymous members of the herd and clip the freeze brands on the ones lucky enough to have more permanent identifying characteristics.

The cows were marching down my university extension specification working alley when one of my extremely pregnant cows decided the extension specs were just a wee bit too narrow.

## Push, pull or drag

We pushed, we twisted, we cajoled. We even teased and taunted her. But No. 22 was stuck as tight as a 32-inch cow in a 26-inch chute. It didn't help that both the cow and the cow pushers had nothing but ice for traction. The four of us looked like fast-forward cartoon characters with all 10 feet pedaling and nobody going anywhere.

We really knew things were tight when the cow pushed her water bag out. Never mind the fact that she was supposedly more than three weeks away from her due date.

The pressure released with that water bag must have been just enough to get her through the alley. One cow through to freedom, one calf about to be liberated.

It looked like we were going to deliver a baby whether we wanted to or not. I'd heard of inducing labor, but usually it's to prevent a mother from going way past term, not to speed things up several weeks early.

## Squeeze management

We got the calf out in good shape, alive and well. If he hadn't been, I'd have probably sworn off of vaccinating or working pregnant cows for eternity.

But, since the calf did come out healthy and happy, I think the "alley squeeze" could be safely used to make ranching a lot more schedule-friendly. Calving time is kind of like milking cows — you just gotta be there. No vacations. No extended trips. No time off.

However, by implementing the labor-inducing squeeze play, you could get a whole week's calving completed in one day, ahead of schedule, and take the rest of the week off to enjoy a little cow-free freedom.

Putting the squeeze on your herd will take a little cooperation from your cows to get 'em shot down a tight, narrow alley. If they're not too willing, a hydraulic pushing mechanism might come in handy to get them through the big squeeze.

If a hydraulic ram is too high tech for you, try greasing the sides of the squeezing alley and use some high-speed bovine velocity to get them through to the other end where tightly scheduled motherhood awaits them.

Now, when someone schedules a bull sale or a ski trip during my calving season, I'll just round up the herd a few days ahead of the event and give my cows a squeeze.

And I don't mean a hug.

# Calving book bingo
## Playing the high stakes odds

I started the spring calving season without one of the most crucial tools of the trade — the official 1998 model pocket-sized calving book.

When the heifers started calving in March, I was forced to jot down the vital statistics of each calf on a piece of scrap paper. It was a poor substitute for the official calving book with its tidy columns, daily calendar, gestation table and calving activity analysis pages.

I was experiencing some of the typical systems of calving book withdrawal. I was making those fidgety motions of reaching for my front shirt pocket like a fella does when he's lost his wallet. I would stutter and stammer when someone asked me, "how's calving going?", because I wasn't able to pull out my neatly organized statistics and tell them with certainty that I had exactly 27 heifers calved out so far.

Luckily, I got to a vet clinic that carried my favorite brand of calving books before the symptoms got any more serious. I'm much more relaxed now that I have that reassuring weight snapped under the flap of my left front pocket.

**Let the games begin**

Now that I'm properly outfitted, I'm able to play my favorite calving book games like "calving book bingo."

The goal of this bingo is to fill all 17 slots on a calving book page with the stats of live calves. If I'm forced to make an entry in the death code column on any one of the 17 rows, I'm out of the game.

But if I can jot in that 17th calf and see that the 16 preceding it are all still alive and kicking, I jump out of the pickup and shout "Bingo!" You have to be careful about how loud you shout, because it could start a small stampede which, in turn, could trample a calf, which, in turn, could disqualify your bingo claim.

Another good game is calving book poker. It requires the participation of a few other ranchers and there are two versions, "bragging poker" and "complaining poker."

Bragging poker consists of ranchers trying to outdo each other with calving season success stories. The winner is almost always some despicable cur who has had five sets of twins and only lost one calf to an act of God. This rancher usually will ante up, raise, and increase all bets, until he lays down his open-faced calving book and says, "I'm running a 104 percent calving percentage boys, read it and weep." I have yet to win a game of bragging poker.

On the other hand, I'm always a strong contender in complaining poker. It's a game of sympathy and it consists of a few guys paging through their calving books and showing how they've never once scored a "bingo."

Blizzards, scours, abortion viruses, hard calving sires and plain ol' hard luck are the things that make for sure victory in complaining poker. Landing less than a 90 percent calving percentage will make you the winningest loser in the circle.

But some games just ain't worth winning. I think I'll go grab my eartag marker bingo blotter and see if today's my day for blackout calving bingo.

# G.I. Joe rancher
## Basic training ranch style

I never figured I had the "right stuff" to make an exemplary candidate for military service, but I'm beginning to rethink that assumption.

My dad was drafted into the Army during the "big one," World War II. He ended up serving in the Pacific theater of that war and his basic training took place near Abilene, Texas.

I asked him once about how tough basic training was and he said, "Oh, it wasn't so bad for a ranch kid, but a few of the city boys had a tough time of it."

I think that was a pretty fair assessment.

### Live fire wires

In all the movies that show scenes of boot camp or basic training, you always see the recruits doing the "low crawl" under some prickly wire or even a little live ammo fire. "Get your butt down soldier, or you'll get it shot off!" is the shout of the burly drill sergeant to the lowly privates.

I don't plan on entering the armed forces any time soon, but if I did, I think I'd be well prepared to do the low crawl. I've been practicing quite a bit this spring, and I've even used my own ranch version of "live fire."

My version is a three-wire, high-tensile electric fence that splits my calving pasture. The top wire's hot, the middle wire's a ground, and the bottom is my juiced up "live fire" wire. Occasionally, I find myself on the wrong side of that fence.

That's when I look for a dip in the ground and assume the low crawl position. And, just like the sergeant says, you keep your butt down or ZAP! – you get a gazillion-volt jolt. Sometimes, it's easier to tuck in your elbows and roll under the live wire. Just make sure you don't get juiced via the nose, or, worse yet, your belt buckle.

Sometimes, recruits use the low crawl to get the sneak on an enemy army. Silent, breathless stealth is of utmost importance. It's a lot like sneaking up on a calving heifer that's in need of a pull.

With obstetrical calving chains in hand, I get directly behind the heifer, outside her field of vision and begin to low crawl toward the oversized hooves protruding from under her tail. One wrong move and that heifer's up and running, foiling your efforts to get the calf pulled without having to chase her all the way up to the barn.

Sneaking up on an enemy guard couldn't be much different.

**Retreat!**

Occasionally, rancher recruits do hear the bugle call of retreat. This is generally spurred by an overprotective cow that is in hot pursuit. Instead of bullets whizzing by your head, ol' mother cow's fire consists of blowin' snot down your back jeans pocket.

We don't have any strategically located fox holes or armored vehicles to retreat to, but bale feeders, loader buckets, pickup boxes and trees usually will provide some timely protection.

Just like the army, fear for your life is the underlying motivator. And although the bark of a 250-pound drill sergeant can be instantly inspirational, so can the beller of 1,200-pound bovine gone berserk.

# Electrical ranching
## Looking for an outlet out on the range

Back in the glory days of the open range, ranchers laid claim to their cattle with a long rope, a good fire and a red-hot iron.

Some of us still do, except nowadays most of the cattle are trailed in along a barbed-wire fence, coaxed into a chute and, instead of building a good hot fire, we look for a rural electric pole and an outlet to heat up the branding iron.

It's not quite as romantic with all that clanging steel and coils of extension cord, but it is effective in permanently marking cattle ownership.

## Character scars

In my neighborhood, most of the young calves still are wrestled to the ground for the spring calf workin', so we don't have a lot of clanging steel, but a lot of the ranchers have switched to electrical branding irons and dehorners.

It's added a whole new element of excitement to the brandings. Not that regular calf workin's weren't already pretty eventful, what with eight or 10 accident-prone cowboys running around with needles, knives and hot irons in a concentrated area.

But add to that mix 40 or 50 feet of electrical cord to trip over and it really gets interesting. However, the tripping is really secondary to the thrills and commotion that comes from trying to dodge an electrical iron flying through the air after someone trips and jerks the cord that it's tied to.

You often can tell how many brandings a fella has been to by checking out the number of brands he carries on his own hide from those airborne irons.

## Gettin' juiced

Last week, I picked up a new electric branding iron for a neighbor while I was in the city. I knew they were in need of a new iron because I had helped them brand their yearling heifers last year.

It was relatively tame since we were just working them through the squeeze chute, but every time my buddy hit a heifer with his old branding iron, she would shimmy and shake like our 1974 Ford Galaxy on the gravel road washboards.

"Yeah, this dang iron must have some kind of short in it," my friend said as he continued to put the iron, and the juice, to the whole herd of heifers. I didn't say anything, but I made sure that I didn't lean against the steel squeeze chute while he was branding them.

This year, I wasn't able to help, but they got a crew together and began branding this year's crop of replacement heifers with that same old electric iron. The first two quaked like a leaf but seemed to recover once they were turned out.

Then they slapped the iron on the third heifer in and bam! She went down like a mass murderer in a death row electric chair. They decided to postpone branding the rest until they could procure a new branding iron.

I've always heard about high voltage electrical stimulation for tenderizing beef in the packing plants. And although I'm not sure if the neighbors tried to salvage any beef from that critter, I bet if they did it would have been tender.

# Freak show barbecue
## Front corral showroom clearance

The front corral here at the Taylor Ranch has one less occupant. Last month, we bid farewell to the 2-year-old steer that I was preparing for barbecue.

In general, he was a pretty nice black steer. He was just a little too head ugly to try and sell at public auction.

When he was born, he was as cute as could be. But somewhere along the line, he got his lip ripped clear up to his nostril. I'm not sure if he got stepped on, caught a piece of wire or just got a poor nose job from an unaccredited plastic surgeon.

Whatever it was, he got ugly in a hurry. We affectionately named him Lippy. He had a constant sneer on his face, and he always was flashing his gums or sticking out his tongue at you. But he meant no disrespect.

He was able to nurse and he could eat grass with the one side of his mouth. It kept falling out of the other side. Consequently, it took him twice as long to get big enough to butcher.

And eating him was kind of our only option. Order buyers really discriminate against disadvantaged, facially challenged calves like Lippy. Rather than let those cigar-chomping, commission hungry thieves steal him for 40 cents a pound, I decided to run him on grass last summer and finish him with a little grain this winter.

I really shouldn't complain about the order buyers, because if it weren't for their discriminating tastes, ranchers never would have any beef in their freezer. By cutting out the limpers, rat tails, stub ears, frozen tails, stags and uglies, they've alleviated a lot of hunger among ranch families. Thanks to them, we sell all the good ones and eat whatever's left.

### Pen of the damned

I've been to feedyards where the front pen up by the office is always full of their finest cattle. Stout, square and uniform in color, they're the first critters visitors see when they pull up.

A visitor may never see the pen that is home to the limpers, rat tails, stub ears, etc., that their order buyers picked up on the cheap. The multicolored mongrels with big floppy ears and hump backs are generally out back.

It's probably a good way to organize things and keep a positive image of the place. The front pen of the Taylor Ranch, however, is more of a freak show than a showroom.

After Lippy left, I still had a calf with a dislocated shoulder, a yearling heifer with a swollen navel and an ornery cow who constantly was kicking at a little dough gutted graft calf. Rounding out the pen was an old hide and bones cow I'd been trying to keep alive. She'd lost all the hair on one side of her face and she was old enough to remember Reagan's first term as president.

Once summer came, I was able to turn my freak show loose. Of course, to maintain the ranch's good image, I found a pasture right next to the road for them.

# Slingin' the bull
## Time to test, ship or tell crude stories

I've been doing a lot of bull shipping lately. Nothing extraordinary about that, you might say, since I'm always slingin' bull in this column.

But the bull shipping I've done lately has been the real kind, like shipping the cull bulls to the sales ring and shipping a few other bulls to the vet clinic to be semen tested.

### Dysfunctional bulls

Topics on bulls and breeding are kind of touchy; some might even consider them crude. But, when you're in the business of breeding and raising animals, it's tough to be politically correct and proper.

Some city people really would raise their eyebrows if they walked into a circle of ranchers who were talking about things like artificial insemination, semen collection, vasectomized "gomer" bulls and bull herd libido.

Then again, one of the more accepted topics on the evening news lately has been male impotency and Pfizer's new drug, sildenafil citrate, or Viagra.

All the talk about Viagra has gotten me thinking about its potential animal uses, in particular for the older bulls that quit romancing the cows and, instead, stand around in the corner of the pasture chewing their cud.

Since Pfizer is pretty involved in the business of animal vaccines, it'd be a natural extension for them to introduce a line of animal grade Viagra for bulls whose sexual get up and go has got up and went.

Instead of culling those 6 to 8-year-old bulls for a lack of libido, slip 'em a little sildenafil citrate and they may just breed forever! I even came up with a catchy name — Boviagra.

### Physical therapy

Of course, not every medical solution comes in a bottle. I heard a story once about a veterinarian who had a natural, drug-free cure for bulls with a lack of lust.

44

The old vet had just hired a young gal right out of veterinary school. She moved into the local community and after a couple of weeks, her new boss got a distress call from a local rancher.

The ranchers says, "Doc, you gotta come out and look at this bull. He's got this dull look in the eyes and all he does is stand around in the corner of the pasture with his head down. The cows are all cycling to beat heck, and he won't even look at them. I can't afford to have a bunch of open cows this fall. We gotta do something."

"I'll be right out," the old vet says. He thought it would be a good idea to take his young assistant along to show her his cure for bull impotency. They met the rancher, went out to the pasture and found the problem bull.

The old vet walked right up to the lackadaisical bull, grabbed a big tuft of hair on its forehead and jerked it up as hard as he could. He tore the hair right out by the roots, but the bull really came to life and headed straight for the cow herd to start doing his thing.

As they drove back to town, the old doctor asked the young female vet if she had learned anything from their little excursion. "Oh, absolutely," she said. "I finally learned why all the cowboys in this area are so bald!"

# Peace of mind
## Doctoring cattle may be therapy for self

It's been a good summer for the drug manufacturers and animal health dealers, meaning it's been a bad summer for pinkeye, the cattle that get it and the ranchers who have to treat it.

For whatever reasons — weather, insects, nutrition, plain old poor management — pinkeye's been running as rampant as poverty here on the Taylor Ranch.

### Blinders

I first noticed my pinkeye epidemic when I was rotating some cows to a fresh pasture. My horse tried to divert my attention away from the cattle by stepping on a hornet's nest, but that was only good for a few minutes worth of saddle-horn-grabbing distraction.

After that, I couldn't help but notice that a good share of the cattle were in need of a seeing eye dog to get them from the salt block to the water tank. The calves had to feel their way around to find the udder and generally were nursing from memory.

Their eyes were red, sore and watery. They resembled a bunch of allergy sufferers in the height of the weed and pollen season.

I decided it was time for some drastic action. Like it or not, I was going to have to quit haying for a few hours and call in the neighbors for some off-season cattle work.

It takes something pretty serious to get a rancher to leave the field during haying season. Like a werewolf under a full moon, ranchers are transformed into hay maniacs under the spell of a full sun. It must have something to do with the four or five weeks of summer we get to prepare for the rest of the year's winter.

Hay maniacs occasionally will drive around the cattle to drop off some salt and mineral, take a rough head count and make sure the bulls still are doing their duty. But cattle aren't supposed to do anything irrational and time consuming like get sick or require doctoring in the summer.

## Good medicine

Somehow, I got a haymaking neighbor to join me in the effort, and we were chasing cows into the corrals by 6 a.m. to beat the heat (and still allow for a good day of haying). After a couple hundred dollars worth of antibiotics, eye powder and fly dope, I figured we had the problem licked.

The cattle still looked like hell as they headed back to the pasture, but time would tell if the doctoring worked.

"So, do you think they'll get better?" I asked my crewmate. "Hard to say," he returned, "the important thing to ask here is do you feel better?"

I had to admit that I did. Like a new mother rubbing some wondrous liniment on an ailing baby, I at least felt like I had done my best to make things better. Call it the warm afterglow of being a top-notch manager.

But after awhile, I realized that if all I accomplished with a couple hundred dollars and several hours of dusty labor was self-satisfaction, I could have gotten the same feeling for a lot less work and money.

Ignorance is not only bliss, it's also real affordable. For the rest of the summer, I think I'll stick with the haying and quit checking those cattle.

# It's a dirty job, but....

# Greasy gears, bloody knuckles
## Shoulder deep in bovine still better than even a trickle of oil and grease

Forget spring, summer, fall and winter. If you raise cattle in the north country there are only three seasons and they're called making hay, hauling hay and feeding hay.

We're deep into the hay making season, and, with a little luck, ranchers will be able to roll up, stack, pile and compress enough hay into an array of semi-mobile packages to keep the herd from turning into Ace Reid cartoon-type skeleton cattle this winter.

Most hard-core ranchers are in business because they like to work with livestock, but livestock need feed. Haying isn't such a terrible activity, but it involves machinery — those oily, noisy, dirty contraptions that roll, grind, shake and somehow turn gasoline and diesel into motion.

Farmers deserve credit because they seem to understand machinery. They deal with a lot of different equipment and have a real knowledge of what goes on under all those hoods and shields. Most cowboys would still rather believe that there are Keebler elves under the hood making that machine move when they're not busy baking cookies. We like our cattle.

### Greasy, grimy tractor guts

Machinery wouldn't be so repulsive to us if it weren't for the one thing that keeps all those bearings, sprockets, gears, chains and steel parts alive — grease. You can call it multipurpose lubricant, motor oil, gear lube or universal fluid. Get it on your hands, in your face or soaked into your jeans and it's all "grease," although it's sometimes prefaced by a number of colorful adjectives.

Ranchers are a funny breed of people. They can be shoulder deep in a laboring cow, covered with manure, blood, urine and other various bovine fluids, and think nothing of the mess. But get them underneath a tractor or some other piece of equipment with oil running down their arms or flakes of grease dropping in their ear and they are thoroughly disgusted.

It's not so bad getting your hands greasy, but "grease transfer" is a real problem. The grease starts on your hands, then you scratch your head a time or two wondering how to put things back together, and you itch your nose, adjust your cap, roll up your sleeve, hitch up your jeans, wipe your hands on your knees for lack of a rag and, before you know it, you're completely black from head to toe. "Grease transfer" makes us and those who do our laundry quite irate.

**The pain of it all**

Of all the pain inflicted on a rancher, machinery inflicted pain has to be the worst.

As a group, we're fairly accustomed to pain. We've been kicked, stepped on, dragged and rammed into rocks and hard places by animals of all ages and sizes. And we bounce back fairly well, a little wiser, a bit more careful and a mite quicker because of the lesson.

But, when that Crescent wrench slips off a burr and we find blood streaming from our knuckles where that little flap of skin still hangs to taunt us, we let loose with a string of observations on that burr's family history and reproductive habits that our mothers would find quite inappropriate.

Physically, the pain maybe isn't so bad, but knowing that we have only ourselves to blame makes the hurt 10 times worse. We could have gotten a real wrench instead of the ranch's favorite Crescent or Vise-Grip, and we could have quit torquing on the bolt before it snapped in two and sent our knuckles flying through a maze of sharp-edged gears. But we didn't, it's our fault and we can't blame it on animals who are less intelligent than we are supposed to be.

Until we find a way to cut the hay with lasers and gravitate it to the hay pen with clean science, we will have to continue on with pieces of grease-coated steel wearing against each other to harvest the winter feed supply. And ranchers will continue to come to the house with bloody knuckles, greasy jeans and a look on their face that says, "I'd rather be pulling a calf."

# small iron!
## Remember the little guys

The BIG IRON machine show will be getting under way this week at the Red River Valley Fairgrounds in West Fargo, N.D. A show dedicated to the success of American agriculture, the most labor-efficient food production system in the world where 2 percent of a population can feed the other 98 percent plus many more beyond our borders. That kind of efficiency is dependent upon gutsy ag engineers who keep designing bigger and better machinery — greater horsepower, longer drills, monstrous combines.

BIG IRON's nice, but what about the contributions made by small iron? Maybe a show could be dedicated to those twerps of tillage, the peons of production. small iron! A show dedicated to some real prairie workhorses like the John Deere "A" and the Farmall "M".

A small iron! show would have to be hosted by a small town. We'd expect to attract a small crowd, and our small budget would be funded by a small fee taken at the small iron! entrance gate.

49

## Fresh paint not allowed

The real danger of hosting a small iron! show is that it might attract those vermin of the business, antique tractor collectors. Don't get me wrong. I'm glad there are people who want to preserve agricultural history, but I've been to a few too many auction sales looking for some bargain horsepower in the form of an "R" John Deere only to be blown out of the water by some antique collector in a blind bidding frenzy.

Right up there with the antique collectors are the suburbanites shopping for a cute little tractor to mow the expansive lawn or till the garden on their "ranchette" or "hobby farm." These people have no sense of what a tractor is really worth when they go to an auction sale either.

It's truly embarrassing for a big, tough farmer or rancher, a real steward of the land, to be outbid by some joker at the auction wearing sunglasses, a tank top and a pair of Bermuda shorts sagging slightly because of the heavily weighted wallet jammed in his back pocket.

Our small iron! show would ward off the antiquesters and the lawn boys by inspecting all tractors entered in the show at the gate. There would be an inspection checklist to certify the authenticity of the small iron tractors as being genuinely employed and used in agricultural pursuits.

- Paint, faded. (No bright green or red air-sprayed units.)
- Hood, rusted. (No pampered, shedded from the elements models.)
- Tires, cracked and wore. (No shiny Armor All coated jobbies.)
- Seat, split with stuffing protruding. (Comfort is not a prerequisite.)
- Radiator and seals, leaking. (Antifreeze and oil are cheaper than a repair job.)
- All moving parts, coated with oil and grease. (The dirtier the better.)

## The supplementary trade show

Along with all the farmers and ranchers bringing in their small iron! workhorses from the fields, we would expect a contingency of spinoff small iron! businesses to show up wielding their wares and offering their services to our small iron! enthusiasts.

These businesses would reflect the small budgets of small iron! farmers and offer a rather unique set of products and parts.

There would be no booths set up for implement dealers doling out brand new replacement parts. For crying out loud, those prices were set with the antique tractor collector in mind. I'm sure gold is cheaper by the ounce than some of the painted-up parts offered by those guys.

We small iron! farmers are much too wise to spend our money on overpriced new replacement parts. Booths at our show would be filled with salvage yard owners and junk dealers. They offer the real bargains. The prices are still pretty outrageous, but you get parts that are pre-worn, pre-grooved and pre-cracked at no extra charge!

The other booths would be filled with suppliers of more universal repair products highly demanded by small iron! enthusiasts. There would be bins of black electrical tape, spools of baler twine and barbed wire, tubes of blue silicone gasket maker, boots and patches for tires and bulk barrels of Stop Leak.

I think there's some real potential for a small iron! show. But getting those old tractors to the grounds could be a spitting and sputtering challenge, and hauling them on those bald-tired machine trailers with no licenses or lights could be risky. We better talk to the Highway Patrol before we print up the posters.

# High tech bogs down
## Mechanized ranchers sometimes need a tug from traditionalists

"Horses are a thing of the past. There's no reason to keep those hay burning glue factories on the ranch. You need to get yourself a four-wheeler, Ryan."

That's what my friends and neighbors who can't ride a horse tell me.

Undaunted by their negative perception of my four-legged friends, I continue to keep a small remuda on the ranch to help chase the cattle, sort off pairs and justify my right to wear a wide-brimmed hat when I go to town.

Horse ownership allows me to correctly answer those who say, "Hey, Tex, where'd you park your horse?" and accept the wishes sometimes directed toward me and "the horse I rode in on."

The most satisfying part of owning a horse, though, is getting to use the horse to help out somebody who swears horses have no place in modern ranching.

### ATH vs. ATV

Sometimes there's a limit to the terrain an all-terrain vehicle can tackle.

That's when the Kawasaki cowboys have to grovel and suck up to us horse owners for some help roping a sick critter or getting an ornery bull out of a pasture.

There's not much terrain that my all terrain horse can't navigate. He's been the transportation mode of choice lately with all the new water holes that sprouted up on our range this spring.

And nothing can satisfy the average everyday equestrian more than coming across someone with a mechanically malfunctioned motorcycle or a failed four-wheeler.

"Hmmm... looks like you're in a bit of a pickle," we'll say with a wry grin on our face. "Looks like you could use a ride. Of course, all that I've got to offer is the back seat on this ol' prehistoric pony."

Funny, though, they'll gladly stoop or step up, actually, to accepting help from a rancher and his hay burner.

**How 'bout a pull?**

The most gratifying scene I've witnessed happened this spring when I was helping a neighbor chase some cows back out to pasture after branding.

A couple of the fellas on our crew hopped on the four-wheeler to help us with the herding. The rest of us were horseback, coaxing cattle through mud, water and muck.

The gate we had to go through had an exceptionally good mud hole for us to ford. The cows made it, the baby calves made it, the old-fashioned horses made it, but the new fangled four-wheeler left its riders right smack in the middle of that mud hole.

Those of us on mud savvy mounts toyed with the idea of letting the two ATV pilots swim and slosh their way to shore.

But our bleeding hearts took precedent and two of the cowboys shook out their lariats and pulled the hapless Honda from its resting place. It would have made a nice photo, I thought, like the sketch I once saw of a team of draft horses pulling a Model T horseless carriage out of a snowbank.

Of course, there wasn't a camera to be found, so the scene will have to live in my mind.

I got a feeling the gratification could continue. I'm heading down to South Dakota tomorrow in my rickety little tin can of a car. Maybe, I'll get to pick up a motorist in distress whose super deluxe Cadillac roadster conked out somewhere between Mound City and Selby.

# Wrecking yards, doughnuts and dynasties

When you find something you like, stick with it. I think that's especially true for makes of cars, colors of tractors and brands of sickle bar mowers.

A little brand loyalty in those areas not only will give you a sense of familiarity in your life, you'll have a slug of interchangeable parts.

Our ranch has been built on dynasties of big old Ford cars and two-cylinder John Deere tractors. And we can prove it with a line of dead LTDs and worn-out Johnny poppers that stretch far into the horizon.

**Rural self-sufficiency**

When you live out in the sticks, you don't want to be dependent on distant parts stores and far-away salvage yards.

If you're in need of an alternator for your car or a radiator cap for your tractor, it just wouldn't pay to drive 30 miles and spend a bunch of money. Take my word. It's a lot handier to just walk out to your own personal ranch wrecking yard and pirate a few parts off the car you went to the junior prom in or the tractor you raked with in the drought of '61.

These "South 40" salvage yards do nothing for the decor of your farmstead, but they're hard to beat for convenience and money savings.

Just don't let it get out of hand. If you tried to stock every make, model and year there was, you wouldn't have any land left to graze your cattle on or put in your crop.

That's why you have to find something you like and stick with it.

I'm learning this lesson the hard way. I've already bought a nongreen tractor with multiple cylinders and odd sized tires, not to mention a non-Ford car with considerably less leg room and horsepower than a '74 Galaxie.

They're not bad machines; we just don't have any spare parts for the darn things.

## Rolling doughnuts

Case in point. Last week, I stopped for something cool to drink at the local watering hole. When I came out, my little non-Ford car had broke a leg.

Now fixing a flat tire on Main Street Towner does not go unnoticed. The cars that stopped claimed they just wanted to help. I think they just wanted to hassle me about the tough luck I was having with my wimpy little car.

The tire change was going good until I popped open the trunk and found this little go-kart tire where the spare was supposed to be. Now I'd heard about these so-called "doughnuts" but never had actually seen one up close and in the wild.

Around these parts, doughnuts are for dunking in your coffee, not bolting on to your car hub. But my options were pretty limited. And I was supposed to be in Bismarck later that night.

I strapped the doughnut to my vehicle and hobbled on down the street. I was able to get the local tire mechanic to come down to his shop after hours (talk about good hometown service!) and get my forlorn flat road ready for the drive south.

Now I'm looking for a five-hole 14-inch rim that I can use for a real spare, so I can toss that doughnut in the bushes where it belongs. But, you guessed it, no five-hole 14-inchers in our little wrecking yard.

If your on farm salvage yard has one, though, I'll gladly trade you a five-hole 15-inch off a '73 Ford LTD.

# Kickin' the dirt
## Keeping an eye out for hidden treasure

It's hard to get ahead when you're always looking down.

There are lots of reasons to be looking down. Some people look down because they're shy, sad, or clumsy and forgot to tie their shoe.

But the reason I'm looking down is because I'm always on the lookout for something I lost in the sand a long time ago.

### A running tally

Losing tools in the sand is figured right into the annual budget around here. Every year, you can count on losing a couple screwdrivers or pliers in the dirt. It's been a real boost to the folks I buy my tools from at the local hardware store.

Being eternally optimistic, I keep a running tally of the tools I've lost in hopes that they'll turn up again. I shuffle around the ranch stirring up a little cloud of dust with each step, hoping I'll kick into some long lost wrench or pocket knife.

Some tools are lost out of sheer neglect like the fencing pliers that are somewhere in the east pasture or the air hose gun in the back of the shop.

Other losses come with good excuses and action-packed stories that detail their demise. I had a good pipe wrench jump right out of the tractor when I was feeding last winter. I think it landed somewhere close to the twine-cutting knife I lost the year before.

There's a castrating knife out in the fine sands of our working corral, too. A calf broke loose from the wrestlers and stuck a foot in the Lysol bucket, losing the knife and cracking our best 5-quart ice cream pail.

### Stemming the losses

After a few trips to the hardware store for new replacement tools, a guy starts to wonder if there's any way to curb these sacrificial tool offerings to the sand god.

One sure way is to quit buying good, name brand tools. The missing tools are always the best ones we have and the most expensive to replace.

If we loaded up our tool box with cheap, foreign junk made from recycled tin foil, I'm sure we'd cut our losses substantially. Of course, replacement costs would probably remain high as we amass a bucket full of bent, broken and warped Taiwanese tools.

Maybe we should just be more careful and conscious of how we conduct our loss-prone lives. We could paint all the tools blaze orange or tie a long string to each of them and hang them off our belt loops.

That would be both unsightly and unhandy.

The sport of looking down is looking up, though. Two days ago, we found that air hose gun in the back of the shop peeking out above the sand. It laid there about 6 or 8 feet from where the concrete ended.

If there's one sure-fire way to cut back on losses in the sand, it's getting rid of the sand. Pour concrete over the whole ranch and just listen for the clank when your tools hit the cement.

But there are some drawbacks to that plan. Concrete is hard on hooves and its mighty poor on grass production. And haying—you probably could  bale in road gear, but it'd be a long, long time before you kick anything out the back.

# Sunshine, timing and luck
## A tricky mix at haying time

"Make hay while the sun shines," the saying goes. If it were only that easy, I say.

These days, it's "make hay while the sun shines if the equipment isn't broke down and your schedule doesn't have you doing something else to earn a paycheck."

Times are getting tough out here in cattle country. The prospect of losing money on every calf we sell this fall has some of us forward-thinking, highly leveraged ranchers out trying to locate a little cash to get us through the cattle cycle.

Guys are out delivering mail, pumping gas or selling cosmetics door to door. Anything to put aside a few dollars for the cows, the family and the banker this fall.

It's taking a lot of time from the hay field, too, which traditionally got top priority when poverty wasn't beckoning at our back door.

These same hard-up ranchers who need to be the most productive also have the sorriest looking, least productive fleet of used-up haying machinery around. So even if the sun does decide to shine, you have to hope it hits on the right day of the week and pray that your low-tech machinery has just one more good day left in it.

**Bad to worse**

This weekend, I had two of the three ingredients needed to make some progress on the winter feed supply. I had Saturday and Sunday scheduled in for some haying and the sun was shining just like the weather man said it wouldn't.

The Friday evening 21-point checklist on the $3,000 round baler found at least one "major flaw." Now a "major flaw" on this ranch means you need to drag the heap into the shop and plug in the arc welder.

So much of Saturday morning was spent sparking, chipping and grinding while the sun shone bright on our old Dakota home. When the time came to roll out to the field, the confidence ran deep as we envisioned the progress about to be made.

Halfway to the hay, though, we hit our second stroke of tough luck. Cruising along a prairie trail, a baler tire and wheel were spotted rolling next to the tractor like a hubcap on the interstate.

Meanwhile, the baler dug a trench about 15 feet long before some sudden braking took place. It was a pretty nice trench, and if it hadn't been so late in the season, I'd have dropped a few potatoes in it to help diversify my income.

So after several hours of parts procurement, torch heat, hammering and wrenching, we had a new stub axle installed on the no good son-of-a-baler and we were off like a herd of turtles.

But, before long, a smoking bearing was spotted and the haying umpire called "three strikes and you're out!"

To the novice, it might seem like the entire day had been a total loss, but not so. The faulty bearing gave me enough time to clean up, pick up some replacement parts and head in to the state fair for some sundown festivities.

Sunshine might be needed to make hay, but it's sure not needed to sow your wild oats.

# Tool chests and file cabinets
## Pails and piles do the trick as well

Organization is a nice concept, but it just isn't feasible in the real world.

I dream of being organized sometimes. You know, everything in its place and a place for everything. Anything you need, you can put your hands on in a matter of seconds.

In my dream world, I envision myself out in the shop turning bolts on the most recent breakdown. Every wrench is in the tool chest in its proper drawer. The bolts are in their bin, the parts are on the shelf and the work bench is spotless.

Looking for a three-quarter-inch socket and that bearing you picked up in town the other day? No time is wasted as you quickly find the drawer with the socket and the bin with the baler bearings.

This dream extends to the office as well. File cabinets line the wall, chock-full of neat little color coded hanging files, alphabetized and categorized through and through.

Say you need to get a hold of the November feed bill from 1992. Just head over to cabinet No. 3, look in the blue receipts file and flip though to the month and year you need.

**Not quite**

Then I wake up. Poof! My whole organized world disappears when my eyes open to the pails of tools and piles of papers that define my lifestyle.

Sure I've got a little tool chest and a couple of two-drawer file cabinets, but they're just about empty because everything is drug out of them.

You just can't get down to work until your tools are laying on the floor where you need them. Likewise, you can't get your bills paid or your taxes tallied until all the files are piled up around you like a fort on your desk.

It makes you wonder if you need those tool chests and file cabinets at all.

**The pail system**

When we're out in the field breaking things, we like to have our tools along so we can do some impromptu tweaking and tuning on the equipment to get us through the day.

That means most of our tools are in a couple of 5-gallon pails in the back of the pickup. "Hey, Dad. This tractor's acting up on me again. Why don't you bring me 5-gallons of box end wrenches and throw in a couple gallons of sockets and screwdrivers while you're at it, huh?"

Then when you're done, you throw in the extra bolts and pieces you couldn't find a home for in the bottom of the pail. You can put together quite a pile of bucket bottom bolts after you've "fixed" a thing or two.

The ag engineers ought to come spend a day or two with me. Most of our equipment probably is running with only half the original components. They could rummage though the spare parts in the bottom of the pails and see what they could have omitted at the factory, saving them some money and saving us all the trouble of removal.

Maybe organization isn't all its cracked up to be. If there was a place for everything and everything was supposed to be in it's place, I'd still be out in the field trying to figure out where all those "extra" bolts went.

# Rancher goes farming
## Fall seeding, cowboy style

I finally lived up to the "farmer" part in the Future Farmers of America that I belonged to back in high school. If the group's name had been the Future Ranchers of America, I could have rested easy years ago.

But farming, that's a game I just haven't had the opportunity to play out here in the blowing yellow sands of south Towner. Cattle ranching is our main game out here where it always looks like the 1930s.

Our township could be the poster child for the Conservation Reserve

Program. People from the valley and other fertile portions of our state like to drive by our scenic sand dunes just to cheer themselves up. "At least we don't live here," they gasp as they speed by.

But I refuse to let our lack of black dirt stop me from realizing my farming aspirations. Learning to do, doing to learn, as the Future Farmers say.

## Seeding time

Most good farmers like to hit the field tilling when things thaw out and the sun starts shining in the spring of the year. I, however, being consistently behind schedule, get around to farming when things freeze up and the sun quits shining.

Farming on the ranch wasn't completely my idea. It was actually part of an experiment suggested by my friends at the local soil conservation office. And it wasn't a very big field we were planning to farm, about six-tenths of an acre.

Just right, I figured. Start small. Leave room for expansion.

The soil guys thought my tillable dune acres would require a specialized, nontraditional crop. They brought out a bag of Dune Wildrye. Guess I won't be hedging my harvest on the Chicago Board of Trade.

But harvest isn't even an option, so that's no big deal. Just fence it out and give it a chance to grow, they said. Lucky thing, no room in my 65-cent calf budget to buy a new combine anyway.

## Conservation cow tillage

Dune Wildrye doesn't need any fancy seeding equipment, either. With a cry of, "As ye sow, so shall ye reap," we just grabbed a couple of fists full of seed and started flinging.

It was quite the romantic agrarian scene. A cowboy and a couple of USDA employees sowing seeds on a balmy November day with snow glistening and a light breeze blowing.

Grabbing a couple of pitchforks, a light covering of hay was applied. Then the cowboy brought out his all-in-one press drill/fertilizer/mulch master. It wasn't a green John Deere or a red Case - International — they were blacks and baldies, mostly Angus.

Conservation cow tillage: hooves uniquely suited to press seed in the ground, nitrogen and organic fertilizer on tap directly below the tail. A no-till drill for the no-budget farmer.

To my farmer readers, custom cow tillage is now available from ranchers looking for new ways to pay for their cows. My herd, one of the few herds in the state with six-tenths of an acre of seeding experience, is now available for rent.

You can rent by the hour, the day or the week, but remember to book your seeding dates early — spring planting is right around the corner.

# In search of heat
## Looking for warmth from a frozen tractor seat

Ranchers will pay just about any price for a little heat in the heart of winter. It's a valuable commodity when you're out feeding cows and we'll do just about anything to locate a little of it.

There's usually plenty of heat at the kitchen table and in our coffee cups, so we do our level best to stay as close to those two items as much as possible.

But before you know it, Regis and Kathie Lee are on, signaling it's time to get your sorry hide outside and start feeding cattle. Then it's time to get creative and look for some heat outside in the cold.

### Breakin' the breeze

We like to think we can tolerate the cold if we just keep the wind off. At least that's the theory behind coveralls, earlappers and whiskers.

But the wind still penetrates, especially if you're perched atop an old, cold iron tractor.

A couple years ago, I was feeding with an International 460. It wasn't the best winter starting machine.

The tractor's sluggish starting nature did bring two sources of winter heat, though. First, the weather usually warmed up about 10 degrees from the time I'd started cranking in the early a.m. to when it actually started running, and after fighting that tractor for about two hours with a battery charger, two headbolt heaters and a half-dozen glow plugs, my body temperature had risen 10 degrees as well, fired by red-hot anger and sheer frustration.

Still, I felt the need for more heat while I was feeding. A grossly overpriced set of tarps and rods called a "heat house" seemed to be the best option. The plastic sheets and plexi-glass slowed the wind down enough to justify the cost and I figured I had it made, maybe....

### Cozy in the cab

Confident with the cattle market of 1993, I upgraded to a winter feeding tractor with four walls and a roof over the seat. No heater, of course, but talk about an improvement from the old tractor tent.

Still, I felt the need for even more heat.

There seemed to be a lot of heat going to waste from the exhaust manifold. If I only could harness it somehow. I soon came up with a cardboard contraption duct taped along the sides of the tractor, shooting that exhaust right into the cab where I could put it to use.

It was no sauna, but it was considerably cozier. Now, when I'm finished feeding, I bail out of that cab smelling like diesel, coughing up fumes and looking a little green.

But I'm a little concerned about the safety of breathing those fumes. I thought I might try packing along a caged canary like the old time coal miners used to do down in the mine shafts. If the canary keels over, it's time to get some fresh air.

I need to work on the details though. The canaries keep freezing to death.

# Cowboys in space
## Better put some ranchers aboard the next shuttle

Looks to me like NASA ought to be out in cattle country recruiting some good ropers and ranch hands for their next big satellite workin' bee.

I'm sure they've all realized that a few good cowboys could have saved them a lot of grief, not to mention a $404 million-dollar herd-quitting satellite.

Some cowboy common sense and reckless bravery sure would have come in handy on board the space shuttle Columbia a couple of weeks ago. Reports say a little ol' half-ton satellite-on-a-rope broke free from its 12-mile-lariat and went skipping through orbit while astronauts wept.

NASA officials decided to just let the $404 million-dollar renegade run off without even sending a few space boys after it. They said the shuttle didn't have enough fuel to take off in hot pursuit.

Things would've been a lot different with a few cowboys riding the shuttle.

### Space roping

First of all, no cowboy worth his salt would even consider trying to swing a 12-mile-long lariat. Some buckaroos will go as long as 60 feet, but 30 feet is a lot easier to manage and gives you a heck of a lot more control of what's on the other end.

Secondly, the tether that the space geniuses came up with was shoelace thin, according to reports. You don't go leading around a half-ton satellite with a spaghetti string!

We rope a lot of half-ton cows and 1-ton bulls for doctoring and such. We demand at least a three-eighths inch nylon or poly rope. Even our pig-gin' strings are bigger than a shoelace.

It wouldn't make much sense to be ill equipped when dealing with a multimillion-dollar ropee. We gear up pretty good just to save the life of a $200 calf or a $400 cow.

### Lots of try

If there'd have been a few fellas from my branding crew on board the Columbia, they'd still be chasing down that satellite.

60

We're not afraid to build a second, third or 93rd loop if something needs catching. Just get the job done.

The NASA cop-out about a fuel shortage wouldn't have carried water in cowboy country. I've known guys whose gas gauge would be bumping "E" north of Bowman and they'd still push on to Dickinson before gassing up.

Articles said NASA "considered" sending a few space boys out with some wire, tape and tools to retrieve the runaway. My crew wouldn't have waited for their consideration — they'd have scurried out there in full force with a pair of fencing pliers, some black friction tape and a ball of twine.

With one guy biting the ear and another one twisting the tail, they'd have had that satellite patched up and contributing to science in no time at all.

So give us a call, Cape Canaveral. We do good work and it'll likely only cost you $35 and three square meals a day. We'll get our ropes ready in the meantime.

# Room for upgrading
## Soupin' up for the race against spurge

The leafy spurge legacy is long and bitter on the Taylor Ranch.

Like everyone else in North Dakota, we can go out in the pasture and show spurge enthusiasts the birthplace of the pesky vermin on our ranch. Some of us mark the sentimental landmark with a steel fencepost, a salt block or an empty Tordon jug (triple rinsed and punctured, of course).

Old-timers get a little teary eyed as they walk down a yellow-flowered memory lane. "I didn't even know what it was when I first saw it. Before you knew it, it was everywhere. If only I knew..." At this point, even the most hardened of ranchers is crying big crocodile tears and wiping them dry with his latest pink pesticide receipt.

### Sprinkling sprayers

Our success in the weed war against spurge is sadly documented along sprayer row in our pasture. The first meager contribution was a lowly 3-gallon hand sprayer made of brass. From there it jumps to the 100-gallon fiberglass tank.

Mounted on a homemade wooden frame on the back of an "A" John Deere, it was long on volume. But the time it took to stop the tractor, put the PTO pump in gear, jump off, unroll the hose, water the spurge, roll up the hose and climb back on the tractor was putting us way off schedule. The dang stuff was going to seed while we were unrolling the hose!

The spurge was really getting ahead of us and we figured it was time to bring in the big guns. Money was no object. We located a pickup sprayer with a leaky steel tank and 30 feet of bent up booms. We hated to spend the

61

big dollars, but we figured the long-term health of the ranch was worth the $75 we shelled out for it.

### Going overboard

The massive $75 spurge-o-matic was working just fine, but it was awful tough on pickups. It was instant death for whatever you strapped it to. Climbing hills, driving over trees and searching for spurge in the remotest of corners, the poor mule of a pickup was overloaded, overheated and, by the end of the tour de spurge, it was just plain over for that rig.

This year, we really pulled out the stops and upgraded to a three-point sprayer that could be put on our semi-reliable, overworked John Deere 4020. With a fairly tight 200-gallon tank and a complete set of rusted up nozzles, we figured it was well worth the three-figure sum we had to plunk down on it.

I hope it does the trick. I don't know if there's room for another upgrade in the ol' checkbook. It looks like the only way to go is up, and I hear it's tough to get a good helicopter for $300.

# Ultra automation
## A world of easy everything

Engineers aren't leaving much for us humans to do anymore.

We now have more automation in our public restrooms than our ancient civilizations had in their entire empires.

I recently made an assessment of the men's room at a big city airport and I realized just how high tech humans have gotten. We've gotten so proficient with the plumbing in our public potties that you couldn't waste a gallon of water if you wanted to.

We've protected ourselves from our own absent-mindedness. It's pretty much impossible to leave the sink running in our new sensor-driven washrooms. No spigots or knobs to turn, just put your hands under the magic faucet and wait for the rains to come.

No paper towels inadvertently falling on the floor because our hands are dried by hot air machines. You don't have to stress yourself pushing a button, either. Just pass your hand beneath the magic dryer and wait for the wind to blow.

Ever forget to flush? Not a worry any more. Simply back away or stand up and listen to the waters fall.

But the most ingenious little lavatory luxury I saw at the airport was the motorized toilet seat wrapper. Designed to take the worry out of sitting on an airport toilet seat, it stretches a fresh tube of plastic on the seat with the flick of a little red button.

As near as I could tell, they put the plastic on to kind of act like a gasket. Gaskets are a good thing on engine heads and manifolds, why not have a gasket on your toilet seat?

**Technology transfer**

I was intrigued and impressed with the magic sensors and high-tech automation in the airport john, but a little confused why we have so much science in something as lowly as a lavatory.

The place where we really need a little automation is out on the ranch.

The first thing I'd do is place a couple of those infrared faucet sensors on my gravity flow diesel tank. My current technology consists of propping the fuel cap under the trigger on the nozzle. That way I can run do a few other things while the diesel's draining.

Of course, I always return when I see I've returned 10 gallons of precious fossil fuel back to the soil beneath the tractor. A few infrared faucet sensors could keep more fuel in the tractor and less fuel on the ground.

But it's the automatic toilet seat gasket machine where I really see a lot of potential for the ranch. There are gaskets that get changed on a regular basis around our place and having a little red button to push would be right handy.

I'll probably pass on the hot air technology, though. Between me and my neighbors who stop by to visit, we've got all the automatic hot air we can handle.

# Forget holiday shopping
Try holiday shop cleaning

The winter holidays are prime shopping time, but here on the Taylor Ranch, the holidays are prime shop cleaning time.

Shop cleaning is a lot easier on the credit cards than shopping. A few dollars for some garbage sacks and a new broom or two is about all it takes.

The best thing about holiday shop cleaning is the availability of free labor loafing around the dinner table. There's nothing like tossing around a few garbage barrels to aid in the digestion process.

**Mr. Clean**

Holiday cleaning is an especially good idea when you have a brother-in-law who both looks and acts like Mr. Clean. Able to push huge piles of refuse around with the greatest of ease, he takes after dirt like a coyote takes to sheep.

Peeking into the door of our shop, he practically threw up in disgust as he examined the intricate pathways carved through the good stuff, garbage stuff and questionable stuff that littered the floor.

What he didn't realize was the great progress that had been made on the Taylor Ranch shop situation in just the last few years. Soon after mortgaging my soul to the FmHA/RECD/FSA, I built a pole barn complete with a 40-foot by 32-foot slab of concrete to start piling stuff on.

The truly amazing thing was that the 40 by 32 shop replaced Dad's 12-foot-by-20-foot model that successfully had gotten the ranch through the advent of the mechanical age.

It's rather interesting to note that we took everything we needed out of the old shop, moved it into the new shop and the old shop still was packed to the ceiling with "good stuff you might need someday."

**Judgment day**

Before you could say, "Wait a minute, that's a good used oil filter," brother-in-law Mr. Clean was making a pile as high as the door to be hauled and burned in the ranch trash hole.

I kinda know how Dad felt now when I threatened to throw away his prized collection of used head gaskets and bent up nails.

I wiped away a fleeting tear as I saw my 73 empty anti-freeze jugs and 42 pieces of two-by-six board that were shorter than or equal to 11 inches tossed in the pile.

But as I witnessed the progress, I began to cheer up and join in the cleaning party. It was truly a miracle shaping up there on Thanksgiving Day — I could see the floor and I could instantly imagine the potential for actually parking a vehicle or two in out of the snow and cold.

After torching the bags of balled up plastic twine and the boxes of boxes, I smiled at Mr. Clean and accepted a crushing handshake of congratulations from him.

Actually, I hardly can wait for Christmas. I think we'll tackle the tack room in the barn. I've got a dandy collection of used A.I. sleeves and empty feed sacks just jumping toward the empty trash barrel.


# Do tractors fit under the tree?
## Life beyond the Santa Claus years

Dear New Holland Headquarters,

Allow me to introduce myself. I'm the guy in the cowboy hat whose words surround the big ad you buy on page No. 7 in *Agweek* magazine.

I write about the lighter side of going broke in the cow business — your advertising copy editors write about the fine attributes of your skid steer loaders, GENESIS tractors with SuperSteer FWD axles and your Versatile 82 Series 4WDs.

First, I must compliment you on your excellent choice of magazines for your hard-hitting advertisements.

Second, I need to tell you why I'm writing. It's getting close to Christmas and since I've gotten older, I've quit writing to Santa Claus. That jolly old elf was pretty good to me, but he never did come through on the big-ticket items I'd asked for.

Lots of toys and games, but never any shiny hand-made saddles or new four-wheel-drive pickups. Now that I've learned how the world works, you know — money, marketing, ambition, creativity — I've opted to write to you instead of Santa Claus during this season of generosity.

## A holiday proposal

I've been thinking about innovative ways your company could get into the spirit of giving this Christmas. Then it dawned on me — a gutsy, glitzy new cooperative advertising campaign between Cowboy Logic, *Agweek* and New Holland.

To start with, I'd get up on Christmas morning, dash out to the shop in my sock feet and find a New Holland Super Boom skid-steer loader, a 70 series GENESIS tractor and a Versatile 82 Series 4WD (which would be too big to fit in the shop, but we could park it outside so we could push a little snow with its shiny new dozer blade attachment).

Then we'd begin our new advertising strategy for New Holland's penetration into the poor, broke rancher market.

## Firsthand testimonials

I'd immediately start writing columns about all the great things I could do with my tough, dependable New Holland equipment. And you could tell your advertising agency to take a well-deserved break. We'd just fill your ad space with action photographs of me tooling around in that new skid-steer loader and those high horsepower tractors.

That Super Boom skid-steer would be a dandy addition to the ranch. I finally could begin lowering the manure floor in my barn and quit bumping my head on the ceiling all the time.

I'm always getting into tight spots when I'm feeding cattle out in the hills, and my testimonials on the turning radius of the GENESIS tractor is bound to boost sales. The Versatile 4WD might be a little more tractor than I need, but it's best to be a little overhorsed when you're baling in the mud and hauling hay in the snow, I say.

Hopefully you'll get this letter in time to deliver the goods before Christmas. If not, I'd settle for New Years. Remember, it's better to give than to receive, and giving me the chance to advertise your equipment will surely make 1997 a prosperous new year for you and yours.

*Author's note: Ford New Holland did come through with a tractor for me, but it was a 3-inch-long toy one. They appreciated my complimentary corporate name dropping, but they didn't think it deserved an $80,000 tractor reward. Oh well, ya gotta try.*

# Pass the hammer, please

## Computer repair is a bit more delicate than tractor repair

It's like a sickness. No matter how little I know about some machine or piece of equipment, I always feel compelled to fix it myself when it's broken.

It could be something in my self-sufficient, "I don't need nobody" nature, or it could be that I'm just too cheap to hire someone who knows what they're doing.

Ever since the days of sod huts and homesteads, us folks on the land have been proud of our hermitlike independence and ability to get along on our own. No need for carpenters or saw mills when you can just cut up a few blocks of grass and build your own home out of dirt and roots.

Our ancestors broke their own horses, patched their own harness and fixed their own wagons. So when cars and tractors came along, they felt obligated to become their own auto mechanics as well.

### New tools, new uses

I, too, am one of those self-taught experts in everything from mechanics to plumbing to electrical wiring. And now, the information age has forced me to expand my list of self-reliant job skills to include computer upgrade expert.

Ambitious, but incompetent, I recently tore into my computer just like it was a hay baler or a John Deere tractor. I even used the same tools, two screwdrivers and a pair of needle-nosed Vise-Grip pliers.

The guts of my computer looked a little more delicate than the other things I work on out in my shop, but I didn't let that shake my confidence. I figured anyone who could put new bearings in a baler should be able to put a new modem and a CD-ROM in a computer.

Like most of my projects, I put the instruction manual aside for later reference, preferring to learn as I go. That way, after I've made a big mistake I can refer to the manual and quickly identify how it should have been done in the first place.

There were a few things that I really liked about being a computer mechanic. First, I stay relatively grime-free, and the less grease I got on me, the better I felt. Second, none of the screws were locked tight with rust and dirt. My WD-40 can stayed put on the shelf, for a change. And last, but not least, I didn't have to stand on my head and scrape the skin off my knuckles to perform any of the maneuvers.

However, some things never change when it comes to my repair efforts. I did my job, put on the cover, powered up the computer, and neither the modem nor the CD-ROM worked.

Now, when that happens in my tractor projects, I either reach for a hammer or reach for a telephone and call a real mechanic.

For the computer, I compromised. I made telephone call, but it was to the supplier to order a computer-sized hammer. Now the only question is how hard I should swing it.

# Meandering
## Rain makes for angular mowing

The shortest distance between any two points is a straight line. It must have taken a real rocket scientist to come up with that little gem of knowledge.

Personally, I picked up on that lesson of logic in high school geometry class and I've never forgotten it. I seem to have lost track of how the scientific phenomena of the universe can be explained with polyhedrons, but I guess some things are just easier to remember than others.

The two points/straight line theorem, however, gets daily use. Whether I'm out driving, fencing or chasing cows, I'm always on the lookout for a straight line.

Lately, though, it's been a real challenge. After the last several weeks, my self-abridged theorem states, "the shortest distance between any two points is a straight line, unless, of course, there's 6 or 8 inches of water between you and the other point. Then the shortest distance is more of a long curving half circle that might actually be as long as the shoreline of Lake Superior."

### Water everywhere

It's been a real year of extremes here on the Taylor Ranch. First, we had the severe blizzard season, then we had the severe scorching drought season, and now we're in the middle of the severe rain and thunderstorm season.

We went from no rain in May to some rain in June to 9 inches of rain in the last three weeks of July. Of course, it's hard for a sand dune rancher to complain about precipitation. The pastures have never been greener and the sight of tall, lush grass warms my heart.

The hay land is another story. Our sub-irrigated hay meadow more closely resembles flood irrigated meadow. No drainage ditches in this impromptu irrigation project, though. Nowhere for this water to go but on my tires.

And nowhere at all to mow straight lines and create nice, straight fields.

## Polygonal fields

Call me old fashioned, but I like square fields. Give me a nice, square 40 acres or a good, rectangular 80 and I'm happy. Heck, I can even accept a 20-acre rhombus. Pretty much any old parallelogram will do.

Just don't make me mow, rake and bale a 17-sided, 33-acre polygon. But, this year, polygons are pretty much the rule on our hay meadows.

Every little dip is full of water and needs to be mowed around, making for a wide variety of corners and angles.

The sharper corners aren't so bad if I'm lucky enough to get the 460 International with the power steering, but there's nothing more frustrating than a bunch of knife-edged, 15-degree corners when I'm navigating the "A" John Deere. No need to work out on the Soloflex machine after a day with that armstrong steering system.

But I should be careful not to complain too much about my moist, 17-sided hay fields. They do tend to produce a few bales, despite their irregular design.

Back in the drought of 1988, we mowed a lot of nice, square fields. Just one drawback — no hay.

# Making a parts run
## When a sprint becomes a marathon

Screeeeeeee! Errrrrrrg! Yup, another bearing had gone on to roller bearing heaven in ol' Yeller, my hay baler.

I was due for a breakdown. The forecast was for rain and I had about 20 bales left to roll up on a piece of hayland that I'd been working on for what seemed like years.

I backed ol' Yeller into the shop and gassed up the car for the next morning's parts run. Just a quick trip to the dealership and I'd be back baling before the neighbors even noticed my withering windrows.

### Nothing new

Running for parts is nothing new for me and ol' Yeller. This wasn't our first rodeo.

I had saved ol' Yeller from the grips of machinery salvage at an auction sale several years ago. It sat in a line of machinery looking kind of forlorn like an abused puppy at the dog pound.

But, like Charlie Brown shopping for a Christmas tree on Christmas eve, I saw potential in this baler that looked about as scraggly and needleless as Chuck's pick of the evergreens. A little tinsel and a few ornaments, and it could be a whole different specimen.

So I did the deal for a mere $3,900, and I smiled all the way home as I drove by the folks out in the hayfields with their shiny $20,000 baling machines. Sure it was rusting, old and showed some wear, but it was mine.

I trimmed my Charlie Brown baler with some tinsel bearings and ornamental sprockets. I even strung a new roller chain on it and I contemplated putting a star up on its top.

The old machine took on a whole new light and it even made a pretty nice bale — fairly round with nice hard edges.

### Ongoing maintenance

But ol' Yeller's service comes at a price. It requires lots of TLM, tender loving maintenance. It's a continual process of inspection and repair.

It's not that I mind a little TLM, it's just that the down time required for upkeep is getting me down because my hay isn't getting put up.

And it wouldn't be so bad if I could just get everything I needed for a repair job in less than eight trips. As it is, I sometimes meet myself coming and going on the stretch of road between me and the parts vendors.

I had my last repair job supplied in a mere three trips and 28 phone calls. But, alas, I'd forgot to pick up the dang spacer thingamajig that goes between the bearing and the roller. It looked like it should cost about 52 cents.

I sure didn't want to drive another 20 miles for a 52-cent part. But, luckily, my guess was wrong. It actually cost $4.13. I still wasn't sure if a $4 part warranted another trip to town.

So, for good measure, I decided to pick up an $80 sprocket and bushing. It was a new record — four trips, a fixed-up baler and none of the guilt of making a $4 parts run.

# Fire in the hole
## Hot slag adds excitement to acrobatic welding

Some occupations just naturally go hand in hand. If you're a politician, you're probably a lawyer as well. If you're a journalist, it may help to be a bit of a photographer. And if you're a rancher, it's crucial to be a welder.

It's just the way things are, I guess, because politicians need to work with laws, journalists need to snap a few photos for their articles, and ranchers always need to patch up and stick together their old junk machinery.

### Holding on

Welding talents are born out of necessity on the ranch.

Long rusty lines of faded green, yellow, and red implements have turned most of us into master metalworkers capable of getting more life from our worn-out, overstressed steel than one would think mechanically possible.

There's nothing I enjoy more than backing up a piece of old junk to the shop and spending a nice, sunny haying day making sparks and burning a little paint off a newly shattered piece of steel.

I take a lot of pride in laying a nice, straight bead of weld atop a crack with a steady hand and pinpoint precision.

However, I have plenty of welds that aren't even worth chipping the slag off of. These are usually the ones that run straight up and down or defy gravity on the underside of some steel plate. We affectionately call these erratic gobs of molten slag "bird crap welds," for their obvious physical characteristics.

## Laying a bead

The other day, I had an especially tough spot on a mower to get at with my magical arc. It was a stand-on-your-head-and-wrap-your-leg-around-the-PTO-shaft kind of a welding job.

I'd just purchased 5 pounds of specially formulated vertical overhead welding rods for the task. I was pretty excited about these new electrodes.

At last, I could weld above my body with confidence. I was sure that these rods not only would allow me to create a stronger bond from my precarious position, they would allow me to work worry-free, eliminating the possibility of hot slag bathing my arms and chest.

I dressed appropriately — helmet, yellow fuzzy chore gloves and a ragged old jean jacket that I put on backwards for the utmost in frontal protection. I wasn't 2 inches into my first overhead bead when I quickly learned that these new and improved vertical rods were anything but spark – and slag-free.

As soon as I smelled burning flesh, I dropped my welding stick, began patting my chest frantically and started to roll out from under the molten mower. Unfortunately, my backward smock had about as much mobility as a straitjacket.

By the time I got the jacket off and shook the slag out of the tails of my shirt, it was a complete loss. Twenty-seven years worth of manly chest hair went up in smoke. What a waste.

Luckily, though, I hear hairless chests are the latest rage in the male modeling world. Now if my pectorals were just a little more muscular.

*Author's note: After running this column I received a really nice sympathy card from the Morrison County, Minn., Farm Service Agency office. The card read "May memories comfort you," and the gals wrote, "We know how important hair on a man's chest is! Hope it grows back soon." Thanks for the sympathy ladies. It has.*

# Tractor shopping time
What's for sale sometimes is the same
as what you've already got

Cattle prices are looking up, so I'm thinking about upgrading some of my haying equipment. Yup, I'm tossing around the idea of going from a 1947 model tractor to something a little sportier from the late 1950s or early 1960s.

Normally, I wouldn't even consider doing something so extravagant, but I don't think the "A" John Deere's are going to make another summer.

The two A's constantly were taking turns breaking down throughout the season, and Dad, the hired hand, the neighbors, all the local two-cylinder mechanics and I took turns tweaking them back into running order.

I don't know what the problem is with those old green machines. They're only 50 years old — they really should run better than that.

## Shopping around

So I've been on the lookout for some new horsepower. And I've been thinking of going red this time around. Now, Dad's always been a green tractor man, but I have no allegiances. Just give me something cheap that'll run and has a parts outlet somewhere in North America.

I've already got one 460 International, so I thought it would make sense to get another. It always makes sense to have pairs of tractors so you can rob parts from one to get the other one rolling. Plus, I already know where to find all the dipsticks and grease zerks on those 460s.

But, most importantly, the 460 fits my price range. On some lots, the only thing you can find for less than $3,000 is a used lawn tractor. And most of them don't even have a 540 p.t.o.

## A real find

Last week, I spotted an old 460 sitting on a dealer's lot between a few of those new $80,000 front-wheel-assist rigs. It was practically calling out to me.

On closer inspection, I found out it was a gas model. I preferred a diesel, but I figured a gas probably would start better when I was out haying on those frosty October days.

The dealer saw me eyeing the old unit. He came out, offered me the key and said, "Wanna take it for a spin?"

I'm more used to turning ignitions with a screwdriver or a pocketknife, but I took the key and said, "Sure, what the heck."

I turned the key and started cranking on the motor. Nothing. We pulled the choke out. We pushed the choke in. We checked it for gas and made sure the gas line was open. But it wasn't long before we ran out of battery.

So we started up an $11,000 tractor to give my $2,500 dream machine a pull. It started and stopped. We pulled it again. Finally, we had it running and I took it for spin. I kind of liked the rough sounding gears, worn-out clutch and sputtering engine, but I had to tell the dealer that I wasn't all that interested any more.

He asked me why and I had to tell him. "We got all the pull-type tractors we need on our ranch. I really had my heart set on a self-propelled unit!"

# A tractor's fate
## Ranch life is a tough life

Tractors, like people, never quite know where life will take them.

I feel a real kinship with my tractor and sometimes I kind of worry about her happiness. I think it's fair to worry about her since I spend more time with her than anyone else I know.

I'm sure that I'm correct in calling my John Deere 4020 a "her." I'm like a ship captain christening his favorite seagoing vessel with a feminine name in admiration of her sleek lines and smooth curves.

Granted, the 4020's curves aren't as smooth as they used to be. A thousand annual hours of hard labor on the Taylor Ranch have really taken their toll.

When I got her at that auction sale back in '93, she was a good-looking thing with low hours and a youthful spring in her step. I do what I can to take care of her, but I can't help but feel like she'd have had a better life if I'd never raised my bidding hand on that fateful summer day.

### Something better

She had been living the good life. A kindly farmer had used her for some light tillage and a little row crop cultivation. Winter was an easy season of pushing light fluffy snow around the owner's homestead.

I wasn't the only guy checking her out at that auction sale. One bigtime farmer with a fleet of four-wheel-drive monsters was eyeing her up and down. He needed a "little" tractor to power a grain auger.

I think there was a hobby guy who needed something to carry a round bale out to his horse and llama every 12th day in the winter, and a lawyer with a ranchette wanted something to clean his driveway so he could get his four-wheel-drive sport utility vehicle out to the highway.

Me, I'd given up on starting my 460 International in anything colder than room temperature. I needed something that would start when it was 20 below zero to feed cows and bounce around on that cab-splitting mine field of treacherous frozen cow pies.

In the off-season, all it had to do was bale hay in axle-deep hogwallows, spray spurge on steep, brushy side hills, push 10 feet of manure through a 9-foot gate and run down the road with 6 or 8 tons of hay dragging along behind.

So I did what I had to do. I stood by it all morning and knocked out anyone else who looked at it with interest. When the auctioneer came around, I had the farmer, the lawyer and the hobby guy tied up and thrown in the back of a silage wagon.

I got her bought, brought her home and the rest is hard-luck history for that poor tractor.

Someday, though, her life will end and she'll take her place as an organ donor in that cemetery of a salvage yard. I sincerely hope that her spirit goes to that light duty hobby farm in the sky because she already knows what hell is like.

# Fully certified
## The private pesticide applicator's rite of passage

It wasn't quite as exciting as getting my driver's license when I was 15, but several years ago, I became a certified private applicator of restricted use pesticides.

Fully decorated and honored with a nontransferable yellow paper wallet card, I was approved by the state department of agriculture and the university extension service to buy a little spray for my leafy spurge crop.

But like all licenses, it expires and has to be renewed. Last week, my number was up and I had to forgo an afternoon of ranching to renew my standing with the pesticide control board.

### Hittin' the books

Private applicator certification is designed to be a three-or four-hour activity with a dynamic multi-media presentation by the county agent and a grueling 30 question written test.

The agent had enough audio, video and slide presentation equipment to open a small electronics store. Looking over the tangled conglomeration of equipment, I finally figured out why we call these people "extension agents." I think it's directly derived from their use of "extension cords."

The meeting wasn't confined to on-screen activities. We also were given a few handouts to read through. The following is the list of light reading materials for wannabe chemical sprayers:   Circular W-253, AE-73 (revised), Bulletin No. 63, A-1099, Bulletin 49, AE-888, AE-1112, AE-1113, AE-1114, AE-1115, AE-1116, A-947 (revised), AE-1052, AE-1041, WC-751 (revised), PP-622 (revised), E-1143, EB-45 (revised) and A-1058.

We also got a few anonymous, numberless documents like the Pesticide Act, Chapter 4-35 North Dakota Century Code with regulations as amended, some ag engineering pesticide calibration formulas and the 152-page manual, "Applying Pesticides Correctly." As a bonus prize, we got a washing machine magnet, a.k.a. HE-382, with detailed instructions on how to launder your contaminated clothing.

The handouts were the key to success in passing the examination. All the answers were there in that 3-inch-thick pile of papers. It was a lot of information for a fella who just wanted to spray a few acres of rangeland for leafy spurge.

### Broadened knowledge

I'm now one of the few cowboys in my neighborhood who can explain the ounces equals gallons method of calibration and give you the details on timing the use of Lorsban 4E-SG for the control of orange wheat blossom midge.

And I picked up one particular fact of interest dealing with the LD-50 ratings of pesticide toxicity. As explained by our agent, an LD-50 tells you the lethal dose of a chemical needed to kill 50 percent of a given population. Or, as he said, "how much of a pesticide would the people in this room have to drink to kill 50 percent of you."

That left me wondering how they discover these LD-50 ratings. I'm not completely sure, but I think they might be doing it at these private applicator meetings with the extension-brewed coffee.

I might have been hallucinating, but I thought I saw a few Tordon jugs sitting next to the Folger's. However, since I'm still around to talk about it, they must not have discovered the lethal dose that day.

Either that, or I'm part of the lucky 50 percent of the population.

# Pull, pull the rope
## The labor of 'labor-saving' devices

If I have to pull the rope one more time on a little engine that drives the gears that runs the blades and tines and sprockets that supposedly make life easier for us, I may just drop from the exhaustion of such an easy life.

We've all had our patience tested by those little one-cylinder wonders that retired the grain shovel, the ax, the grass scythe and the garden spade. Hopefully, we all kept our manual implements on hand to get the tasks done in the event of internal combustion failure.

### Swing the saw

Take my chain saw, for example.

I've always appreciated the simple, sweaty labor of swinging an ax and felling the trees that threaten my fences, or cutting the sticks that show promise as gate posts or corral rails. Despite my fondness for the Paul Bunyan romance of old-fashioned logging, I decided that my time was too valuable to chop at trees when I could buzz them down with a chain saw.

So instead of spending an hour clearing timber with an ax, I find myself felling trees in a mere 15 minutes with my handy dandy chain saw. Of course, I spend at least 45 minutes mixing gas and two-cycle oil, filling the tanks, adjusting the chain and fine tuning the choke.

When pulling the starting rope for 10 minutes straight, I usually can tell by the smell that my anti-perspirant has lost all its anti-ability — not the sweat reduction I expect from such a labor saver. I really could use three hands to operate the outfit. I've contemplated holding the saw against the tree while engaging the sprocket and pulling the rope to then turn the chain and cut the tree.

Most times, I scrap that idea and decide to just swing the saw at the tree like an ax. When that fails to work, I take a few steps back and throw the dang thing at the tree. Timberrrrrrrrr!

Yard and garden miniature two-cycle motors may be temperamental, but nothing can beat a 3-horsepower lawn mower engine for sheer frustration. Small engine mechanics make a pretty comfortable living off of guys like me who give up on motors that usually only need a spark plug, some fresh gas and the secret $10 tuneup.

I'm convinced that there is a secret reset button on lawn mowers and only accepted members of the small engine mechanics fraternity know where it's at. Ten dollars later, the motor is purring like a kitten, reset for another 25 hours of trouble-free operation.

Nothing has given me as much trouble this year as our garden tiller. I gave it my own Taylor tune-up – change the gas, change the oil, clean the air cleaner and check the spark plug. But since I couldn't locate the secret reset button, it barely would run.

My poor mechanical methods proved to be a real boon for our garden, though. Since I never got the garden tilled, we never got the tomatoes planted. Yes, a temperamental tiller saved our garden from sudden death in a late frost.

Thanks, Briggs & Stratton.

# Onedownmanship
## Outdoing by underdoing and suffering

You've probably heard of oneupmanship, the practice of outdoing someone else by going one up on them.

But, among my cohorts in the ranching business, we tend to practice "onedownmanship." It's the art of underdoing a fellow rancher and going one less.

In short, we live to suffer, and then we like to brag about it.

### Tractor shopping

A prime method of suffering is achieved by putting together the oldest, most obsolete line of haying equipment possible.

We're really big fans of the International "M," the John Deere "A" and other letters of the alphabet made famous by tractor manufacturers. It's even better when we can get our hands on something that no longer is made so we really can suffer as we search for parts. Olivers, Minneapolis Molines and Co-ops are especially prized.

Sometimes, we'll amplify our suffering by choosing to forgo the fixing of certain luxuries like mufflers, radiators and seats.

Then we can really brag to the neighbors about how we can't hear anymore because of a perforated muffler, how we always carry an extra water jug for our radiator and order our Stop Leak by the case and how our lower back has been thrown completely out of joint by not replacing the back rest on the seat.

We also work as a self-regulating support group to make sure no one steps out of line and buys something a little too new.

The other day, one of my friends was looking into a tractor that was just 35 years old. By the time I got done chastising him about the outfit's power steering, live power takeoff and dual hydraulics, he was too embarrassed to even think about buying it.

Friends don't let friends buy something too modern or dependable.

## Win/win situations

Not everybody in agriculture follows the philosophy of onedownmanship. Some farmers and ranchers actually buy new equipment and, believe it or not, they even like to show it off.

I went to one farmers place recently to check out a hot lead on an "A" John Deere that he was ready to sell. The two I have are starting to show the wear of 10 million hard hours, so I thought it might be time to bring in a new recruit.

The seller was a pretty large operator and I don't think he understood my excitement over his "A." Before we went to look at the Johnny Popper, he took me to the shed to show me his "two new toys."

There stood a big, brand new green combine and four-wheel-drive tractor. I guess they were kind of nice, and I reckon they should be since he had nearly $300,000 invested in the two rigs. I tried to hide my distaste for such new equipment and politely muttered, "Well I'll be darned, those look like a heckuvadeal there."

Then we got to the real iron, the mighty "A" that was up for grabs. After a little haggling, we got him down to $900.

The deal was struck, and, although it seems odd, everybody was happy. Me, I had a new "A" to rub in the face of my friends who've really had a tough time finding any 1940s-era haying equipment, and the seller, he had $900 to put toward another $130,000 tractor that he could show to his friends. There's nothing like achieving a little win/win in the business of agriculture.

# Looks ain't everything

# Sunny side up
## Turning and burning under the big orange fireball

There's a few things fair skinned, Norwegian cowboys ought not do in the good ol' summertime.

Never leave a building bareheaded, never wear less than one long-sleeve shirt on your back, and never, ever wear shorts unless you're in bed under the covers. Unfortunately, I broke every one of these sacred rules last weekend, and I've got the scars to prove it.

I spent the Fourth of July in Detroit Lakes, Minn., and I've come to the conclusion that fun in the sun isn't so fun if you've spent the last 25 years of your life covered up by denim.

I've been working for years on a suntan that extends down to my neck and as far up as my wrists. But a little peer pressure had me thinking that my tan lines were a bit too conservative.

So I decided to loosen up a little. Now I've turned the remainder of my body a bright cherry red and I still don't fit in with the beach crowd.

### Brown as a berry

Cowboys may be "brown as a berry from riding the prairie," but no self-respecting cowboy was ever out riding the range bare chested in a pair of shorts. Then again, most cowboys don't spend much time at a beach where "coolness" is inversely related to the amount of clothes you wear on your back.

I went with the standard blue jeans, long-sleeved shirt and cowboy hat my first night on the shoreline of Detroit Lakes. Needless to say, I wasn't perceived as being too cool by the girls whose bikinis weren't big enough to make a decent shop rag.

So the next day, I went with shorts, a T-shirt and a cowboy hat. Still not too cool. Must have been the hat.

By the next day, we were tubing on the Ottertail River and I'd lost all my ranch inhibitions, not to mention my common sense. I was floating down the river wearing nothing but a pair of swimming trunks.

Sunglass sales were brisk along the river that day. Anyone caught without a pair was quickly blinded by a blur of white skin maneuvering the current in a black inner tube.

### Well-baked body

By the end of the tubing run, I was grilled to a nice crisp medium well. Someone should have grabbed a spatula and flipped me over midway down the river.

78

The massive amount of sunscreen I smeared on my lily white rancher body didn't do a whole lot of good. Maybe without the SPF 15 sunscreen, I'd have burned 15 times worse. That would have put me in the french fry category.

My only prior experience with tanning is with cattle hides, and those cattle whose hides get tanned usually have gone on to the great beyond. Me, I'm not quite ready for the great beyond yet, so I'd best keep my hide raw for awhile.

# North Dakota's love connection

Ah, spring is in the air.

When the meadowlarks begin to sing and a young man's heart turns to calving out cows and planting crops.

In other parts of the world, spring is the season when a young man's heart turns to love and romance. But out in the countryside, a man's got to get the farming and ranching done before he can think of anything as frivolous as courting.

But once the calves are on the ground and the seed is in the dirt, thoughts surely will turn to attracting the attention of the opposite sex.

And when that time comes, things get busy for the Towner Area Young Rancher's Bachelor Club (TAYRBC) as we strive to meet our membership goal of zero. The group's goal may seem a little regressive, but just like golf scores, low is better.

## A social crisis

The TAYRBC was formed several years ago to tackle the bachelor crisis head on in Towner, N.D., population 667 (348 married people, 282 children, 46 bachelors and too few bachelorettes to even bother counting).

In the past, local bachelors were a rather unorganized lot with little coordination or group strategy. However, once the boys in Herman, Minn., made the headlines with their "Today" show interview, the local bachelors decided it was time to unite and make some headlines of their own.

Like our counterparts down under in Australia who sponsor "B & S (bachelor and spinster) parties," single young males in our hemisphere are beginning to organize events called "Bachelor Days."

Herman's gathering probably has gotten the most press, but I've heard talk of an up-and-coming annual event in Napolean, N.D., that could give Herman a run for the money.

In Towner, though, we've decided to let those other guys handle the carnivals and street fairs. We've opted to concentrate on nutrition and lobbying.

In particular, we're working hard to bring back the old-fashioned basket social. You know, where the single gals would fix up some tasty vittles in a picnic basket and the local bachelors would bid on the meal and its anonymous preparer. High bid got both the food and the female company.

The basket social may be tough to revive with the general loss of food preparation skills in our population. I know if I had to prepare the basket, bids would come mighty slow. There's something about a TV dinner that fails to attract a frenzy of big-dollar bidding action.

Of course, if the basket preparer's identity isn't so anonymous and the desire to dine with him or her is strong enough, it is possible to get caviar bids on frozen fish sticks.

Our second area of concentration is in the lobbying arena. Like most groups, the TAYRBC has an extensive government affairs strategy.

But rather than waste our time in Washington, D.C., or at the state Capitol in Bismarck, our bachelor lobbyists spend the lion's share of their time pleading to local school boards and the hiring departments of rural hospitals.

There aren't a lot of job opportunities in small rural communities for the career women of today. One thing we do have, however, is schools and clinics. And if there are any hiring decisions to be made, the TAYRBC wants to have some influence on whether they hire an old married guy or a young female college grad.

Over the years, school teachers and nurses have not only made ranching a lot less lonely, they've kept a lot of outfits from going broke when cattle prices headed south.

It's not just a matter of loneliness, it's a matter of economic revival.

So if you know of any young ladies battling spring fever this season, have them contact our vice president of member relationships. If everyone pitches in, we can get that membership figure to zero and burn our charter at the last bachelor's wedding.

# Wedding shopping for those who have everything
## Everything you ever needed for ranchin'

There seems to be another little burst of weddings coming up this fall that I ought to attend. Going to weddings means buying wedding presents and picking out appropriate presents can be a problem.

Most couples are bound to get at least five toasters, 40 or so bath towels and enough cute little wall hangings to pull the sheetrock right off of the walls if they were all nailed up. Because of this madness, I prefer to buy wedding gifts that are a bit more unusual and much more useful.

## His and hers accessories

It isn't unheard of for me to head to a wedding with an inconspicuously wrapped pair of his and hers cattle sortin' sticks for the prospective ranchers and ranch wives. His and hers sortin' sticks will be remembered for years to come as they eat dust, slosh through mud and dodge ornery cows together.

Sortin' sticks can be used by ranchers to point out the blaze-face cow in the middle of the pen for their new wives to peel out of the herd. You know, the one with the bad eye and the upside-down eartag that used to read 826.

"You can't miss her, there she is right there," he'll say as his wife begins to wish she'd married an accountant.

By the same token, when the rancher starts waving his stick wildly and yelling, "Why'd you let her get by you?," the hers model sortin' stick can be swatted across his backside right before she gives it a bionic toss over the fence and informs him that he can sort his own dang cows. His and hers sortin' sticks are a definite wedding gift couples can bond over for years to come.

Another classic wedding gift for the agriculturally inclined is a pair of his and hers Vise-Grips. These tools will give couples a chance to get a grip on their new tandem lifestyle and help hold them together through the tough times.

His Vise-Grips can be used to enhance their marriage by allowing him to complete those "honey do" projects around the home. These are the projects that are suggested with a "Honey, can you do this?" or "Honey, can you do that?"

Her Vice-Grips probably will be needed to improvise when the "honey do" projects go continually undone. She can lock them onto the faucet to replace the broken hot water handle or use them to hold together the broken bathroom door knob. She also might need them to get out of the field pickup because the inside door handle is missing and the window won't roll down for her to use the outside handle.

## New breed of registries

Many couples register at different stores for their potential wedding gifts. This cuts down on duplicate presents or towels that don't match the overall bathroom decor. People buying gifts do need to know where the couple is registered or else they'll make those interior decorating faux pas anyway.

I'm sure that registering at big department stores is a handy thing to do, but for me, I'd rather they registered down at the local vet clinic or livestock supply store. If the couple is getting married in May or June, why not get them a new multidose syringe and a couple hundred doses of seven way to get the calves vaccinated at branding time. Fall weddings could call for nice gifts of pre-conditioning vaccines or a 5-gallon can of pour-on to rid the cow herd of any lice infestations.

As far as matching and decor goes, registering at the livestock supply store would deter unsightly mistakes like getting a squeeze chute that didn't match your head gate or was incompatible with your crowding tub. Imagine the horror of getting a bunch of red, green and brown portable panels that not only clashed, but wouldn't even match up on the ends.

The right formulation of cattle minerals and coordinated bale feeders are sure to get newly - married ranch couples off on the right foot.

Just remember, if you're wrapping up some vaccine to give at the next wedding, throw in an ice pack.

# Free help and easy plans
## Saving time usually spends it

Never pass up a shot at free labor. When my brother-in-law comes out to visit and innocently asks, "is there anything I can help you with today?" I practically trip over myself getting him into the shop, out to the barn or into the pickup, so we can get right to work.

The nice thing about my brother-in-law is he's everything I'm not — big as a horse, strong as an ox and as patient as an oyster.

His arms are as big around as my thighs and he's got biceps on top of his biceps. But this ex-Marine who works out at the gym every morning is more than just might.

When a task has gone completely haywire and I'm ready to call it quits out of sheer disgust, he just buckles down and gets the job done. He could spend a whole day untangling extension cords, taking knots out of shoelaces or driving rusty nails into hard oak railroad ties.

The last time he came out, I knew just where I needed his strong arms and cool head — out on the fence line.

### The easy way

If you've ever seen a group of western jokesters called the Riders in the Sky, you've heard the saying, "that would be the easy way, but it wouldn't be The Cowboy Way."

Well, I thought I had a plan for rolling out three new barb wires that would be the easy way, but it turned out to be the cowboy way. In retrospect, the plan had all the intelligence of a bowl of oatmeal.

82

The plan was to have three rolls of wire spinning on a pipe in the back of the pickup. We'd just pull the wire a quarter of a mile to the corner post.

It would have made more sense to tie the wire off and drive the pickup, but there were too many trees to motor a vehicle along the fence. I figured two guys should be able to pull a couple hundred pounds of measly wire.

Dragging barbed wire through the brush and across the knolls wasn't as easy as I thought. Those three wires were doing all the work of a chain saw and a ditch witch with us providing the horsepower.

## Twisted and tangled

After an hour or two of wasted effort, we figured something must be wrong. Retracing our steps, we found a tangled-up ball of brand new barbed wire that just about brought tears to my eyes.

I was ready to start cutting and splicing, but my patient partner talked me into helping him untangle the mess. That was pretty brave of him since his fencing attire for the day consisted of shorts, a sleeveless T-shirt and a pair of tennis shoes.

When we got done a couple hours later, he looked like he'd just run crossways through a keg of nails. But success was ours—we'd just turned a three hour jog into a six hour marathon. The cowboy way.

WARNING. Do not attempt this stunt at home. The characters described are untrained professionals. Stupidity fencing is not recommended for those under the age of 12 or over the intelligence threshold of 35.

# Identifying the individualistic
Heavy metal rockers and cattle have a lot in common

You meet some interesting people when you're out on the road.

The other night, I found some real interesting folks at a rock 'n' roll bar in southern Dakota.

The band was banging away on some tunes that would have sent a gopher to his hole. They were louder than an "R" John Deere and the guitars were squealing like a roller bearing gone bad. No wonder it was called heavy metal.

My friend and I stood there and amused ourselves by trying to guess the gender of the people who were walking by. It was considerably more difficult than gate cutting the steers from the heifers back at the ranch.

Most of the females had crew cuts, the fellas had hair like a sheepdog. Some didn't have any hair at all.

But they were darn sure supporting the cattle industry. Their leather wardrobes had contributed greatly to the high value of cowhides and I think I heard one of their softer melodies attributed to a band called Meatloaf.

## Permanent I.D.

We correctly had guessed the gender of at least one gal and struck up a conversation with her. With calving season soon upon us, our visit quickly turned to systems of identification.

We considered her to be an expert on things like eartagging since her body had been pierced numerous times. Her pierced belly button quickly caught our eye and we quizzed her about its practicality.

She said the procedure involved taking a piece of balin' wire, jabbing it through the navel and tying it off with a bead. Now she couldn't wear anything but half shirts for six months, or else it might get irritated.

That seemed a little impractical here in the frigid Northern climates, but it beats having an irritated belly button I guess.

She said she used to have her nose pierced, but gave up on that. I imagine our winter cold and flu season with its runny noses made a chilly navel seem like a better option than a snotty nose ring.

She had a variety of holes cut in her ear lobes from top to bottom to complete her sense of individuality. No other hardware or tattoos were visible from our vantage point.

I think the next time I go to that dance hall I'll bring a few of my calves with me. I think they'd fit right in.

Cloaked in leather with a plastic ear tag, a metal Bangs vaccination clip and a purebred ear tattoo, they should get right through the door. A nose ring for the bulls, a brisket tag for the replacement females and a freeze brand or a fire brand on the hip should make them just as individualistic as the rest of the customers. But it might be tough getting the cattle to dance to any melodies by Meatloaf.

# Cashy cowboy clothes
## The high cost of old fashion

It's getting pretty costly to be a cowboy these days.

If anyone deserves a break on the cost of their wardrobe, it's cowboys and cattlemen. But it costs us more to be us than almost anyone I know.

The point really was driven home last week when I decided I needed a new pair of cowboy boots.

My old pair was pretty well depreciated. They'd split a couple holes in the side, the heels were just barely hanging on, and the soles (third set) were relying on my threadbare socks to keep my feet off the ground.

There's only so much you can do with saddle soap and shoe shine, so I decided to buy a pair of boots that wouldn't show everyone in church the bottoms of my feet when I knelt for communion.

I figured I deserved a minimum amount of quality, so I passed over the boots made of cardboard and plastic and went for the ones that had a little more of a connection with my colleagues, the cows.

## Sticker shock

I know guys who sold whole calves last spring for less than the price of one pair of boots. I'm sure they sold the hide right along with the rest of the calf, too.

I used to think city kids who spent more than $100 on a pair of tennis shoes were crazy, but you can't be too vocal when you spend almost twice that on a pair of boots that you can't even play basketball in.

But tennis shoes aren't too good for high-impact ranching, either. Sandals aren't worth a hoot for fencing and penny loafers just won't stay on when you're walking through knee-deep muck and manure.

Saddle shoes may sound like ranchy footwear, but you'd get some mighty strange looks if you put on your hat and jeans and wore them to the big cow town hoedown.

With all that practicality and peer pressure staring me in the face, I had no choice but to stick with my heritage and buy the boots.

## What to be

The accessories were just as outrageously priced. Good leather belts and silver belt buckles had price tags like ransom notes and the latest western shirts were made for celebrity incomes. You'd have to sing like Garth Brooks or George Strait to afford the things.

Felt hats were priced a lot higher than the rabbit skins and beaver pelts they supposedly were made from. I've trapped a few furbearers in my day, and I dang sure didn't get the 20X price for the beavers caught in my trapline.

As cashy as it's getting to be a cowboy these days, I'm thinking a lifestyle change might be in order. The new "grunge" look seems to hold a lot of budgetary promise.

Rummage sale season still is going strong and I probably could put together an entire grunge wardrobe for less than $10 from the tip of my scruffy goatee clear down to my untied canvas sneakers.

# Hard luck groomsmen
## Under the dark cloud

The Towner Area Young Ranchers Bachelor club got one step closer to its goal last weekend. The Club's goal, of course, is zero membership, and last week, another one of our comrades cashed in his TAYRBC membership card.

As is the tradition, the TAYRBC served as the color guard for the event. Kind of like when a Marine gets married, except we didn't have the swords to hold over their heads as they walked down the aisle. We tried to whip out our jackknives and use them to form the archway, but it wasn't nearly as dramatic.

The crew standing up in the front of the church with our former bachelor brother had the congregation whispering to each other in a mild state of shock.

"By golly, them boys clean up pretty good," they murmured, remembering the times they couldn't recognize us for the dust, mud, grease and manure we wore. It's amazing what a little soap and water and some rented clothes can do for a guy.

The bride was kind enough to let us wear our boots instead those rock-hard waxy tuxedo shoes. That was a real comfort, considering the amount of time we spent standing up front shifting our weight from one foot to another. Kind of like a restless horse tied to the hitching rail all day long.

### Typically Towner

Us groomsmen members of the TAYRBC did the best we could to walk when we were supposed to walk, stand when we were supposed to stand and dance when we were supposed to dance. It didn't even take a whole lot of prompting from the bride and groom's parents.

But just when we began patting ourselves on the back for our stellar performance, the south Towner black cloud suddenly appeared over our heads, or actually over our limousine.

For us, riding in a limo was like putting a bunch of rangey feedlot cattle in one of those fancy aluminum show trailers that go around to all the bovine beauty contests. We adapted fairly well, even though there were 10 of us in the capacity nine unit.

None of us groomsmen had a very long history of driving dependable cars, so we really were enjoying a ride in what we thought had to be the most dependable vehicle we'd ever ridden in.

No sooner had we kicked back in comfort and confidence than our limo was stalled on Broadway in Minot with both the hood and the trunk popped up. We wouldn't have been surprised if we were driving one of our old patched up jalopies, but we expected more from the stretch limo.

We took it all in stride, though, as we grabbed the cables and recruited a jump start from a two-door Grand Torino with clear plastic and duct tape for a driver's side window. Kind of humbling, but very effective.

It cost us though. We had to trade him our only jar of Grey Poupan.

# Spring stowing
## Easier than spring cleaning and less damaging

Spring is here. The time of year when the meadowlarks sing and the ranchers mop their brow and say, "Whew! I made it through another one!"

Spring is always a welcome time. It's victory time — victory over windchills, snowbanks and ice.

For me, spring is most welcome because it means my old threadbare coveralls made it through another year of hard use. Every fall I drag out those brown duck bibs and make the call — buy new or run the trusty Carhart cuvvies another year.

My decision is usually a little sentimental and a lot financial.

It's hard to break tradition and abandon my old insulated friend with all the right creases in all the right places. They've been with me a long time, seen me through some tough weather and walked home with me a time or two when I was stuck in a snowbank.

They wear the scars of battles with barbed wire, ornery cows and father time.

And, financially, it's tough to trade up until you've completely depreciated the old. Not just "they're kind of faded, full of holes and missing buttons" depreciated.

Coverall depreciation means everything but the zippers have completely evaporated and the pocketful of fencing staples you've been carrying around fall to the ground for lack of a pocket to suspend them.

### Secret of longevity

So as long as there are a few threads hanging together on the old standby bibs and a big price tag on the replacement bibs, I keep on keeping on with the old standbys.

It's surprising how many years you can get out of a pair of coveralls if you take the time to properly care for and store them. When spring comes around, you can't just carelessly toss those things in the washer and fold them away in your footlocker.

The key to conscientious coverall care is keeping them dirty. Nothing can wear out a good pair of coveralls like the vicious spin cycle of an automatic washing machine.

And when those soapy suds go to work you remove all the grease, grime and slime that help hold those threads and seams together. Manure, especially, is the glue that binds.

Plus, you get the added benefits of a weatherproof, protective coating. Kind of like paint on a house, wax on a car or a good coat of varnish on the front deck. Coveralls without a crusty coating are like a roof without shingles.

The "don't wash, just stow" theory goes way beyond coverall care. Try it on your tractors, cars and machinery. Nothing reduces the life of moving metal parts like cleaning and scraping. Take away that protective layer of grease and sludge, and you're looking at instant deterioration.

So I'll be putting my coveralls aside this spring, manure and all, for another summer of storage. They may smell a little gamey right now, but in six months, they should be aired out, crusted over and ready to wear.

Kind of gets me excited for next winter.

# Summer headgear
## Covering up a sun-sensitive scalp

I'm a hat wearer. Spring, summer, winter or fall, I always can be found with some sort of lid on my head.

Some of my best friends wouldn't even recognize me without my hat. The only folks who know what I look like without my lid are people who either have seen me in church, at the supper table or in bed.

Those who have seen me cranially naked know that my days of hard-to-manage hair are long gone. At a mere 27 years of age, I can boast a hairline that's receding like the farmland along Devils Lake.

And when a fella starts seeing more hair in the drain of his bathtub than he does on the top of his head, it's crucially important to keep the old noggin undercover. Especially when the summer sun is shining.

Usually, I wear a wide-brimmed straw cowboy hat, the ultimate in ultraviolet protection. But, in a pinch, a baseball cap will do.

The other day, I was out mowing and the wind was blowing along at about 40 knots. It made one side of the field pretty tough to cut and it made straw hat wearing a real challenge on all sides.

I finally lost my bangora straw hat completely. It hit the ground right in front of the mower and I quickly learned what a sharp sickle can do to a bangora straw. I retreated to the pickup, looking to trade up to more windproof headgear.

### Looking for a spare

I ransacked the pickup in search of a replacement lid. I own hundreds of baseball caps advertising everything from saloons to cattle dewormer. I couldn't find a single one of them.

I knew I couldn't go without. The risk of sunburn ran high. And if the mosquitoes tapped into my skull, I'd be $2^1/_2$ quarts low on my "O" positive by nightfall.

Finally, I found an old, dusty bandana under the seat. I swallowed my pride, shook off the bigger chunks of dirt and tied it around my head.

My hired mowing companion told me I looked like Aunt Jemima. I felt like pouring maple syrup on his head.

I thought I looked more like the surfer dudes I've seen in the movies. "Whoa, cowabunga! This field is bitchin, dude," I said as I climbed back on the tractor.

I couldn't find any waves to ride, but I did stand up and assume the surfer stance on the 460. The surf really was pumping, I was on the endless wave — until I hit a badger hole. I ditched my board and sat back down.

I got into my surfer relaxation mode and began to inhale. "Whoa, dude. This is some really good grass," I exclaimed as I cut through a thick patch of smooth brome and big bluestem. I didn't even have to smoke it to get its comforting benefits.

After a day of surfin' the hay fields in my bandana headgear, I went home and looked in the mirror. Upon seeing my reflection, I went out to the pickup and stuffed a couple of baseball caps under the seat.

# Incognito
## Abandoning the facial hair challenge

You'd have never known it from looking at the picture by my column, but for the last couple months, I've been flirting with facial hair.

I hadn't tried growing a mustache since I was 18 years old. Back then, I wanted to look older. A mustache was a lot cheaper than a fake ID for fellas anxious to pass for 21 and get into the good dance halls.

It was a pretty weak attempt back then, but I figured I'd give it another go this summer.

### Mixed reviews

I started the mustache after a speaking job last spring. From then on, I knew that I wouldn't have to be seen in public for several weeks. I estimated that would give me adequate time to incubate and nurture a healthy little caterpillar beneath my snout.

As I neared the date of my 10-year high school reunion on the Fourth of July, I was kind of glad to have my new mustache. My classmates all had spouses, children and family pets to bring to the event. The least I could do was tote along some new facial hair for them all to admire.

Since then, I've rolled out the new "me" at the state fair, a couple of speaking gigs and numerous on-the-street encounters.

I thought the hair on my lip would allow me to go incognito and slip through the crowds without recognition. But most everybody recognized me just the same. I thought the mustache would make me look a little meaner and more menacing, but my signature grin crept out from beneath the fur and gave away my identity anyway.

Like a president judging his approval rating in the face of scandal, I diligently polled all bystanders to get a feel for the popularity of my new upper lip.

Comments were wide ranging. I was compared with everyone from Sam Elliot and Tom Selleck to Charles Manson and Adolf Hitler. Personally, I thought I most resembled Wyatt Earp, only not dead.

## Cutting room floor

After a three-month trial run, I decided to drop my newfound whiskers and send them down the drain of the sink.

I made the decision to clip based on several factors.

First, it seemed like the mustache was hastening the hair loss on top of my head. It might have been my imagination, but it really looked like I was getting some kind of migratory effect that moved the active follicles from my hairline to my face. I definitely couldn't afford that kind of redirection of active hair growth.

Second, my new habit of mustache tweaking was taking too much time away from the things I really needed to get done. Stroking that 'stache and twirling the ends of it was making my column a full day late to the editors and delayed my entry onto the hayfield by as much as an hour after the noon dinner.

The last straw, though, was a seasonal consideration. You see, it's corn on the cob season, and if you've ever watched a man with a mustache eat a big buttery, messy cob of corn, you'd shave, too.

# Head-scratching thoughts

# Need time to think?
## Try therapeutic hay hauling

All across corporate America, stressed-out executives and schedule-crazy professionals are looking for places to get away from it all and "find themselves."

Even in North Dakota, corporate hideaways are springing up along the banks of the Missouri River and in the hills of the Turtle Mountains. They hope to entice the big city suits to the tranquil countryside where they can slip into some denims and forget about their phone, fax and appointment calendar.

Even us simple folks out here in the country find ourselves suffering from mental fatigue and the stress of time and financial management. In short, we get sick and tired of there not being enough time in the day or enough money in our checking account.

We're supposed to be out here in the country chewing on a blade of grass with a clear mind and a look of peace and love on our face. In actuality, we've got stress in amounts that would make even the busiest executives wince with pain. We've got too many jobs crammed in too little time, too many bills relying on too little income.

Could us folks in boots and jeans find common ground with the people in tailored suits and power ties? Could we find understanding in each other's face as we compare their appointment calendars with our seasonal schedules, their fears centered around profit and loss statements with our dreaded FmHA Farm and Home Plan, Form 431-2?

### A Tom Sawyer trade-off

I was out hauling bales in my John Deere 4020 last week pondering these very questions. My 4020 is a prime place for problem pondering because there's not much else you can do out there once you've mastered the art of holding the steering wheel straight.

This tractor has no radio, no music or disc jockeys to keep you company as you roll down the open road. The cab is in no way soundproof. It's not even mothproof or mouseproof. But it is somewhat windproof, which is a great luxury to this rancher who used to spend the cold weather months bucking the wind atop a 460 International with a ski mask and a scarf.

Despite the downfalls of a noisy, radioless 4020, it's an extremely therapeutic place to gather your thoughts and "find yourself." Not long after I had "found myself" somewhere in Smokey Lake Township pulling a trailer hauling 11 bales, I realized I was being somewhat selfish by not sharing the remaining 63 loads of therapy with my white collar friends in urban America.

Tom Sawyer was able to earn a little extra cash by letting other kids in on the fun of whitewashing a picket board fence. I probably could boost my ranch income by letting stress-ridden executives in on the therapy available in my radioless 4020.

They could get away from the office and telephone calls by confining themselves to my stressproof tractor cab. While they let themselves unwind, I could kick back and watch my hay get unloaded. This definitely would qualify as a win-win situation.

Everyone would be happier. My guests could enjoy the fine prairie scenery and tranquillity it affords. I could enjoy the free time I get while someone else gets my work done and I'd really enjoy heading to the bank to deposit the therapy fees paid by my hay hauling house guests.

**The expansion phase**

Once my clientele is built up and news spreads of the mental relaxation available out here on the prairie, I'll have to get a couple more radioless 4020s to facilitate my booming customer base.

If my patients can't come during hay hauling season, I may have to find other activities to satisfy their hunger for soul cleansing. I believe people could learn to love feeding cows, calving heifers, fixing fence and baling hay.

We wouldn't even have to limit our services to corporate executives. We could be just as helpful to the everyday working class people looking for a change of pace and scenery. Lovelorn teen-agers really would find a mile of down fence helpful in clearing their minds and solving their problems.

If you have a cousin out East who is in need of my services, give me a call. But hurry, it looks like I'm going to have to haul my own hay this week.

# A new and improved CRP
## Introducing the cow reserve program

The controversy in the 1995 farm bill seems to be the plight of the Conservation Reserve Program.

Some folks get the letters mixed up and call it CPR, but considering the new life it's breathed into the bankrolls of some retiring farmers, maybe cardiopulmonary resuscitation isn't so far off.

In our country you can rent all the erodible land you want for $10-an-acre — we call it pasture.

If it's too light to farm, you leave it in grass and run cows on it. The government, however, decided to pay $40 an acre rent for it and run wildlife on it. Only a government that pays $600 for a toilet seat would pay $40 an acre for $10-an-acre blow sand.

**Switching gears**

Since the cattle market went south this spring, producers have been looking for ways to make a little dough. I propose a healthy dose of governmental intervention.

How about a new and improved CRP, the Cow Reserve Program? Ranchers could put their cows in the program, feed them, care for them and collect a payment at the ASCS office. Good cows produce a calf a year, and last year, steers brought $550 a piece. That would equate to a fair government payment (multiply times four) of about $2,000 per cow per year.

We still could ride the range and keep an eye on our retired cow herd. There'd be no calves to work, no bulls to take care of, no mental marketing stress or calf weaning headaches.

The CRP cow herd would serve as a great beef reserve for the world food supply. At the drop of a hat, we could turn out bulls and nine months later, we'd have a new supply of protein on the ground; 15 months later, we could invite the countries of the world to a barbecue funded by our taxpayers.

**Red tape or red ink**

Passing legislation for a Cow Reserve Program could be tough. Environmentalists would have a fit if the government proposed paying ranchers to keep a bunch of methane belching, range destroying, wildlife harassing cows out on "their" pristine prairie.

With some time and money spent on the lobbying process, they probably could weigh down the legislation with enough rules, regulations and stipulations to make it ecosuitable. Cows forced to wear methane filters on both ends, bureaucrats hired to evaluate the greenness of grass on a weekly basis, wildlife stocked at a rate of 10 animal units of wild critters for each animal unit of beef.

By the time the program got approved and funded, all the time saved by ranchers would be spent in town across the desk from someone at the ASCS office with a 3-inch file of forms. Our money earned in Cow Reserve payments would be spent on gas getting to the ASCS office and a bar tab racked up when we get out of the office and need to air out our grievances.

On second thought, scrap the idea. I just decided I'd rather put up with red ink than red tape. I'd rather ride the roller coaster of free markets than put myself under the steamroller of governmental market manipulation.

# Cashing in our time savings
## Time saved just seems to disappear

The shortest day of the year is upon us. As I write this column, I'm only a day away from the winter solstice, Dec. 21, the first official day of old man winter. Of course, as far as I'm concerned, winter started in November when the snow came, the mercury dropped and I traded in my Stetson for earlappers.

Dec. 21 is the day when the sun barely clears the southern horizon, scampers across the sky in a mere eight hours and 27 minutes, then drops like a ton of bricks, about the time "Jeopardy!" comes on, approximately 4:54 p.m.

The days were already short. The thought of facing the shortest day of the year had me in a cold sweat since we never seem to get all our daily chores and projects done, even in June when we've got more than 16 hours of sun time at our disposal.

I began making preparations to get the jump on the shortest day of the year so I could make the best use of my 8 1/2 hours. I put new batteries in my flashlight, checked the light switches in the barn and set the timer up on my tractor plug-in.

I was even ready to sacrifice my mandatory two pots of morning coffee so I could get out earlier to complete a few chores.

### A hedge on time

Then it struck me that I didn't need to get all fired up about getting everything done on the shortest day of the year. I had a hedge on time that would make the day a breeze.

All year long I'd been saving time with new gadgets and technology. I'd been getting more and more efficient with each improvement made to the ranch. All I had to do was transfer some of the time I already had saved up and make use of it when I really needed it.

I went to make a withdrawal on my savings account, but when I got to the teller, she told me my account was as empty as the checkbook of a rancher waiting for his new operating loan.

How could this be? I'd fixed up the corrals so it would take less time to sort and work the cows. I'd bought that hay baler so I could get hay up quicker and I had given my calves all the shots possible so I wouldn't have to spend much time doctoring them.

The computer on my desk was supposed to make recordkeeping and income tax preparation a snap. The propane stock tank heater eliminated the time I used to spend chopping ice.

### Bummed out

I was pretty bummed out when I realized all the time I had saved was gone like yesterday's calf check. I really was looking forward to putting those time savings to use this winter.

I'm starting to cheer up a little though. I've got a new plan and a new place to look for some extra time.

I know I can count on my Uncle Sam to provide for me. He must have a pile of time in storage after all the years of Daylight Savings Time. I'm sure they've stored all that daylight we've been saving when we set our clocks ahead each spring.

Maybe I'll go hit him up for a loan at the federal time bank.

# Change comes slowly to traditionalists
## No turning back; we're knee deep in the 1990s

As usual, I've written the first 10 checks of the new year like I've written the first 10 checks of every new year. No, not with an overdrawn balance; I mean with the year scratched out where I'm supposed to put the date in the corner of the blank.

I've been reminded by the man or woman at the checkout counter that it's now 1995, not 1994. I make the usual small talk with them about my mental incapabilities and they assure me that I'm not the only stupid person who's made that mistake.

Change comes slowly to a traditionalist like myself, but I'm finally getting into the swing of the new year and accepting the fact that 1994's a goner.

### Facing the facts

I'm kind of like the fella who swam halfway across the English Channel and realized he couldn't make it so he turned around and swam back. Now that we're halfway through the decade of the '90s I feel like I should turn back and return to 1990 rather than risk the chance of going forward into the year 2000.

If I could go back to 1990, my pickup would have fewer miles, my tractor would burn less oil and my cows would have more teeth.

I could roll back the depreciation schedule on all my worldly possessions and enjoy that new car feeling. Not that I've ever had a new car but I have experienced the new car feeling when I bought my used "new to me" vehicles and implements.

A real problem I have with accepting the passage of time is realigning my thought process when it comes to the years cars were made.

I still think a '78 Bonneville is a pretty new car. An '85 Oldsmobile would be newer than I could ever hope to own.

Now that I've accepted being knee deep in the decade of the '90s, I have to realize that what I thought was a pretty late model vehicle is really just another piece of junk waiting its turn to join the long line of four doors parked back in the hills.

## The positive side

There's a positive note to my realizations though. Not too long ago, I used to envy my friends who drove '88 Berettas and '89 Cougars down the main drag of our little town.

Now that those cars have been pretty well depreciated out, I stand a pretty good chance of walking onto the lot and purchasing one of those beauties of yesteryear. I can cruise the highways in the exact same cars I was drooling over several years ago.

Sure they may have 120,000 miles on them, but it's the thought that counts. In my mind, the status wouldn't be much higher if they'd just rolled off the showroom floor. I'm not really comfortable in a car unless someone else already has loosened the piston rings and slackened the stress points.

I'll be bathing in glory as I peer at the ultra modern dashboards of these '80s model roadsters. More gauges and gadgets than a country boy knows how to use.

Having an '80s car could make being a '90s guy a pretty livable situation. As a matter of fact, I can't wait to enter the 21st century. Have you seen those 1995 models coming off the assembly line? Just wait til they rack up a few miles, dents and dings. By 2005, they'll be within easy reach of my transportation budget.

# Beware of farmers and ranchers
## Tinkering patent busters head to ag shows

Winter is ag show season here in the heartland. Equipment vendors, gadget gurus and sales reps of all kinds hit the circuit each winter in hopes of moving their wares and making an honest living.

Long winters and the threat of cabin fever drives farmers and ranchers away from the cows and into their pickups to head to the show. They do their morning chores and hit the road to check out the new lines of equipment that they can't afford, see the gadgets they don't need and tease the salesmen looking for the big sale.

In the process of teasing the salesmen, farmers gather more ballpoint pens than they can lose in a year's time, more ice scrapers than they have windshields for and more info sheets in their plastic bags than they'll read in a month of Sundays.

## A tough sale

Farmers and ranchers are a hard sale. Sure, they need the products that are offered at the ag shows, but it really goes against their grain to buy something that they could have built in their shop at home.

It's a pride thing. Rural folks are an inventive bunch and they hate to admit someone else can provide them with a product that didn't originate on their work bench.

Most of the folks at the ag shows are farmers themselves and, like most farmers, they need a way to supplement their income. They figured they could take the better mouse trap they built on the road, get on the gravy train and pay the mortgage on the homestead.

The peddlers forgot their roots, though. The farmer customers appreciate the ingenuity of the inventive peddler but their frugal nature won't allow them to appreciate the retail price tag that the peddler hopes will pay his bills.

## I could do that

Salesmen, beware of the farmer of rancher who shows more than a passing interest in your product. He'll be asking questions galore and you'll think you've got a live one on the line when actually he's just forming a mental blueprint so he can head home and build one out of scrap metal and trailer house axles.

Pointer No. 2, salesmen — beware of the farmer or rancher accompanied by a kid packing a tape measure. He'll be diverting your attention with those blueprint forming questions. Meanwhile, Junior will be scurrying around measuring angles and jotting down figures to back up Pa's mental imagery.

Attentive eyes will be checking thicknesses, lengths and distances. He's sure he can build one cheaper at home because he won't have to hire $35-an-hour welders, pay for any fancy decals or paint jobs, or foot the bill for a traveling sales force.

## Real bargains

After a day of wandering the ag show, picking up freebies and garnering ideas, the amateur engineers will head home.

But first, they'll swing by the tube and steel place to pick up some extra box tubing and angle iron for their new project. Then they'll swing by the welding store for an extra tank of acetylene and a box of good arc welding rods.

When they get home they'll devote the next month to design and building. After a couple hundred hours, and $1,000 worth of materials, the project will be complete.

When the smoke clears and the slag is chipped, he can step back and say, "I'm sure glad I didn't give that slick salesman $900 for his rig at the ag show!"

# Plastic plentiful on the prairie
## Hay may come and go, but plastic is forever

Nobody likes a litterbug.

When I'm driving down the road, nothing irks me more than seeing someone's plastic pop bottle or candy wrapper in the ditch.

Don't they know that those plastic pieces will be litter on the prairie for billions and billions of years? You know they'll be there forever because the only garbage folks pick up, as a rule, are the aluminum cans because they've got a little resale value.

Plastic, however, just stays and stays and stays. It doesn't rot, it doesn't break down, it doesn't do anything but sit there and witness the rise and fall of mankind. It remains as a kind of sad legacy to our civilization.

So it's with great guilt that I confess to all that I have joined the ranks of the despicable plastic litterbugs.

### From the top

Round balers revolutionized the haying business, but they brought their share of problems, too. The hay goes up faster with less labor, but when it comes time to haul them home, most fellas gladly would trade their bales in for stacks.

They say the work's only half done when you've got your hay baled up. If that's the case, my work's still only half done.

We had some good fall rains (we never say we got too much rain here in the sand dunes) and found most of our hay bales were sitting in mud or water.

It was a Catch-22 or maybe a Catch-222 considering all the angles in our dilemma. We had to wait for the ground to freeze to move the hay, but before the ground froze, the snow came and kept the ground from freezing. When it did freeze the bales froze in about 6 inches, too. The snow still kept coming, making the whole hay hauling process a real pain.

This is where the litterbug part comes in.

### That dang twine

Twine is a key ingredient for a good bale and a frustrated rancher. We use plastic twine, not because it's environmentally friendly, but because it's the cheapest—pure economics.

It's also the strongest, won't rot when it gets wet and it helps you get more hay home and leave less along the road ditches. That is unless its froze down in six inches of ice.

99

When that's the case you're lucky if you can keep a single strand of twine on the bale before you get it on the trailer heading for home.

Prying bales out of the ice is a delicate process. You start by grabbing the bale with the grapple fork and gently try to coax it loose with a little hydraulic to and fro.

Before long the ice proves thicker than your patience and you're backing up and ramming the bale with your tractor to try and bust the biscuit loose. You kind of wonder how strong your loader mounts really are as you're heading full tilt towards an ice bound bale.

The end result is a grapple full of what once used to be a round bale. You leave all the twine and a liberal amount of hay on the field for seed next year.

**Wasted effort**

As I pull my trailer load of crippled, busted-up bales home, I wonder why I put any twine on them in the first place.

I could have saved a hefty chunk of change if I just kicked them out of the baler without any twine at all. That would have made them easier to bust out of the ice, too.

As it is now, I have to go to bed at night realizing that I've added to the problem of plastic profusion on the prairie. It's a definite black mark on my character.

On the bright side, at least I won't have to cut my hands in two trying to pull the twine off while I'm feeding. Next summer, I'll make up for it by jumping off the mower tractor and balling up my winter refuse.

Keeping the ranch plastic-free is a full-time job. Now, if I could just get the cows to quit losing their plastic eartags.

# Sport is what you make it
## Remedies to wile away the workday

It's sometimes hard to tell where work ends and sports begin.

Usually, whenever you add the element of competition, everyday work becomes a competitive sport.

Running to catch your bus can be exhausting work, running to catch the person ahead of you in the Boston Marathon is great sport. Driving to work during rush hour is stressful, driving a race car in the Indy 500 is stress relieving.

Roping calves for a branding is working, roping calves in a rodeo is sporting. Seems like most forms of work drudgery can be transformed into sport enjoyment if you just make the things you do everyday a contest.

Calving is starting to lose the excitement it had when I first started. This concerns me because there's not enough profit in this cattle business to keep a guy enthused, so he should at least enjoy himself.

So, in order to keep the level of enjoyment high in the latter days of the calving season, I decided to spice things up with a little competition and sportsmanship.

## Self-competition

The tough thing about adding competition to calving chores is the lack of people to compete against. Sure I could call up the neighbors and tell them to come over every time I'm feeling competitive, but it would take a lot of scheduling and planning.

It's easier just to compete against yourself and then tell the neighbors how well you've actually done. You then could throw down the gauntlet and challenge them to match your feat or beat your self-proclaimed record.

Just about anything you do on a daily basis can be sporterized to add excitement to your calving chores, but I've got a few favorites I'd like to share.

## Fun calving contests

The most thrilling of calving sports is the "tag, vaccinate and weigh a calf before its mother knocks you flat and tap dances on your head" event. This one can really get your adrenaline pumping and the high stakes in this game make it pretty exciting.

Losing could mean being out for the remainder of the season, a devastating loss if you need to hire a replacement player for $50 a day. Winning gives you a calf with identification, immunization and a head start on good performance records.

Maybe that game is a little lopsided in its costs and benefits. It may be better not to take part in this event at all if you see El Toro Cow pawing the dirt and sizing you up every time you get near her baby.

A less deadly calving game that is loads of fun is "loading your ear tagger and filling your syringe while on the go atop a green broke filly." This is an efficiency event. Kind of like city folks using their cellular phone or shaving with a cordless razor on their way to work in the morning.

It, too, has its dangers though. You run the risk of vaccinating your palm or ear tagging yourself. But body piercing is "in" you know.

My last calving game is a distance event. Every good rancher likes to fling the afterbirth away from a cow if he finds her chewing on it out in the pasture. "She might choke on it," they say. But they really just want to see how far or how high they can send the placental projectile. It's an exhilarating sport, not unlike the discus event in track and field.

And office workers think waste paper basketball is fun.

# Shooting the bull
## The disappearing art of storytelling

Have you been to a good bull sale lately?

I just got back from a bull sale in Dickinson and I've decided the world would be a better place if we all took a day off and went to a bull sale once in awhile.

Bull sales do more than provide quality cattle genetics in a fair bidding situation. They provide cattlemen an excuse to get off the ranch and catch up on the news, the gossip and the latest jokes circulating around the cattle business.

Going to a bull sale not only gives you the opportunity to buy a bull, it gives you a golden opportunity to shoot the bull, too.

### A culture of storytellers

Ever since the television, VCR and video game joystick invaded our homes, conversational skills have suffered.

The art of conversation and storytelling has taken a back seat to sitting in front of a glowing screen, watching folks shoot each other, cheat on their spouses and smoke drugs. Kids' goals of growing up to be a doctor or a fireman have been replaced with the goal of reaching the next level of the latest video game.

Now, rural agriculture may be the last stronghold left in the storytelling culture of America. This culture still thrives at country elevators, vet clinics and bull sales.

Whenever farmers and ranchers get together, you'll learn about humorous brushes with financial or physical disaster, the latest antics of someone's cane-raising kids and the most recent Ole and Lena joke.

Stories don't necessarily need to be fresh either. Like good wine, they often get better with age. The best stories are the fifth-hand versions heard from a friend of a friend whose cousin was there when some other guy first told it at the local coffee shop.

And most folks have a favorite story they like to tell when a group of ranchers circle up in front of the sale barn. Kind of a signature story that has been perfected after telling it a couple hundred times.

There's a lot of strategic maneuvering in good storytelling, too. Sometimes you can steer the conversation, creating an atmosphere where your favorite story just has to be told.

Other times, someone will be gracious enough to provide you with an introduction like, "Hey, George, why don't you tell that one about your dog that opened the gate for ya when you were chasin' the cow." Then the stage is set and the spotlight is on you.

### Encouraging trends

I think storytelling and conversation are poised for a comeback.

As I rolled down the highway to Dickinson with two other bull sale fans, I realized car pooling is a trend that could really boost the art of shooting the bull. People commuting to work everyday could open up their vehicles to a couple of traveling partners and learn the joy of good stories and enjoyable conversation.

And not all technology has been detrimental to the telling of stories. I can see the potential for spreading a little bull on the information superhighway. All good country roads have a little manure on the edges and I don't think the superhighway will be any different.

Although nothing is as good as hearing a story in person, online e-mail and instant messages could provide a proving ground for good stories, allowing them to grow and be perfected.

And if I might suggest a new Internet extension to the list of .com, .net and .edu, I would add ".bs" for story tellers only.

# Cowboys and culture
## Penetrating the disgusting market

Watch out world, I'm climbing the ladder to high society.

As a matter of fact, I just topped the rung on that ladder that says, "you have to eat something considered disgusting by most to be a part of society's upper crust."

Disgusting food is an accepted barrier to high society. We've all seen those diamond-clad folks riding around in limousines. Seems like they're always eating something that would gag a maggot.

Fish eggs (caviar). Raw fish (sushi). Snails (escargot). Raw oysters (expensive slime).

Well, I'm here to tell you, us folks in the ranching business have been holding the key to high society for a long, long time.

Our link to the upper class comes from used-to-be bull calves and we call this delicate fare "Rocky Mountain Oysters." But don't let the pretty name fool ya. We're just trying to fit in with our high-class friends who call a slimy little rodent like the muskrat a quaint and palatable "marsh hare."

### Picnic in the pens

For years, ranchers have been eating Rocky Mountain Oysters at barroom gatherings and neighborhood get-togethers. Sometimes we'll eat 'em right at the scene of the crime.

Last week, the neighbors were over helping me work some calves. We worked up such an appetite we had to whip up some Rocky Mountain Oysters right on top of the branding iron oven to help keep our strength up.

These dainty appetizers were about as fresh as fresh could be. Lightly roasted on a piece of rusty tin that was precisely heated by a propane blow torch, these oysters couldn't have been fixed any finer.

Lacking any salt or pepper, we just sprinkled a little sand on them and called it tasty. Our senses were piqued as these oysters tantalized our taste-buds and burnt our fingertips.

Australians might be known for saying, "Ay mate, throw another shrimp on the barby!", but we easily could compete with some snappy lit-tle saying like, "Hey pard, throw another nu...," well, you get the idea.

### Premium byproducts

Everyone agrees the beef industry needs to be innovative to survive.

I've got an innovation that not only will allow ranchers to rub elbows with the high and mighty, it'll expand our markets and make use of a pre-viously wasted byproduct.

What we need to do is slip some Rocky Mountain Oysters in between the caviar and escargot at a few ritzy gatherings where the folks with fat wallets hang out. Once these big spenders develop a taste for our premium byproduct, we'll be on easy street.

The more we charge for our product, the more attractive it'll be to these folks who insist price determines quality. If we charge about $500 a pound, the demand should really take off.

And if each bull calf produces about 6 ounces (that's three ounces each), the byproduct income will more than make up for the market drop that has us selling our dollar-a-pound calves for 70 cents.

The value-added options are endless. One niche could have us run-ning a few cow calf pairs in the Beverly Hills. We could let the folks play cowboy for a day, helping to gather the cows and work the calves. Then they could experience for themselves the taste of fresh Rocky Mountain Oysters cooked on the branding iron oven.

Of course, before we commit, we'd have to "testes" the market (get it?).

# Let the judgers be judged
## True value is the only way to judge

You're not supposed to be judgmental of others, but last week being judgmental was part of my job as beef umpire and cow referee for the North Dakota Junior Beef Expo in Williston, N.D.

I hate to judge anybody by appearance, but steers and heifers in the show were having a hard time with the personality and talent categories.

Appearance meant more than shiny hooves and a nice hairdo. A steer could have been having a bad hair day and if he was thick, meaty and put together right, he got the official nod.

## In the mirror

Cattle judges and livestock show officials are a necessary evil during the summer run of county fairs and 4-H achievement days.

We're brought in to put our opinions on the line.

But, in all fairness, judges should be judged if they want to maintain any credibility.

I don't mean being judged on our judging skills. I mean being judged on the same criteria as the animals we evaluate in the show ring.

At 6 foot 2 inches and 170 pounds soaking wet, I'd make a darn poor feeder calf. Tight gutted, hard-doing and light muscled, it'd cost more in feed and groceries to put any gain on me than I'd be worth in the market.

## True value

Sometimes you've got to make these livestock officials toe the mark outside the show ring.

I know both guys and gals highly trained in livestock evaluation who do a nice job of evaluating animals.

But catch the single, unmarried cattle judges when they're on the lookout for a dance partner and you'll see an entirely different set of priorities.

Sad to say, the cattlemen are looking at the frail, shallow, light-boned ladies who just wouldn't survive in most ranch environments. One good drought with short grass and long walks to the waterhole would finish most of them off.

The cattlewomen, likewise, are flirting with some sorry-looking double-muscled dudes.

A few years down the road when the structure gives out and they can't even follow a lawn mower around the yard, the gals are going to wish they'd snagged that long, lean cowboy.

The tide may be turning, though. There's a new mode of thought that could put the show ring and the nightclub on equal footing.

Value-based marketing could have all of us getting beneath the skin, crediting both animals and people for what they're like inside.

The heck with hide color and fluffy hair coats. No more feed bucket thickness on steers, or humans built with silicone and plastic surgery.

True value and real worth — the only way to judge cattle or people.

# Save blood, ban bugs

## Summer insects hold some entertainment value, but not much

There'll be no need for me to head to the blood bank for my bi-monthly donation this week.

My blood thirsty friends, the mosquitoes and wood ticks, already have drained at least a pint from my veins. I'll have to wait the mandatory eight weeks for my next batch of juice and cookies at the local blood drain.

The mosquito population has done exceptionally well this year with all the standing water and recharged stagnant ponds. Wood ticks have enjoyed the moisture, too. Lots of tall grass in the pastures and meadows have made for some nice tick habitat.

### That's entertainment

I was visiting a friend of mine down in South Dakota last week and ended up staying overnight in a cabin they had out in the sticks. Or should I say a cabin they had out in the ticks?

The road proved a little tough to navigate when we decided to head up there, so we parked the pickup and hoofed it a quarter of a mile to the lodge. When we got there, we popped the top on a couple of cold ones and commenced to swapping stories, playing guitar and cranking out some old cowboy tunes.

My friend on the guitar was as good as any pied piper or snake charmer you'd ever meet. We were pickin' and a grinnin' and a pickin' wood ticks as they headed up our legs dancing to the beat of "Amarillo, By morning" and looking for a good vein to tap into.

It was good entertainment in a cabin with no electricity, television or radio. It soon turned competitive as we tallied up the ticks each of us picked off and burned on the stove like heretics in old European days.

The grudge match soon ended and my lucky friend beat me seven to five. I demanded a rematch, though, because he got to break the trail through the grass and got first crack at the local population.

### B*zzzzzzz*....Swat!

Mosquitoes are a real favorite in the summer months. Rumored to be the North Dakota state bird, they're great material for tall tales, short stories and long strings of cuss words as they swarm the state looking for blood-laden victims.

Mosquitoes can turn otherwise sane folks into babbling idiots as they start swatting the air, jumping up and down, fussing and fuming. Their

106

antics often attract neighboring swarms of mosquitoes who relish in the antagonization of a live one.

More patient folks will sacrifice some blood just to get revenge on these proboscis-packing needlers. Giving their enemy a chance to settle in and draw a little "O" positive plasma they'll pounce on him like a tiger, leaving a big red handprint on their forehead and a malicious vengeful grin on their face.

I've seen some people beat themselves silly sitting in lawn chairs in the evening just so they can rid the world of 15 or 20 skeeters. The human casualties often outnumber those of the enemy.

There are even stories of small children being carried off by the larger skeeters. And some guys out mowing hay are beginning to carry a shotgun on their tractors so they can pick off the more aggressive ones before they get a chance to bite.

Just remember: It's not so bad getting picked up by a pair of big skeeters. It's getting dropped that hurts.

# Slowing down
## Forget the rush, we've got nothing but time

It never pays to get in a hurry.

At least that's what the highway patrolman down in South Dakota told me last week. He drove the lesson home with a big fat speeding ticket, a self-addressed, unstamped envelope and a kind farewell.

Any benefits of getting to my next destination on time were erased with a flick of the pen. Hurrying can cost you about $5 for every minute you're trying to make up for in South Dakota.

The slowing down theory may work as well on the ranch as it does on the open road.

### Low-impact ranching

Most of the heavy-duty breakage around our ranch happens when I'm in a hurry. Usually, I blame the breakdowns on some sinister plot to keep me from getting ahead or finishing on time.

The vaccinating syringe always explodes when I'm rushing to finish the last pen of calves and running low on the vaccine that costs $2 a dose.

The car overheats when I'm already 10 minutes late for a meeting.

The hydraulic hose on the tractor blows when I'm trying to finish baling a field before an impending rain storm.

The computer crashes right before I think about saving the file and the deadline is approaching at a rapid rate.

So, maybe if I just slowed down a bit and took my time, fewer things would break and my stress level would plummet like the 1995 cattle market.

Backing off a gear or two on the tractor probably would save countless spindles, axles and bearings I'm sure. Ease up on the cow herd when you're chasing them and they're much less likely to go through the fences and bust down the gates.

And reining in the Chrysler would save me a little cash on speeding tickets.

### Jumping the gun

Excess speed with tractors, machinery and cars can bring some real problems and repair bills. Pushing the cattle a little too hard or fast will bring you splintered corrals and mangled gates.

Slowing down can do as much good on the money side of ranching as it does on the production side.

When you live on borrowed money like I do, it makes good sense to slow down the bill paying process. If the payment isn't due until the 20th of the month, mail it in on the 19th. Taxes due on March 1 can be mailed before midnight of that day instead of rushing to the post office in January.

I already got a letter from my lender reminding me of a note coming due Dec. 15. They won't need to worry about me rushing in any time soon. I'll see them on Dec. 15 and not a day earlier.

Cattle marketing is something that will deserve some time this fall, too. No jumping the gun and dumping the calves for 65 cents a pound. Hang tough, take your time and hold out for a dollar.

Slowing down and holding out on this calf market could make for a future grass shortage though. All of us hold-outs are going to need some extra range to run our growing herd of staggy 4 and 5-year-old steers on after a couple years of slowing down our marketing strategy.

I hope that lender's note said the payment was due on Dec. 15 four years from now.

# A wasted effort
## Accomplishments hard to measure

Whenever things get you a little depressed, look around and you're bound to find somebody worse off than you are. It's comforting to know that someone else's misfortunes can always cheer us up.

It sometimes seems like I never get anything accomplished. I don't spend a lot of time idling around watching wire rust, yet it's tough to pinpoint what the day has accomplished at times.

Then I drove down the highway and saw the guys with the orange tractors mowing the ditches and medians. I had to chuckle and ask myself, "How'd you like to spend the whole day mowing hay you'd never get to bale?"

It must be tough for the highway department to measure the accomplishments of their haying season when it's left to wilt in the swath along the road. Clean winter roadways offer some reconciliation but a couple stacks of good round bales would be a lot easier to identify with.

## Tough occupations

The highway department mowers aren't alone in trying to identify some blurry goals and accomplishments.

How about the folks building bombs for the government that'll sit in some warehouse and never get detonated? Or the workers assembling a super collider, a star wars defense system or a prairie water diversion project that may never be utilized?

Farmers can seed conservation reserve ground that they'll never get to harvest and bureaucrats can write and file forms that nobody ever will read.

Seems like poor Uncle Sam has a lot of deadwood on the government tree.

If the budget needs cutting, we could start by not paying anyone to do anything that doesn't need doing. Sounds simple, but I'm sure the brotherly order of bureaucrats would raise quite a stink and launch a campaign to shore up the necessity of their jobs and the protection of their turf.

## For citizens, too

Maybe this isn't just a problem of government. We could cut costs in private society by concentrating on accomplishment and goals. The "use it or lose it" mentality practiced in the handing out of government grants can be found out in the countryside as well.

We probably don't need to buy things just because they're on sale. I've saved so much money buying sales items, I'm just about broke. And all I've accomplished is the need for another loan, but at least they were running a special on interest rates that week.

Don't get your windshield replaced just because it has a little crack in the corner and Gonzo's Glass Garage said he'd waive your $100 deductible. The only "waiving" going on will be a wave goodbye to lower insurance rates when your glass man inflates his charges to cover the "rebate."

Prices always seem to float a little depending on who's paying for it. A water hole can cost quite a bit more if its cost shared by the government, while discounts may apply if you pay cash for it yourself. We always seem to push for a little better deal if we know we have to pay for it ourselves.

I guess waste, goal-less tasks and fraud do accomplish something. They keep a portion of the population employed and keep the great American economy rolling.

One final positive thought on the highway department's fall "haying" operation. At least they don't have a bunch of hay bales to haul in before the snow starts to fly.

# The big picture
## A new theory on holistic management

I've always been real interested in resource management. Comes with being a rancher, I guess.

I was so interested that I bought a book on holistic resource management last winter. I was hoping to learn how I could do a better job of managing resources for the good of the "whole" here on the Taylor Ranch.

Unfortunately, there's been so many holes in our ranching operation, lately, that I haven't had the time to read about whole management. I think a lot of people are in the same boat I am, and it may indicate that a new school of holistic thought is forming in the countryside.

### Managing with holes

My new theory of holism came to me in the east pasture a couple weeks ago. I was out looking for holes in the fence that needed mending when I drove right into a canyon of hole that the bulls kindly dug along the pickup trail.

That bull hole practically swallowed the whole pickup and I spilled a whole cup of hot coffee on my lap. Needless to say, I was wholly upset with the dirt-digging bull, the worn-out suspension in the '67 Ford and the new scar tissue that was forming on the inside of my thigh.

My theory of hole management was further reinforced last week when I was driving Ol' Brownie, the wonder Chrysler.

I pulled her up to the drive-up window at the bank to get a little spendin' cash. While I was trying to talk the teller out of some money, I noticed a whole lot of smoke billowing out from under the hood.

The teller gave me my cash and asked if I'd like to talk to one of their loan officers about a car loan. Wise guys....

The smoke got me wondering, though, if there was a hole somewhere under the hood that might need managing. I pulled up to the gas station and checked her vital signs. Sure enough, the transmission fluid was sorely lacking.

I gave her two whole quarts of brand new transmission fluid and realized I'd just found the newest hole in my operation. But with all that new fluid in the transmission, I figured I could put off any hole-patching plans for awhile.

I drove to Bismarck to catch an airplane, and left Ol' Brownie at the airport parking lot. But when I got back, I had even more holes to fix. The back tire was flat as a pancake.

## Getting published

With all the expertise I've gleaned on hole management, I've been thinking about submitting a paper on holistic theory for academic publication.

I'm sure there'll be a lot of professors out there who'll try and shoot holes in my theory, but I think with all my recent experience, I can manage.

# Yogurtburger hotdish
## A meating of the mindless

Yogurt ain't just for breakfast anymore.

Made of cultured (i.e. rotting) milk, yogurt used to be just for the horizontally challenged and the deranged segment of our population that was looking for a little variety in their usual nuts and twigs diet.

Nowadays, yogurt is all over the place. Who'd have ever thought bacteria would get to be so popular?

Nothing's sacred. First, they went after the ice cream stands. "I scream, you scream, we all scream for live and active cultured soft serve frozen yogurt with acidophilus and artificial color."

There's something wrong with a population that'll replace one of the world's most perfect foods with something as wimpy and retentive as yogurt. They won't catch me betraying the American tradition of ice cream. Keep those sundaes, shakes and triple scoopers coming my way.

But now the yogurt lobby has gone too far. The gooey little ladder climbers are trying to scale the food pyramid and push meat right off the steep side.

### Yogurt and potatoes?

The United States Department of Agriculture recently suggested yogurt as a meat alternative in the school lunch program. That's right. Yogurt — the other, other white meat. Also announcing strawberry yogurt — the other red meat.

Personally, I think the idea's crazier than a room full of federal bureaucrats, but I'm sure the government's just looking out for us. Maybe I should make the switch.

In fairness, I decided to test it out a little.

I started by cutting myself a nice thick, juicy slab of yogurt and throwing it on the grill. I like my steaks done medium, but I barely got the

111

beller out of my yogurt steak before it all ended up as meat substitute soup on the bottom of the grill.

I got the same results when I tried a little yogurt stir fry. My yogurt kabobs were a complete flop. Just couldn't keep the slimy buggers on the stick.

I thought my new meat substitute might be better uncooked. I laid a nice quarter-pound patty of it on a big sesame seed bun. It looked promising until I took a bite. My burger alternative squirted out the side and hit the floor in one fairly unattractive heap.

Yogurtburger was even beyond the saving graces of hamburger helper. I guess there's some hamburger you just can't help.

**No thanks**

Satisfied that I'd given yogurt a fair trial, I decided to stick with real meat. Real beef with real nutritional value. Things like iron, zinc and niacin that you just can't find in a cup full of yogurt. Plus it's sugar free — something 10 out of 10 dentists likely would promote.

And if the people who prepare the meals in our school lunch program think yogurt is easier to prepare, all they have to do is come take a look at the bottom of my grill and see for themselves. Meat won't let you or your health slip through the cracks.

*Author's note: Not surprisingly, I got an e-mail from a vegetarian reader who was rather appalled at my yogurt attack. Of course, you can't expect protein, niacin, zinc, iron and thiamin-starved people to have a very healthy sense of humor.*

# Commodes go high tech
## When you gotta go, go in style

Not so long ago, finding a top-notch rest area meant spotting a two-holer with a finely sanded finish or a good grove of trees within walking distance of the highway.

Times are changing, though.

Now, we demand more than just relief. We demand art, education and entertainment.

North Dakota is meeting those demands with some creative commodes along Interstate 94 and U.S. Highway 2. These sentries on the Plains are anything but plain.

**Move over, Sears**

Education and art are nothing new to the outhouse world. Generations of people got most of their reading education in the old outhouse with a Sears catalog. The missing pages could be really frustrating for beginning readers, though.

Artistic impression could be found right on the outhouse door. The crescent moon cut into most doors is a a carpenter's tribute to toilet art. Many young poets got their start in the outhouse with a pencil and some catchy rhyme beginning with, "here I sit...."

But art and education have gone to new heights along the highway. We now have rest areas with a theme, kind of like Disney World. We have a rest area with a riverboat theme, one with a railroad theme and a third with a Native American theme.

## Paradoxical potties

I think its great that we have rest areas with Western frontier themes, but I'm not sure if some state-of-the-art rest area with unique architecture and a nice narrative plaque can tell tourists what life on the frontier really was like.

If tourists really want to understand the life of the Old West, they might want to get away from the infrared flush toilets, hot air hand dryers and quilted toilet paper.

The bathrooms on steam locomotives and the riverboats, were probably about as comfortable in frontier days as today's bathrooms in jet airplanes and Greyhound buses. These new rest areas are probably much roomier and more stable than their Old West counterparts.

There wasn't a heck of a lot of comfort to be had on the plains of North Dakota for the Native Americans, either. I'm certain that a few chokecherry bushes and some tall grass was the extent of their privacy and luxury.

So if we really wanted to give our tourists a snapshot of the Old West to take with them as they "go through" and "go in" our state, we probably could do it for a lot less dollars than what the new rest areas cost.

I haven't priced it lately, but I'm sure it'd be pretty cheap to outfit all our new "frontier experience" rest areas with a few chokecherry trees and some tall grass.

With the new low costs, we could even space them a little closer than every 150 miles. One outcome would be certain — we'd have tourists around the world talking about the rest areas in North Dakota!

# Golf plays a role on the ranch
## The challenge of real ranch golfing

I've only played golf twice in my life, but I think I've already gained enough experience to design my own pro course for real pasture pool enthusiasts.

I could spend a lot of time preaching about what a waste of time it is for strong, healthy people to run around chasing after a little white ball, but I think my time is better spent figuring out how I can make a few bucks off those silly club swingers.

It's true — the real money is in recreation. When you look at what people spend for custom-cut golf clubs, turbo-charged golf carts and those nice shirts with the embroidered pony on the front, it's plain to see that money is no object for these hard-core recreationalists.

## Golf course economics

When I counted the number of golfers out on the back nine and divided their green fees by the number of acres under their feet, I realized that I could make a lot more money running 200 head of golfers than I could running 200 head of beefers.

You don't need near as many acres for 200 golfers, you don't have to feed them in the winter, and you don't even need to take out any salt blocks, unless, of course, you want to get them all thirsty and increase demand for the over-priced beer back at the clubhouse.

On a per-acre basis, you won't find anyone who'll pay a higher rental rate than a recreational pasture putter. Uncle Sam wouldn't even pay that much for CRP. Plus, you can hay golf courses every year, and you don't have to wait until July 15 to do it.

It doesn't take near as much fence to keep in a golfer, and best of all, you can sell them a dozen golf balls, let them lose them in the water trap, pick them up and sell the same dozen back to them a second time. All you need is a pair of overshoes.

## The challenge of it all

I'm certain I could give competitive golfers their money's worth at the Taylor Ranch pasture pool pasture.

I doubt they've ever seen a sand trap as severe as the ones we could put together in the south Towner sandhills. Instead of a water trap, we could have a leafy spurge trap. Ever try and hit a golf ball out of a thick, tangled stand of 3-foot-high spurge? They'll be packing weedeaters instead of a chippin' wedge.

Animals could be a real challenge to the Arnold Palmers out on my course. You never know when a golf ball might drop in a badger hole or a coyote den. And you never know when a bull or an overprotective cow might take a disliking to you.

Just in case, you might want to keep a one wood handy and be ready to use it.

# What money can't buy

## Harvest time brings small pleasures from a big garden

The only two things that money can't buy are true love and home-grown tomatoes.

I think that pretty well sums up one of the basic laws governing modern mankind. It tackles values, economics, greed and the agronomics of home gardening all in one sentence.

It's harvest time on the Taylor Ranch vegetable patch, and although I'm allergic to hoeing and fundamentally opposed to getting down on my knees to pull weeds, I have no problem at all with harvesting (that means eating) the fruits of my mother's and father's labor.

Luckily, they put up with all my excuses for not spending any time in the garden, and, true to the basic notions of parenthood, they're still willing to share the harvest with their last born.

### New or old?

I don't know if there's anything so celebrated in the world as the arrival of "new potatoes" on dinner plates across the prairie.

The phrase "new potatoes" always kind of struck me funny. You don't hear folks at the supper table talking about "new milk" or "new bread." I guess it's just a difference in terminology. We have "old milk," but we call it cheese, and we probably do have "old bread," but we know it as turkey stuffing.

But potatoes are potatoes and you either eat 'em old, eat 'em new, or cut 'em up and plant 'em.

Old potatoes are kind of like long winters. Several months of "old potatoes" really can have you craving some fresh-from-the-sand spuds like a cow craves green grass in the spring.

Having your own garden and being able to sneak out and dig some new potatoes before they ever hit the store shelves makes country living all the more worthwhile.

### Fruit or vegetable?

Biting into a bright red, vine-ripened tomato more than likely will bring up the age old question, "is it a fruit or is it a vegetable?" Personally, I don't much care what you call it, just keep the salt and pepper handy.

The taste of your own tomatoes more than likely will spoil you, though. You'll find yourself sneering at those pathetic counterfeits you find in the grocery store and spitting out the little red rocks they try and pawn off in your salad at the restaurants.

Potatoes and tomatoes can make gardening pretty worthwhile, but some of the other vegetables are a little harder to get excited about. I'd say that peas, carrots and sweet corn are near the top of the list for tasty garden fare, but there sure are a few on the bottom of the list that I could live without.

Have you ever heard anybody say, "The only two things that money can't buy is true love and home-grown zucchini?" I tell you what. If true love was as easy to come by as home-grown zucchini, we'd be living in a pretty loving world.

# Keeping an eye to the sky
## Looking for UFOs to reduce the IOUs

Tens of thousands of normally normal people are packing up the family and driving to Roswell, N.M., this week to celebrate the 50th anniversary of the famed "Roswell Incident."

For those uninformed about the unidentified flying object incident, Roswell, N.M., is the friendly little desert oasis where friendly little aliens crashed their saucer and visited us earthlings back in 1947.

It's been the subject of movies, books and countless news reports. Believers claim there's been a huge coverup on the part of the government. The government claims the alien visit was merely Air Force parachutes and crash dummies.

Most of the citizens of Roswell are believers, especially the business people and entrepreneurs. Selling everything from alien dolls to UFO underwear, they approach all life forms, be they outer space alien or mere traveling tourist, as another lucrative sale.

One especially lucky local actually owns the land where the flying saucer ceased flying. Like me, he's a rancher. Unlike me, he's found a use for grazing land with much more per-acre profit potential than cattle.

### Tourist ranching

Instead of grazing cattle, gazing tourists can be seen dotting the rancher's landscape. I think tourists are my kind of livestock. They pay for their own food, take care of themselves, and you don't have to chase them. They pretty much go where they're told.

Fencing costs, however, are about even. Cows need pretty sturdy fences to hold them in; tourists need fences that are horse high and pig tight to hold them out. Tourist fence does carry the added cost of a coin-operated turnstile at the entrance gate.

Cows never leave money at the entrance gate. The closest they come to that activity is leaving a few bills and liabilities at the exit gate.

For all I know, aliens could have very well landed in Roswell. And if they really did, I'm just glad that they decided to land on a rancher's property and not some rich guy's mansion grounds. If anyone oughta find a little profit in the alien business, it's a hard scrabble, desert rancher.

Financially, one acre of tourism beats the living heck out of a thousand acres of ranching.

### On the lookout

Nope, I don't blame that rancher one bit for charging tourists a few bucks a head to see the UFO crash site. I'm just keeping an eye to the sky in case some benevolent alien decides to bless the Taylor Ranch with a small crater and some outer space rubble.

A couple days after turning out the bulls for another breeding season, I was sure I'd found the planet's latest UFO crash site. There was a big hole in the sand and pieces of tin and rubber scattered throughout.

But, on closer inspection, it turned out to be bull hole and what used to be my best mineral feeder. Oh well, maybe next time.

# Battle of the birds
## Classic clay pigeons

There's really nothing likable about a pigeon.

In the cities, you'll find them roosting on the skyscrapers, sitting on the park bench and waiting for some hapless lost soul to share a piece of bread with them.

If the folks breakin' the bread had to put up with a barn full of used-up bread crumbs that came from the opposite end of the beak, they'd probably switch them over to poison oats in a hurry.

There's nothing about a barn full of birds who are doing their best to whitewash your floor and texturize your saddle that is worth perpetuating. The last thing you'd want to do is provide the paint can for the air brush they keep under their tail feathers.

Our barn is generally home to only sparrows and swallows, but lately, a half-dozen pigeons decided to join the roost. With winter coming on, I can't blame them, but I darn sure don't welcome them either.

Swallows I can tolerate; they eat lots of mosquitoes and head south for the winter. And I can even live with the sparrows because they're pretty little and that means little droppings.

But there's something about a big, ugly pigeon who leaves a big, ugly trail behind himself that just makes me turn a little barbaric.

117

**Better than clays**

I don't have enough leisure time to join a skeet club or go to a trap shooting range, but I did bust a few clays with a buddy up by Crosby once. I have to admit it was pretty exciting. "Pull!" "Ka-boom!" "Smash!"

We went through enough clay targets to surface about two miles of country roads and retired to the clubhouse for a cold one.

Ever since then, I thought it'd be nice to drive back up and bust a few more pigeons, but it's a long way from the ranch to Crosby. But now I had the real thing roosting right up in my rafters. Pigeons just waiting to enter the wide world of sports and show the clay counterfeits what a real bird could do in front of a Remington pump.

Most trap ranges have some high school boy pulling the pin on the clays. Lacking anyone like that to help me out, I recruited my 64-year-old mother to go upstairs in the barn and send the pigeons my way.

"Pull!" I said. "Pull what?" she said. "You know what I mean, chase out a pigeon," I said, jacking a shell into the chamber. I heard "shoo bird" and "get out pigeon!" Still nothing to shoot at.

Then I heard her toss something at the lethargic target and out he flew. "Ka-boom!" Flap, flap, flap. "Ka-boom!" "Plop!"

It seemed like dandy sport to me, but the jury's out on whether or not we'll have target practice on a weekly basis. Me and the dogs were enthusiastically in favor of it, but Mom cast the deciding "no" vote. Looks like I'll be getting a box of clays and a bag of dog food instead.

# Praise the lord
## And pass the lutefisk

Different religions worship their supreme beings in a lot of different ways. The Aztecs used to sacrifice a couple of their best warriors on top of their Mexican pyramids, the Hindus pay homage to their holy cows and, in Towner, the Lutherans like to get together and eat a few hundred pounds of lutefisk.

Lutherans have a strong connection with food of any kind and whenever more than two get together, it's bound to be potluck. Maybe this isn't universal among Lutherans, it could just be our local church's strong Scandinavian connection to the seven-meal Norwegian day.

Being three-quarters Norsk myself, I adhere strictly to the breakfast, midmorning lunch, noon dinner, afternoon lunch, supper, evening lunch and bedtime lunch rotation. Every meal is washed down with lots of strong coffee so we can stay awake until the next feeding.

## Cod of life

Last Sunday, the men of Zion Lutheran Church in Towner put on their annual lutefisk feed (No. 5 in the seven-meal schedule). And I was one of the chosen few tapped by the parish elders to serve the holy cod.

People of all walks put their differences aside that evening to commune and partake in the eating of lye-soaked fish smothered in butter. Norwegian Lutherans, German-Russian Catholics and a even few Presbyterian Scots coughed up $8 a head and bellied up to the tables for a healthy dose of lutefisk and lefse.

Eating lutefisk truly is a religious experience. Getting the slimy stuff to slide down your throat without gagging is a true test of faith, kind of like walking barefoot across hot coals.

Serving the tables was a fast and furious experience. You really had to stay on top of things and make sure the platters were full of fish. If you didn't, you'd have some crabby Vikings to contend with.

At one point in time, I barely could keep my assigned table afloat with lutefisk and all the fixin's. If I had checked IDs, I'd probably have found that table to be inhabited by nothing but Olsons and Larsons.

### Fish tales

After the crowds subsided and the dishes were washed, crews sat around the remaining coffee pots and recounted mighty tales of lutefisk consumption.

One table had the converted German who brought his own bib and must have put down at least 20 pounds of the Norwegian delicacy. Another crew talked of the Scandinavian farm wife whose butter consumption likely funded the retirement of two, maybe three, local dairy farmers.

But we were all a little disappointed with our aging consumer base. Seemed like the younger generation just didn't show up in mass for the annual ritual. I tried to carry the weight for the rest of my generation, but one skinny cowboy can eat only so much lutefisk.

And I may not need to eat it again for some time because all I have to do to relive the experience is conjure up a good healthy burp.

# Post-election trauma
## New jobs for the recently unemployed

Another election has come and gone.

As I write this column, the election results have yet to be announced.

The only election result leak I've heard at the time of this writing is that Dole was rumored to be carrying North Dakota and Minnesota by more than 99 percent. Word has it that the ballots were misprinted and they left the "D" off of his name. Apparently, all the Scandinavians thought they were voting for Ole!

I doubt that we'll send Ole to the White House, or even Lars for that matter, and that no matter who wins, they'll keep on doing what they've always done and always said they wouldn't do.

## Money, money, money

As someone who's never had any money, I have to really admire the politicians, both winners and losers, for their ability to attract money.

The bottom line is looking pretty grim on the Taylor Ranch these days and I've been giving some thought as to how I can provide a little employment to the Election Day losers. I reckon they're in need of a job, and with all the contacts they have, I bet they'd do a great job of scouting up some funds for the old homestead.

A "good" politician could raise all kinds of cash for the ranch. They'd go right after the big tobacco companies for a donation, telling them how we allow smoking from one end of the ranch to the other.

They'd hit up the National Rifle Association for some cash to help support our stance on responsible gun use during hunting season. And they'd easily talk the Pro Life faction into lending us a hand since we give every unborn fetus calf the chance to be born. As a matter of fact, we encourage it.

But I wouldn't take on this political hired hand unless he or she could play both sides of the coin, talk out of both sides of their mouth and capture even more dollars to put the ranch in the black.

I'd want them to go after the tobacco-free lobby as well. Maybe throwing a $1,000 a plate smoke-free dinner in the east pasture touting our fresh, clean air.

The political hand should be able to loosen the purse strings of the anti-gun lobby by showing off the complete absence of automatic weapons on our place, unless of course they count the pickup that automatically backfires every time you shut it off.

And to attract the Pro Choice checkbook, our hand gladly would fill them in on our cows' right to choose, letting them know that our cows are free to slip on the ice, eat a poisonous plant or contract BVD if they choose not to go full term with their calf.

The only difficulty I can see in this plan is getting them to put the new found funds in the ranch checkbook and not embezzle it off to some Swiss bank account. Good help is hard to find, but honest politicians are even harder.

# Temporary fix
## Less than permanent, less than perfect

You get what you pay for.

Whether the investment is made in cold, hard cash or back-breaking sweat, that saying holds pretty true.

It generally doesn't pay to cut any corners. Most bargains are only bargains for the near term. Cheap stuff usually lasts about one day longer than the warranty.

It's not only sub-par supplies and jobber repairs that give in early because of low-level investment. Most of my quick-fix, "temporary" solutions to permanent problems have the same short life span.

### Just for now

Most of our ranch has been built with the idea of, "I'll just tack this up for now and we'll really build it right when we have a little more time." Our corrals, barn, house and fences are a testimony to this hopeful attitude.

We have old machinery lined up in the pasture that is held together with spot welds, barbed wire and baler twine, awaiting the day when we have a little more time to really fix them up right.

Even the cow herd's kind of tacked up with our "just for now" philosophy. There are a couple cows that oughta be shipped, but they do know the range, so we decide to run 'em another year. We'll throw the chlorine in our gene pool when we have a little more time.

Temporary fences soon become full-fledged sorting corrals, welded up shafts become trusted components of machinery miracles and short-term cows become foundation dams too dear to part with.

### Portable problems

Last fall, I made a real effort to permanently patch the holes in the corrals and reclaim the temporary panels that were wired in as a short-term solution two or three years ago. My reclamation project yielded 12 truly portable portable corral panels.

It's been a good winter to have a little mobile fence. With all the permanent corrals buried in snow and the gates four months away from swinging, it's nice to be able to build a new pen on top of the snow with those little green panels.

Rather than dig out our loading chute last week, I opted to set up a "quick fix" loading area to get a few cull cows in the horse trailer. The cows didn't have much respect for my temporary set-up as they temporarily knocked them down, not once, but twice, before I gave up and shoveled out the real loading chute.

I had the same luck with some temporary grain storage I tacked up in the pole barn to hold a semi-load of supplemental cow chow. The pellets were piling up nicely in my planked-up, plywood-clad holding area until the last couple hundred pounds caused it to burst at the seams and send pellets flowing hither and yon.

My temporary grain corral did teach me a couple things about wooden structures-though. I now know why No. 2 lumber costs less than No. 1 boards, and I have firsthand knowledge of how to bend plywood to make a wooden canoe.

# Little hobby or big jobby?
## It's all in the eyes of the beholder

I've been feeling a little stressed lately. It's the often-heard story about life and work in the '90s. Too much to do in too little time. I've fully entered the rat race, and I'm convinced that the rats are winning.

The other day, I was feeling blue and bending the ear of my boyhood buddy and confidant, Sonny Outlook. As usual, he wouldn't put up with my complaining. He figured I was way off base for even bringing up the subject of work-related stress.

"You know, I used to have some hobbies. Now I barely take enough time from work to eat and sleep," I told him. Sonny scoffed at my meager problems, slapped me up along side my jughead and told me to come to my senses. "Waddya do that for?" I asked my suddenly abusive pal. "You were whining," he retorted.

Sonny had a point. I was whining, but I figured I'd earned the right to complain a little. I'd been working 80 hours a week — ranching, writing, speaking, working off the ranch to support the ranch. I wanted a little sympathy, but Sonny wasn't budging one bit.

"You've got more hobbies than you can shake a stick at," he told me. I challenged him to name even one. "Just tell me what you did yesterday," he asked.

"Well I rode horse out to check the cows. I found a hole in the fence and a bunch of cows were out. So I chased the cows back in, fixed the fence, then rushed back home to get on the tractor and mow hay all afternoon. At night I did some research, put some thoughts down on the computer, returned some phone calls and paid some bills."

"That day was chock full of hobbies, you moron," Sonny informed me. "Come again," I said, "It sounded like all work, no play to me."

Sonny claimed it was practically all play, no work. "First you were horseback, that makes you an equestrian. And looking for cows — I'd call that hunting. You're a real sportsman. Chasing those cows back in would qualify as cow cutting or team penning — huge recreational horse hobbies.

Fixing that fence is the kind of stuff basement shopsmiths live for — swinging a hammer, building and admiring the finished project. What'd you see while you were riding?"

"Just the usual," I said, "Grass, trees, some weeds and flowers. Lots of birds — meadowlarks, bluebirds, hawks, ducks."

"Aha! Exactly what I thought. Not only are you an equestrian, a hunter and a shopsmith, you're a bird watcher and a botanist," Sonny said. "Okay," I returned, "give me your read on the haying and the evening office work."

He said that was easy — more fun, more leisure, more hobby time. "I drove by the meadow while you were out mowing and I see you were using that old John Deere A," he said.

"Yeah, I was bouncing around on that old, rough-riding junker," I confirmed. "You know, a lot of people have made a hobby out of collecting and working on those two-cylinder Johnny poppers. Some people even enter John Deere slow races to entertain themselves, and I saw you shifted down to first gear in that wire grass." I could tell Sonny was on a roll.

"And I had no idea you were such a fan of entomology, Ryan, until I saw you drive into that cloud of flying ants. Then once you got out of that fine insectary, you got right into a swarm of mosquitoes and even got to study a few horseflies."

"But I was especially impressed that in the middle of it all, you shut right down and had yourself a picnic under that big, blue summer sky."

"You mean the summer sausage sandwiches, Fig Newtons and coffee I gulped down in the shade of the pickup where the temperature was only 96 degrees instead of 100?" I asked my power of positive-thinking pal.

"Absolutely," he confirmed, "and you topped it all off with an evening in the intellectual arts — reading, writing, creative thought, comparing philosophy with distant companions over the telephone."

"How about paying those bills? I suppose you'd consider that a practice in penmanship and calligraphy, maybe licking and sticking that sheet of 32-cent postage would make me a stamp loving philatelist?" I pressed Mr. Feelgood.

"Don't be stupid," he said, "you gotta do a little work you bum."

After it all, I decided that my old friend, Sonny Outlook, had a point. The real truth of the matter is I need fewer hobbies.

# Hold the sprouts
## Bacteria even affects grazers

As if the beef industry didn't have enough trouble, the E. coli bacteria has risen to the top of the trouble list, shoving aside such trivial matters as producers who won't work together and consumers who'd rather buy chicken.

The outbreak of E. coli in a batch of frozen hamburger patties from Hudson Foods has been a media feeding frenzy. And it should be. The bacteria can be deadly. It has killed people and it's especially dangerous to the very young, very old or immunity deficient.

Just one more little challenge for the cattle business. But there's hope. Consumers can watch their bacteria worries go up in smoke if they just cook their burgers a little longer and a little hotter, 160 degrees to be exact. So, turn up the grill.

## Hold the salad

I'm confident that cattlemen will take care of their E. coli problem and find new ways to make beef even safer, but I'm a little worried about the folks in the alfalfa sprout business.

Or haven't you heard? With all the talk about the Hudson burgers and the high drama of USDA "swat teams" out combing the beef plants for invisible bacteria, hardly anyone has heard about the alfalfa threat.

It's not the kind of alfalfa scare I'm used to either. To me, alfalfa scares are things like winter kill, rain on the windrows or getting the bill for the seed when the little legumes already have droughted out.

The alfalfa scare is also about E. coli and some sprouts that sickened four times as many people as the Hudson burgers. But their ill-fated trip to the salad bar failed to make the front page, it was too full of tainted burger stories.

But folks should be just as worried about their salads. It's tough to cook the bacteria out of salad fixin's. Imagine alfalfa sprouts after they've been cooked to 160 degrees. Not too appetizing.

This could be a vegetarian's nightmare! Cutting off their salad would be like weaning me off beef. It could get pretty ugly.

## Worried cows

I'm already seeing the effects of fretting salad eaters. My favorite vegetarians — my cows — are going berserk over the alfalfa sprout issue.

Just the other day, I was driving down the road and found my cows out picketing a hay field. Like a bunch of disgruntled UPS workers they were marching around with wooden laths stuck between their cloven hooves.

The signs said, "Alfalfa kills," and, "Cows deserve safe forages." The most active picketers were those most susceptible — the baby calves, the old gummer cows and the immunity deficient, you know, those animals that just won't respond to LA-200.

They'd heard about the alfalfa scare and they had a long list of demands that ranged from a vigorous forage testing program to a new hay bale cooker for any suspect alfalfa. It was understandable, but their worries were unfounded.

124

I assured them that all the ranch's alfalfa had fallen to the June drought and that they'd be getting nothing but sterile slough grass and CRP hay this winter. Another crisis solved.

# Standby to win

## Does the prize patrol van venture out on gravel roads?

Things are looking up here on the Taylor Ranch. The calves look pretty good, we'll be done haying by Halloween, and I've been put on "standby alert" to win $3.5 million in the Publishers Clearing House sweepstakes.

I'm pretty confident about the calves weighing up good and the hay being wrapped up, but I'm a little less sure about the multimillion-dollar superprize.

Just in case, though, I got my claim ready to mail. My superprize claim number stickers are properly affixed, my prize delivery location approval sticker is stuck, I initialed three times and signed the form on the bottom line. The only thing I didn't do is order any magazines. That could be my downfall.

### A few edits

The Publishers Clearinghouse even showed me the exact script and storyboard that's already been written for the big day. It may have to be edited a bit, though.

"The PCH Prize Patrol is in Towner, N.D., to surprise our newest winner!" My new 911 address must have tricked them into thinking that I live right in the greater metropolitan Towner area. I'll have to inform them that 1363 54th St. N.E. is actually 17 gravel miles away from the city limits.

The next line goes, "It's pretty early. We just might have to wake up Ryan M. Taylor!" For starters, they could get a little more personal and just call me Ryan, for short.

And that crack about waking me up can be deleted. The winning announcement is scheduled for Oct. 15, the same day I was planning on weaning the calves. I should be out saddling a horse by 7 a.m., so they'll probably find me out in the barn nursing a travel mug full of coffee.

The storyboard wraps up with, "Good morning, Ryan M. Taylor, you've just won $3.5 million!" Again, they can just call me Ryan. I notice the picture above this line in the script shows the prizewinner with his arm around some gal. The neighborhood really would be buzzing with gossip if the prize patrol found me with my arm around some gal at 7 in the morning. They'll have to settle for a picture of me standing next to my horse.

**Extra luck**

At about the same time I got my standby alert letter, I got another letter in an unmarked envelope that said, "This is not a chain letter!!! This paper has been sent to you for good luck." How fortuitous.

It told about all the cars, jobs and money it had brought about for others who had made 20 copies and passed the good luck letter along. "Send no money," it said. I liked that.

So I invested $10 in 20 copies, envelopes and stamps and addressed the letters to the folks on my Christmas card list. That should get me knee deep in luck I would think.

I hardly can wait for the big announcement on Oct. 15. I just wonder if the prize patrol boys can handle a sorting stick and help me wean the calves.

# Signs of aging
## It's more than just gray hairs

I don't know if it's the years or the miles, but I've really been noticing the effects of aging lately.

I'm getting used to my general loss of hair, but now I've got to deal with the graying of what little hair I've got left under my hat. My growing clump of gray strands is best seen under the glare of high-power fluorescent lights, but it is definitely there.

I figure that at this rate, I'll have that distinguished "silver fox" look by the time I'm 30. Of course, things are pretty competitive on my skull — the hair could all fall out before it has the chance to turn gray.

I'd like to blame it all on the steady burning stress of going broke in the cattle business, but, in all truthfulness, the causes are probably genetic.

Most of my older male relatives have a nice, lustrous sheen to their chrome domes and a few of my cousins got that salt-and-pepper look to their hair well before the age of 40. Surprisingly, most of them don't even run cattle. Of course, grain farming, construction and office work are plenty stressful, too.

**Sure signs**

Although the graying and hair loss are fairly visible, the most evident signs of aging can be seen as I work around the ranch. It's those everyday actions that really tell the tale.

Just the other day, I shut the gate behind me when I went out to check the cows. A younger person with more hair and less gray would have left that gate open, preferring to spend an hour chasing in cows rather than spend 30 seconds shutting the gate. This is a true sign of maturity amongst cattlemen.

Then I went to visit a neighbor and I left the vehicle running the whole time I was there. A younger person would have shut that pickup off to save the gas burned in an hour-long idle, but us old guys really appreciate getting into a warm vehicle.

When I was younger, I used to have a pretty bad temper. However, now that I've aged, my fuse burns a whole lot slower. Patience is most certainly a virtue that comes with age.

For instance, the calves wouldn't budge when I tried to chase them out of the feeding pen this morning. Rather than yelling and screaming and busting a cold sorting stick across the feed bunk, I just hung in there for the five minutes of coaxing needed to get them out.

And when the pickup wouldn't start and the battery went dead, I didn't even kick it in the fender or cuss its manufacturer. I just walked to the shop and got the battery charger. Now that's a sure sign of maturity.

So I've decided getting older ain't so bad after all. My receding hairline, graying follicles and calm, cool demeanor kind of suit me. Now I can concentrate on finding some big fat profits in agriculture before I retire. I guess a good sense of humor must come with age, too.

# Good nutrition
## Ranchers know their cow's diets better than their own

I was eating my breakfast cereal the other morning when a thought struck me. As healthy as I am, I'm really quite ignorant of my daily intake of nutrients.

I came to this conclusion after reading the nutrition facts on the side panel of one of my favorite cereals, Fruity Pebbles. I already had completed the maze and the word games on the back panel, and I'd long since dug into the box to find my free Fruity Pebble prize.

The only entertainment I was left with was to review the 10 essential vitamins and minerals that Fred and Barney were sending my way via the artificially flavored, wholesome, sweetened rice cereal.

I had no idea Fruity Pebbles were so good for you. They're practically the perfect food.

### Well balanced cows

As usual, I went out to feed the cows after I finished eating my healthy, sugar-loaded breakfast. I rolled out several bales, ensuring that the cows were eating enough pounds of hay to equal about 3 percent of their body weight.

The hay had been tested for its nutritional worth and I was careful to use the right quality of hay for the cows' current needs in their last trimester of pregnancy. I poured a bag of mineral supplement in a tire feeder to take up any nutritional slack and make sure the cows were getting plenty of essential minerals and vitamins A, D and E.

I could tell you their approximate dry matter intake, how many pounds of protein they were getting and what the diet's energy level was. I could recite the grams per pound of calcium and phosphorus and the parts per million levels of zinc, copper and selenium.

Funny thing, though, I couldn't tell you diddly about what I put in my own body that day, aside from that little dab of information gleaned from the Fruity Pebbles box. Ironic, isn't it, that I had no idea how much iron was in my diet?

**People rations**

Of course, if I feed my cattle complete rations and then eat the beef from those cattle, I should have a fairly well balanced diet.

But, as good as beef is, I admit that man cannot live on meat alone.

You can get close to a complete diet if you throw in some Fruity Pebbles, a few spuds and some candy, but there's still one thing missing — a good block of "a little lick'll do ya" supplement. Sure, there are multipurpose pills out there on the market, but why can't we get the same convenient block form our cows do?

I think there's a huge unmet demand for desktop lick blocks. Feeling sluggish? Just unleash your tongue and have a couple super-fortified licks right there on your desk.

And if you prefer the granular form, put a small rubber tire feeder on your desk and fill it up from time to time. The tires would have to come from toy tractors, but they'd be easier to work with than the life-size ones.

Yes sir, desktop lick, available in block or bag. Finally, a sensible way to complete the diet, and all within reach of your tongue.

# Shake your booties
## Getting the other shoe to drop...with ease

Last week's blizzard was pretty mild compared with last year's storms, but it lasted long enough to exhaust some supplies on the ranch.

It had been awhile since we'd been to the grocery store and I was needin' to get there pretty soon. It wasn't the dwindling supply of milk or bread that had me worried, it was the shortage of plastic grocery sacks that was beginning to worry me.

I can get along without milk for a few days, but I need a steady supply of plastic sacks to get my five-buckle overshoes to slip over my boots. Plastic grocery bags are a footwear staple around here for tight overshoes.

Forget about whitewashing the inside of your overshoes with Grandma's superslick corn starch. Don't even think about drafting an innocent bystander to help you get that size 11$^1$/$_2$ overshoe peeled off of your size 12 clodhoppers. I've seen people thrown through Sheetrock walls while wrestling with overshoes.

## Easy on, easy off

My trick of the trade? Just stick your boot into a nice slippery grocery bag and slide it right into the tightest of five-buckler rubbers with ease.

And exit is as easy as the entry. No more using your semi-clean hands to pull off those slimy, manure-laden overshoes. A little fancy footwork and a good sense of balance and you'll have 'em slipped off with nothing but pure foot power.

There is a downside, however. Bag fatigue. Plastic grocery sacks are generally plentiful, but they're not that well built. You'll have more hole than bag in a week or two, so keep plenty on hand.

That's why I always say "plastic please" when I'm questioned at the checkout line. But once you're hooked on plastic, blizzards and limited trips to the grocery store can make you pretty nervous.

## Other options

There are other kinds of winter footwear that can make you less dependent on cheap plastic bags.

But most of the other systems are a real drag for sock wearers. Insulated pack boots will have socks with the best of elastic pulled down and balled up in the toe of your boot in no time flat.

The same goes for slip-on rubber "dairy boots." There's nothing more uncomfortable than walking around with your over-the-calf socks situated not only under-your-calf, but under your ankle, in front of your heel and barely hanging onto your big toe.

Those shoes might be all right if I had a pair of those sock garters. I've never had a pair, but I understand they're kind of like suspenders for socks. I saw a lady in a movie who was playing the part of a call girl wearing a pair, but they just didn't look like my style.

So I think I'll just stick with the boots, bags and overshoes for now.

One last tip — don't try to substitute paper bags for the plastic. They may be made of a renewable resource, but they tear real easy and they don't do a thing to keep your feet dry if you spring a leak in your rubbers.

# Mailbox surprises
## Reader generosity shines bright

My trips to the mailbox have been a lot more exciting since I started writing "Cowboy Logic" four years ago.

I don't usually ask for gifts outright in my column, but some readers have figured out a few of my needs and popped a package in the mail to help fulfill them.

Fortunately, I haven't gotten any mail bombs or other life-threatening materials, like a vile of calf scours bacteria or a package of sprouting leafy spurge seeds. No, just good, useful kind of rancher stuff.

### Good-will gratuity

One of the first things I remember getting from a reader was a base-ball cap. Most of us farmers and ranchers live for free caps. We hang 'em up in our houses, stuff a few extra ones under the pickup seat and keep a few in the shop just in case the one on our head gets doused with oil when we're pulling the drain plug.

We've been known to drive 100 miles to an ag show just for the chance to snag a few free caps and here I was getting one delivered right to my mailbox!

It came from Dale Lincoln out in Arthur, N.D., and it had a ranchy-looking longhorned cow on it with the caption, "Friends don't let friends eat chicken!" It's a ranch favorite.

Two winters ago, I wrote about a new advertising scheme for Ford New Holland, the folks who buy the space under my column every week. I proposed a Christmas season swap — a couple big tractors and a skid steer loader in exchange for my never-ending devotion, a weekly testimonial on tractor toughness and some action photographs of me and the new tractors that they could use in their ad space.

A few weeks after that column ran, my mailbox held a couple boxes from a regional New Holland sales office in Minnesota. No tractor keys or certificates of ownership — just two baseball caps and a 3-inch-long toy tractor. At least it was a front-wheel-assist model.

### Recent gifts

This past winter has been a real generous one. After I wrote about my new 911 street address that put me on 54th Street (but still 17 miles from town), I got a big, shiny green street sign from fellow farmer and entre-preneur, Dennis Erickson, in Gully, Minn.

130

It came complete with personalized reflective lettering so I could find my way home in the dark. It's proudly mounted at the end of my driveway and working nicely.

Just last week, though, I got a dandy package from Mary Kjerstad in Quinn, S.D. The box seemed light when I picked it up, and I immediately knew what it had to hold. Hearing my plea for plastic grocery sacks to put inside my five-buckle overshoes, Mary sent me a real nice collection of 29 plastic bags.

She hoped I didn't mind mixing brands of bags. Not to worry, I'm not too proud to wear a Cash Wise Foods on one foot and an IGA Foods on the other. I'm just glad to have them.

Now, if I just had a few more brown paper sacks to wrap gifts in for upcoming weddings, birthdays and anniversaries....

# Sighting in
## A keen eye, a straight line and a flat planet

There are a few things ranchers take a lot of pride in, and near the top on my list is a straight fence.

A straight fence is a real test of personal skill. No amount of money or new machinery can make it any easier for one person to accomplish. As far as a solo test of skills goes, a straight fence separates the men from the boys.

### Fence off

I had a couple jags of new four-wire barbed to finish putting in this spring, and, as luck would have it, I was able to talk my visiting brother-in-law into giving me a hand.

He'd already helped me set the corner posts and string out the wire when he was here for Thanksgiving last fall. Now, it was already Easter, and I was ready to start setting the steel posts in the freshly thawed ground.

If it weren't for family holidays and my visiting brother-in-law, I sometimes think I wouldn't get anything done. Lucky for me, his heart is as big as his ex-Marine biceps.

There aren't many physical contests that I can beat my brother-in-law at. The odds are just plain against me and my lanky physique.

So I challenged him to the only physical game I had a chance at: a fence off. It involved a little strength to pound in the posts, but we would judge it on both speed and finesse. First done and straightest would win.

He could pound a post in with two licks compared with my six, but when the dust had settled, the skinny cowboy was victorious.

Brother-in-law was still 50 paces from the railroad tie finish line, and his string of steel posts were as crooked as a dog's hind leg.

"Nice try. You gave it a good effort," I said as I patted him on his Charolais bull-like shoulder. After pulling and resetting a few posts, we had him straightened out. I accepted the title of fencing champion graciously.

**Round earth rationale**

I was back on the fence line last week, but without any major holidays going on, I was forced to fence alone. It was an easy job, a mere two-wire electric cross fence with posts spaced every 100 feet or so.

I began pounding posts and things were looking good, at least in one direction. Looking west, I was as straight as an arrow. Unfortunately, I was "lined up" to miss the east corner by about 10 feet.

As defending champion of the ranch's straight fencing title, I improvised. I began pulling a few posts and reset them to give the fence a nice bowed, artistic arc. I got the fence to hit the corner, but, overall, the cross fence had quite a curve to it.

However, I'm certain that the blame for that midfence bulge does not rightfully rest on my straight shoulders. And after giving it some thought, I realized exactly why I'd missed my mark.

Thanks to Christopher Columbus and his round earth theory, I have a rock-solid alibi for that crooked cross fence. It's clearly evident to me that I was straight, but the darn earth had curved on me.

# Lack of luck
## The life of a door prize drop out

I went to the annual meeting of my rural electric cooperative recently, hoping to cash in on some of the spectacular door prizes that were up for grabs.

Top prize was $3,000 in cash, with a name drawn from the entire membership list, but you had to be present to win. Other prizes for those in attendance were handy things such as water distillers, electric grills and donated gift certificates. I was one person in a crowd of more than a thousand, but like most compulsive door prize gamblers, I thought that I just might get drawn and be the lucky one in 1,000 winner.

I should have known better. When it comes to door prizes and raffles, my luck runs about as deep as a shallow mud puddle. Once again, I didn't win a dang thing, but I'm still hopeful for the next meeting or the next book of raffle tickets that comes my way.

That's how it is with us addicts. Like a junkie hooked on heroine, I'll drive to the next meeting, register my name at yet another sign up table or buy just one more raffle ticket, to get my fix for the week.

It's a horrible, vicious cycle.

Of course, the first step in conquering an addiction is admitting that you have a problem. I not only admit it, I'll even write about it.

**Worst best odds**

Last fall, I went to a meeting put on by our local veterinary clinic. The overriding purpose of the meeting was to give us a little education on animal health, but they drew us in with a free steak supper and a table full of door prizes.

The steak was good. Free steaks always are. And the odds looked pretty attractive for me to finally take home a door prize. Good weather and fall chores made for a low turnout at the meeting. I counted 14 ranchers in the chairs and tallied up a dozen door prizes that ranged from leather gloves to multi-dose syringes and tempered steel hitch pins.

This was my big break – an 86 percent chance of fulfilling my door prize desires! I waited anxiously as they drew one name after another from the registration slip coffee can.

Believe it or not, they drew for all 12 prizes and I got passed by all 12 times. Two people went home prizeless – me and my neighbor who rode in with me. All we had in front of us at the end of the evening were empty plates and chewed-up foam coffee cups. No gloves, no syringes, not so much as a hitch pin.

I was devastated. That evening, I was convinced there was absolutely no hope for me in the world of door prize success. Not only was I inflicted with terrible luck, I was the carrier of an apparently contagious poor luck pathogen and I'd passed it on to an innocent neighbor. He'll probably never ride along with me to another meeting again.

If you have a door prize addiction, be sure to seek help before it breaks up your neighborhood, too.

# Nodak three degrees
## A bond with everybody in much less than six degrees of separation

Remember the Kevin Bacon "six degrees of separation" craze that was sweeping the country a few years ago? I think it was a book or a board game or something where people could name any actor or actress and connect them to Kevin Bacon with fewer than six other actors and movies.

So, any actor you name could have starred with another actor, who, in turn, could have starred with another actor who had starred with the actress who had played opposite Kevin Bacon in some movie. I think that example would be about four degrees of separation.

It's an entertaining enough concept, but I don't think it has anything over on everyday life in North Dakota and the rest of the rural plains. I would bet that just about every North Dakotan could be connected in three degrees of separation or less.

A friend of mine from Minnesota gave me this example. A friend of hers from Mandan had some car trouble in Fargo. A young fella stopped to give her a ride, they struck up a conversation and found out that her brother's best friend's brother was his roommate. A mere three degrees of separation!

## Training grounds

While citizens in other parts of the country somehow survive on anonymity, North Dakotans thrive on familiarity. And it has gotten to be a fanatical game for the inhabitants of this state with a population of just 640,000 people.

Years of training through youth camps, high school activities, 4H and FFA, the state's university system and careers requiring a lot of in-state travel have got some people connected to everyone else by a mere one or two degrees of separation.

The goal of these stellar players as they met people from around the state was to make sure that they knew at least one person from every town, big or small, in North Dakota.

I consider myself a pretty good hand at "Nodak Three Degrees of Separation" because of high school FFA travels, college extracurriculars and my personal rancher and writer network of contacts.

## Playing the game

There are some places where the game is just naturally played, both in and out of state. I'm sure I'll get a couple of rounds in at the State Fair next week, but I've also had some good matches at the departure gates for Minot or Bismarck in the Minneapolis airport.

The game is fairly simple and goes something like this: "Hi there. Where are you from? Oh, you're from Bowman! I bet you know so and so, he was my roommate in college." Score! One degree of separation.

If your counterpart is worth their salt as a true Nodak, they will find out your hometown and immediately identify a few people that they know from your locale, keeping the score fairly even.

However, if you're from a large metropolis like Towner, you could get outdone by someone from a smaller town. They could know several people from your city, and you could appear quite inadequate with folks in their area. That's where it pays to do your homework.

Luckily, I'm well covered for most towns like Amidon, Dodge, Monango and Gilby, but I do have a couple of weak spots. So, if you're from Burt or Norma, you just might have me beat.

*Author's note: I did get a letter from someone in Norma, N.D., so I've now shored up that weakness. However, I'm still a little lacking in Burt.*

# Information gaps
## Small town info networks better at speed than accuracy

There used to be a game we'd play as youngsters where one person would make up a short story, tell it to someone else, who would tell it to another person and another and another.

After the story made its way through 10 or 20 people, you'd ask the last person who'd heard it to tell everyone their ending version of the story. Usually, it would be about as close to the initial story as a New York Times article would be to the National Enquirer's version.

The game had the politically incorrect name of "Chinese Gossip," but regardless of the game's racial label, it proved a pretty valid point about how stories can get out of control when they're passed from person to person.

### Hometown hearsay

The game just as easily could have been called Dakota gossip, or Norwegian or German gossip, or "good people concerned about their neighbors" gossip. The end result is still a whopper of a story that's far from the truth.

Picture this. A morning thunderstorm with lots of lightning went through my area. In the afternoon, I spotted some smoke coming from a neighbor's hayfield.

I drove out there and found four round bales struck by lightning. They were blazing away. The fire wasn't spreading much, but if the wind decided to come up, there were another thousand bales in the area to fuel the fire.

I figured it probably would be a good idea to get a water truck out there to put it out, or else we'd be feeding the cows charbroiled bales all next winter. So I called the fire department and told them not to get too excited, but we could use a little water on some burning hay bales.

### Coincidental calls

I didn't know when I called the fire department that an ambulance had headed to our neighborhood just a little earlier.

My neighbor had gotten bucked off a horse and took a bad bounce. He cracked a few vertebrae and the pain was so intense that he went unconscious. The unconscious part especially had his family pretty worried. They called the ambulance for a little assistance.

Sending an ambulance south of town caused a flurry of activity in the neighborhood. Everyone dropped what they were doing to try and find out where the siren was heading.

Some of the neighborhood investigation is really quite sophisticated. One of the more informed farmwives in the area even keeps a police scanner on her kitchen counter to keep up on local emergencies.

But even the scanner failed to solve the mystery. Phone lines were buzzing as everyone called everyone else to track down who had gotten sick or injured. Nobody thought to call the house of my relatively young, healthy neighbor with the newly cracked vertebrae.

Finally, the solution to the puzzle made it to the local grocery store where my injured neighbor's mother was shopping. She hadn't been home to get the news from her granddaughter so she was unaware of the afternoon's excitement.

"How's your son doing?" someone asked. "Gosh I didn't know anything was wrong with him," she said, unaware of the horse wreck. "Oh yes," the other local super sleuth returned, "They just took him to the hospital in the ambulance. He was struck by lightning!"

# Odd urban and rural observations

# Hats are in the heartland
## Going east to find out what's west

I was out in Chicago last week, getting eye to eye with some of the folks who get our cattle to the last link in the beef chain.

The Food Marketing Institute gathered up some 30,000 retail and food service people for their Supermarket Industry Convention and another 5,000 export buyers for the U.S. Food Export Showcase. All that on top of the 4 million inhabitants who already were crowded up against the shore of Lake Michigan.

Chicago was a nice town to visit. The people were generally friendly and there was certainly no shortage of things to do and see. But the poor people have a couple of real geographical misconceptions they need to overcome.

### Mid what?

First off, Chicagoans keep saying how nice it is to live in the Midwest.

Midwest? How do they figure? It's a mighty long day's drive east of where I call home and I thought I lived in the Midwest.

I might grant them the middle, but definitely not the west.

The newscasters in that area are even more mixed up. They report on the "life in the heartland." There's body parts I'd compare that big city to, but the heart isn't the first one that comes to mind.

If it was the heartland, it wouldn't appear to be a very healthy one. The streets making up the arteries were so clogged up, they reminded me of the overweight fellow who figured grease was one of the four major food groups and defined exercise as reaching for the remote control.

I'd hope the heartland of America would more closely resemble the Dakotas — strong, free flowing and full of health. My heartland's blood pressure is low, its beat is slow and steady, and it does it all with honest exercise and a steady diet of beef, bread and potatoes.

I won't compromise my definition of the heartland — America's health is riding on it.

### All hat, no y'all

The second big geographical misconception they have in Chicago is that everyone who wears a hat comes from Texas.

Now I'm pretty proud of who I am. I wear what I like to wear and I do what I like to do. And it sure let the wind out of my sails to be walking tall like a good North Dakotan should and have some half-wit city dweller ask me, "Are you from Texas?"

Since when did Texans have an exclusive on wide-brimmed hats? Just because I see someone wearing a parka, I don't ask them if they're from Alaska. And if I see someone with orange hair and tattoos, I don't automatically assume they play basketball for the Bulls.

But after you explain to the first 20 confused souls that there's a land called Dakota where cowboys call home, you get a little wore down. So when confused soul No. 21 asked me if I was a Texan, I just smiled and said, "No, ma'am, I just stole the hat from one."

# Commuting on the rolling prairies
## Miles converted to hours put us at par with our city cousins

Unless you're independently wealthy, unemployed or farm for a living, you get to enjoy the daily drive from the home where you work, sleep and eat to the job site where you work, sleep and eat.

The daily commute is a big issue for our friends in the cities where everything is measured in minutes, not miles. The drive time can compound stress, burn up dollars and waste precious time for busy people.

**But how far is it?**

It's hard to get a straight answer from these folks when you ask them how far they are from somewhere.

"How far is it between your home and the office?" I recently asked a metropolitan friend of mine. "It's about an hour," he replied. "No, I mean how far is it?" I repeated. "Well, 45 minutes in good traffic, an hour and 15 minutes if the streets are busy," he said.

I could see I was getting nowhere. The poor guy must have had some terrible teachers in elementary school when he was growing up.

I learned early on that a mile was 5,280 feet, a township was six miles by six miles, and a section of land measured one mile square.

These numbers were real distances and I was able to answer questions of distance with clarity and certainty. Near as I could tell, an hour only measured about 15 inches around on our kitchen clock, and barely an inch on my wrist watch. Time and distance were completely separate measurements in my mind.

Apparently, this buddy of mine from the city hadn't learned his distances. I wouldn't dare let him survey our ranch without a better understanding of measurements than that.

I still was trying to make sense of my friend's explanation of distances in the big city when he started asking a few questions of his own.

"How far is it from your ranch to a major city?" he asked. I figured a major city meant a population of more than 5,000, so I answered, "Oh, it's about 60 miles from the ranch to Minot. They've got it all — malls, movies, tap beer."

"Sixty miles! How can you stand to live in such desolation? I couldn't imagine that kind of a commute for the necessities," he said. "Yeah, it's pretty tough," I said, "It's not like living in the big city where work is only an hour away."

"How long does it take to drive that far?" He asked. "There must be an awful lot of traffic lights in that many miles."

"It only takes about an hour, but the lights can slow you up at night," I said.

"Do the traffic lights get really busy during the evening rush?" he asked. "Oh, there are no traffic lights," I said, "but the northern lights can come out at night, and then we like to slow down and admire them as we drive."

# What truck?
## Picking up on pickup lingo

I was talking to an urbanite last week about different modes of transportation. "You must have to drive a truck out there on the ranch," he said.

Immediately, my mind conjured up images of 18-wheelers, big long-haul reefers and the neighbor's 1949 Ford that I meet on the gravel in the fall when he's hauling his harvest into the local farmer's elevator.

"No, I've just got a pickup," I told my city friend. "We don't do any grain farming and I don't own a single David Allen Coe tape. Heck, I don't even know any fancy CB radio lingo — you read me, good buddy?"

But my friend still insisted that I owned a truck, even after I explained to him that the ranch vehicle I owned only had four wheels and didn't have to pull over at the weigh stations along the highway.

I told him that the box was only 8 feet long and 18 inches deep. It didn't have a hydraulic hoist and it couldn't haul very many bushels of anything, just a little barbed wire, a few empty oil jugs and, occasionally, a ton of salt blocks.

"That's what we call a truck. They're cool, everybody drives one in the city," he said. "Those aren't trucks, they're pickups," I told him. "And why do you people think you need to have a pickup to drive on the pavement? Worried you might need to haul a couple bags of lawn clippings or a new foot stool from the furniture store?"

He went on to tell me how the city's a real jungle that demands a big tough pickup truck. Gotta have four-wheel drive because if you look real hard you can find a spot of mud or an occasional snow bank to go through.

"You need the clearance to drive over speed bumps, and I don't know how I'd get my Jet Ski to the lake or my snowmobile out to Yellowstone without that bumper hitch," he told me.

"Gosh, I feel kind of silly needing my pickup just to drive 17 miles of unplowed roads in the winter and axle-deep mud in the spring. I can sure see where you need that three-quarter-ton to pull something as heavy as a snowmobile trailer. My half-ton feels the same way when it's hooked up to 9,000 pounds worth of cattle," I related to him.

He showed me a couple of showroom shots of his truck with its chrome trim, fancy wheel covers and leather seats. I showed him a couple pictures of my pickup. "Tough looking truck," he said.

"What happened to that back license plate?" "Bumper trailer," I said. "What happened to the tailgate?" "Neighbor's gooseneck," I returned. "And the grill?" he asked. "Chasing bulls." "How about the creases in your running boards?" "High centered on a sand dune," I explained.

"Hmmm, that's quite a pickup," he said, giving in to my terminology. And all I could say was, "I wish I had your truck."

# Gettin' there is half the fun
## ...and all of the challenge

Can you get there from here?

This question doesn't get posed much in the cities where paved streets run every which direction and are spaced about every 100 yards or so. But out here in the sticks, "gettin' there from here" can be a pretty tall order, especially from about November until June.

The routes of travel are pretty limited in a lot of rural areas. There's a usually a pretty good road running north and south or east and west to the nearest highway, but the next closest path of least resistance may be six or seven miles away.

Rerouting out in the country can be about as circuitous as flying to Billings, Mont., from Minot, N.D., via Minneapolis, Minn.

### A formidable moat

We've got one of those pretty decent gravel roads running north and south by our place. It's kind of the main artery circulating through about 12 square miles of sandhills and sloughs.

I was doing a little scouting the other day, checking the road out for mud depth and puddle circumference before taking a little trip southward to Bismarck. I was tooling along about 45 miles per hour and dang near got a radiator grill full of mud and an intensely close look at a washed-out culvert.

I put the brake pedal through the floorboards, left a little tire-width trench in the road way and dug my fingernails into the vinyl cushioning on the steering wheel.

This culvert had washed out before about 12 years ago when I was merely a lad. Back then, I had ridden my bike with the banana seat and grippy tires down to the washout and thought it was pretty cool.

Now, 12 years older, I looked at the same washout and thought it was much more inconvenient than cool. I did think it still had some cool attributes though.

It served as kind of a protective moat on the south side of a kingdom made up of five neighboring ranches and ourselves. I smiled at the thought of insurance salesmen, Jehovah's Witnesses and other pesky peddlers driving up to this formidable moat with no drawbridge to be found.

Then again, what if the same moat discouraged Ed McMahon from wheeling up to my doorstep with the Publisher's Clearinghouse prize van? Ahh, I'm sure any van packing a check for $10 million could clear a 10-foot gap in a gravel road.

## Backtracking

I still made my southward journey to Bismarck, but I racked up an extra 20 miles doing it. On my trip, I encountered a few other amusing signs of spring travel.

I saw a few side roads were washed out and blocked off with wooden laths and some of that yellow ribbon that says, "Police line-do not cross." The only crime that had been committed though was done by Mother Nature, and nobody dares take her to court.

It's nice to live in a state where police line ribbon is used on muddy roads instead of bloody crime scenes.

As I roller coastered over the frost heaves on the paved roads of my little traveled route I encountered a "Bump Ahead" sign about every quarter of a mile. I realized the meaning of the signs as I failed to take the cruise control off and ended up "Bumping Myhead" on the car roof about every quarter of a mile.

But the award for budget savings and county government efficiency goes to the county commissioners who scrapped the idea of putting up 72 "Bump Ahead" signs and 72 correlating "Bump" signs.

Their sign read, "Rough road next 18 miles." I appreciate their honesty.

# Hats off to salespeople
## Rain, snow, sleet or hail, sales must be made

This week's Cowboy Logic Award for valorous rural service above and beyond the call of duty goes to two feed salesmen who did something the mail, the school bus and the gas truck couldn't do — they penetrated the south Towner system of road ruts and washouts.

The business of sales is tough enough, what with growling farm dogs and some customers just as friendly, but throw in a set of roads like ours, and that commission-based pay scale starts looking pretty low.

I'm not sure how these two fellas got their little white car out to our place, but the freezing temperatures were a big help I'm sure. Without the mud to contend with, they could concentrate on keeping their car perched atop the narrow ledge that ran astraddle the bottomless frozen rut.

It must have been a company vehicle.

### Poor timing

Timing is key in the sales biz.

The two feed pellet peddlers caught me at a pretty bad time.

The needle on my sleep gauge was bobbing toward "E" after a long night on prolapse patrol. Three calves, 20 degrees worth of mercury, across-the-board cattle markets and one heifer's uterus had all recently dropped.

The only thing I could do anything about was the prolapsed heifer; the rest were controlled by contractions, God, the cattle cartel and the chicken eaters of the world.

Tough events preceding a sales call, no matter what you're selling. This particular day on the ranch didn't make things any easier for guys trying to get you to pump a little more money into your cows.

It'd be like selling a set of fuzzy dice to the fella whose car just blew up or a new saddle to the cowboy whose horse just died.

### The good effort

My hat went off to these guys for their perseverance in the face of poor roads. Of course, regardless of my feelings, my hat would have went off to them anyway because the wind was blowing about 100 miles per hour.

I almost felt sympathetic enough to buy a couple tons of some feed with a catchy name and an impressive guaranteed analysis, but my feed bin was already full.

Salespeople, as a rule, are a pretty amiable bunch. It's the nature of the business I guess. I've made a few sales calls in my day and, ever since that time I've lived a vow of friendliness when it comes to those hard-working, road-weary individuals.

If I hadn't been so busy with some immediate calving duties, I'd have given these boys a hot cup of coffee and a few minutes to gather their senses while the shocks on their car took a breather.

But as it was I couldn't do much more than trade a few minutes of chit-chat by the corral fence for a couple business cards and a feed tag on some range cake.

Company of any kind is appreciated out here in the boondocks. Feed salespeople willing to visit about the cattle business are usually more appreciated than those of the insurance nature whose conversation always turns to the subject of your death or dismemberment.

And although I'm glad to be hospitable with those who show up in our yard, I don't go looking for them on the highway, handing out directions to the place. So if anyone selling vacuum cleaners or encyclopedias asks you where the south Towner Taylor Ranch is, tell them, "They're right along the paved highway just north of town. You can't miss it."

# Farmers are off and tilling
## Roadway fields a little rocky, but it might make a crop

Farmers in our country are just a little too anxious to get a crop in this year.

Why just last week they were out with their discs and harrows working up the roadways.

I never question the action of farmers because I don't know enough about the cropping business to make any judgments. Our ranch was blessed with sandy land and about a quarter-inch of topsoil, so I don't do any farming myself, aside from tilling the garden.

But I was a little skeptical when I saw my neighbors tilling the roads. Sure the fields were still too wet to get any machinery on, but they really must have wanted to get a head start on the season to shine up their equipment on the gravel.

If they continue down this path, I wonder if they'll seed spring wheat or barley? Maybe oats? It might be best to check some university trials to see what crops and varieties yield best in gravel and clay.

**Past the fence rows**

At first, I figured these guys were helping me and the rest of the neighborhood out by leveling the ruts in the road and speeding up the drying process on our muddy paths. But then I saw an ad in a farm magazine that showed a tractor and a cultivator tearing up an asphalt street.

Geez, I figured, this must be the latest phenomenon in farming. America can show the rest of the world the power of modern farming techniques by sprouting grain in the gravel, producing bushels on the byways.

The early '70s saw farmers planting "fence row to fence row." The heck with stopping at the fence rows, there's a lot of good land lying idle in section line roads and highway medians.

## Traffic trials

I've seen guys try to put a crop in gravel before. Certain sections of the road between two fields will get seeded when the drills are moved. I'm not sure if the seed was flowing, but if it was, the milk trucks and school buses did their best to help pack it and seal in the available moisture.

I think the traffic got to a point, though, where the crop was ruined. There are a few little-used prairie trails that could grow a pretty good crop though I think. A good no-till farmer could even achieve a pretty high percentage of residue cover on those roads.

The higher traffic roads, however, could require some creative crop-saving techniques. If the farmer really wants to boost the yields on these major roadways, he may want to set out a few orange pylons and "road closed" sawhorses on the ends of the "field."

And just in case some illiterate driver steers around the barricades, it might be worthwhile to take out a little crop insurance.

They may want to check and see if their roadway crop insurance covers livestock damage, too. Chances are, if a few tender green shoots sprout up on any of my roads, there'll be a few barbed-wire-immune cows out there pulling up the tasty seedlings by the roots.

But all these plans may be a little premature. This year, it looks like the roadway crop already is ruined.

Things looked pretty promising until the county road grader came out and leveled everything in its path.

But it's still early. I think they might get a chance to replant.

# Ecolawn care
## Country solutions for city problems

I always get a kick out of city folks and their passion for lawn care. They're constantly out watering, fertilizing and herbiciding their little piece of nature so the grass will grow faster and thicker. Then they can mow it and mulch it more and more often.

It seems like a pretty vicious cycle to me as they strive for the most meticulously manicured lawn on the block. It pits neighbor against neighbor, facing them off with fertilizer spreaders, lawn sprinklers and riding lawn mowers.

What a waste of gas, grass and resources.

## Move over deer

It seems especially odd that folks work so hard to get a good stand of grass when their concrete deer and plastic pink flamingoes can't even make use of the fine grazing.

I say we should save the concrete for the sidewalks and replace those stoic deer with something a little more lively, entertaining and beneficial.

Move over deer, here come the horses and ponies.

We've parked our lawn mower and converted our yard to a horse pasture. We not only have the pleasure of watching our lawn get automatically mowed for us, we have the enjoyment of watching our lawn decorations eat the flowers, rub on the trees and get chased by the dogs.

I think the system would work equally well in our large urban centers where the population's concern for the environment is only surpassed by their concern for themselves.

There's a lot of grass in the yards of our cities and a lot of people driving to work every morning in their little smogmobiles.

Why not run a horse or two in the back yard, save the headaches associated with lawn care and use that critter for transportation to and from work?

Fossil fuels are a limited resource, but grass grows year after year. Think of the savings — no gas going through the weed trimmer, the lawn mower or the station wagon; no exhaust fumes or pollution; and free fertilizer!

## Giddyup, Yuppies

Picture all our young urban professionals going to work on horseback. It'd be good exercise for them and they'd look a lot healthier if they spent a little more time out in the elements putting a little color on their pasty complexions.

Most large corporations have extensive yards themselves that could use a little grazing. New fringe benefit packages could include horse day care and grazing allotments for the employees.

It'd be a real cost savings for the corporations. Cut the groundskeeping crew and all their expensive equipment. Quit pouring concrete for parking lots; just let it grass over and string a little fence around the perimeter.

There'd be saddle racks next to the coat racks and boot scrapers over by the welcome mat.

Stress could be greatly reduced for our strung-out young professionals. Horse travel potentially could move faster than rush-hour traffic. Plus, it'd be much more peaceful to have horses nicker back and forth to each other, instead of having traffic-jammed cars honking, crashing and backfiring.

We'd have a whole new class of working men and women in our cities, and you know what we'd have to call them. That's right, make room for the Giddyuppies.

# Postal service lingo
## Deciphering government speak and bureaucranese

I got an envelope from our mail lady a while back. Her correct title probably would be mail carrier, but we affectionately call her the mail lady.

She's a good, friendly gal who dutifully delivers our mail, smiles often and waves when you pass her on the road. Nice qualities in a governmental employee.

What we got from her was an order envelope for stamps and such that she would bring to us out in the boondocks, saving us a trip to town.

The amusing part of the whole deal was the sentence following "Dear Customer," on this PS Form 3227-R. It said, "This envelope is provided, in conjunction with the U.S. Postal Service and the National Rural Letter Carriers' Association National Joint Steering Committee on the Quality of Working Life/Employee Involvement Process...."

No kidding! I've seen some long names for organizations before, but this one really took the cake.

How would you like to write a check out to that outfit? You'd need a check blank as long as your arm to fit that whole name behind pay to the order of. The Postal Service thought of that, though, and indicated we could just make our checks out to "Postmaster." Whew!

### HC, RR, or 980 St. W.

It was a nice offer on behalf of the Postal Service. But after reading it, I was surprised that we had gotten one. You see, it was from the Rural Letter Carriers' Association and our mail lady is a Highway Contract Carrier.

I know this because our address changed from Rural Route 1 to Highway Contract 1 a couple of years ago. Apparently, though, Highway Contract carriers' have been authorized to deliver stamps to the country-side under the guise of the Rural Letter Carriers' Association.

The RR to HC conversion, has been pretty traumatic to the folks out here on Towner No. 1, though. Whenever we order something over the phone, it takes a little explaining for the person on the other end of the line to understand you when you say, "our address is HC 1 Box 71."

"What was that address?" they ask. So I start talking in military code then. "That was HC. You know like horse cow 1." Then they kind of begin to understand what I'm saying.

Their misunderstanding could just be due to my Towner accent, which is probably why I get mail addressed to Brian Taylor, Horse Cow 1, Tower City, N.D.

It could be worse, though. I could have one of those new fangled street addresses like some of my other ranching friends around the state.

I know some folks who live at 20700 249th St. N.E., and they're 20 miles from a little town that probably didn't even realize it had 249 streets. I doubt if there's more than 10 streets surrounding its grain elevator, post office, bar and church, and they're not even all paved.

Better yet are the nice green street signs erected out in the country-side. They make a dandy photo opportunity, standing next to the 249th Street sign surrounded by pastures, grain fields and dusty roads. Snap one and send it to your relatives living on 249th Street in Chicago. Bet they'll enjoy it.

# New year's fortune
## Savings and satisfaction ahead

I was a little worried about my financial future after tallying up my year-end pluses and minuses. The bottom of my tally sheet had a pretty siz-able number inside a pair of brackets — brackets mean a big fat minus and denote red ink for those of us without a color printer.

But then I got a letter in the mail and all my financial fretting flew right out the window. The folks at FORTUNE magazine were ready to lend me a hand and extend to me the tools necessary to make 1996 a banner year for both me and my banker.

I had no fear that this might be a letter they'd send to just any overex-tended rancher in Smokey Lake Township. The letter said, "We're con-ducting a nationwide search to attract leading business professionals and key decision-makers, and your name was referred to us from the Towner City area."

Wow! All those leading business professionals to choose from in the entire U.S. of A. and little ol' me was referred by the Towner (population 669) City area! It's not often that us Towner suburbanites in Smokey Lake Township get referrals from the big wigs in the Towner City area.

## Not for everybody

This offer definitely wasn't for just any Jack out in the countryside. The envelope said, "the enclosed Professional Discount Voucher is for the express use of the person named herein and is non-transferable."

The publisher had authorized Brian Wolfe, consumer marketing director, to give me 74 percent off the newsstand price, send me free guide full of breakthrough ideas and unconventional tactics and guarantee my satisfaction because of my "status as a business professional" (in the Towner City area).

I could see that making that kind of offer to the general public probably would lose fortunes for FORTUNE magazine. But cutting someone like myself in on the deal made a lot of sense.

I'm sure their advertisers would be phoning in almost immediately and increasing their promotional budget with them once the big orders started rolling in from the Taylor Ranch.

Brian said FORTUNE would help me grow my business (heavier calves and taller grass), motivate my staff (optimistic cows and horses chomping at the bit, ready to work) and maintain my edge (not settling to be just another broke cattleman, but be the best damn broke cattleman there is).

## What the heck

Even with the professional rate, I had second thoughts about spending any money on anything, what with the cattle market down in the basement and all. You can't fall for every smooth-talking salesman whose snake oil, or magazine subscription, will cure all ills.

But, then again, like Oscar Wilde said, a cynic is someone who knows the price of everything and the value of nothing.

So, without cynicism, the new year brings new optimism, new hope and, most importantly, a new operating loan. A professionally discounted FORTUNE magazine subscription could be the first chip off the old 1996 borrowed capital block.

Besides, I spotted the little box to check that said "Bill me later." It's a popular option for us leading business professionals in the Towner City area.

# Community super heroes
## Those few who go so far

If you need something done, ask a busy person. Communities and organizations around the globe can back me up on that statement.

If you need a director for your board, an organizer for your school reunion, or someone to be in charge of any one of a number of thankless tasks, ask a person who already has 10 or 12 irons in the fire.

More than likely that person's fire is hot for a reason. The people stressed out over their single iron or two probably are stressed because their fire has gone cold. The only reason some people have "too many irons in the fire" is because someone else doesn't have enough in their's.

## Community Superman

As organized as a speeding appointment calendar, able to complete tall tasks in a single evening — it's a committee chair, a board member, a city councilman — it's Community Superman!

Disguised as modest farmers, school teachers and small town business-owners, these Community Superpersons can be seen slipping into a meeting room five minutes early for a quick change into their super hero garb.

Beneath their plaid flannel shirts and denim jackets, is a set of bright red long johns emblazoned with a large golden "C." The letter stands for community, but it also could stand for contributions, charity or just plain crazy.

Once they've donned their big "C" long johns, they can be seen dashing from meeting to meeting, volunteering to beat the band, saying an enthusiastic "yes" to anyone and everyone who asks them for help and never complaining when they've been drafted to do things they'd really rather not.

Scheduling takes on new importance because the same 20 people end up doing the work of an entire community. They need to make sure their school board meeting doesn't conflict with their church council, commercial club, economic development board, farm crisis group or pancake supper committee meetings.

They can tell you what day of the week it is by merely remembering what meeting they have to go to that evening. With careful planning, they spread the commitments throughout the month so they can keep all their irons equally hot.

## Give 'em a break

Do you have a Community Superman or Superwoman in your town? Chances are you have several. Trouble is, using only several people to make life more enjoyable for everybody can cause a community to burn out their best.

When people take on a position of leadership in a community, they take a risk. They risk being judged by those who prefer to judge rather than take part. Making a decision and charting a direction runs the risk of being heckled by those afraid of decisions who have no direction.

Those who hang around in the safe zone are really in a stagnant zone, and making things happen in the outback of America demands courage, risk and people willing to put on the "C" suit and do the work.

If you haven't taken part in your local community or industry organizations, give it a try. Lighten the load for those special few in the "C" suits. Who knows, with a little volunteering and a few meetings on the calendar, you might become a "C" person yourself.

# Crime free in the heart of Texas
## Reverse psychology may work on would-be thieves

You look pretty silly walking off the plane in south Texas with your winter parka on.

The temperature was 30 below zero when the plane left Bismarck, N.D. San Antonio welcomed me with 70 degrees.

I'm sure there were a lot of happy cattlemen from the Northern states when they jotted down the dates and the place for this year's National Cattlemen's Convention.

### People everywhere

A cab driver told me there were more than a million people crowded around the home of the Alamo. Another 7,000 had come in from ranches and feedlots to boost the local economy while boosting their morale and knowledge of the cattle industry.

Coming from a state only half as populated as this one town, I felt small. I had to wonder what crime was like in a town this big.

I saw my first "club" in the pickup of a friend who drove from Houston. I'd heard about these gadgets in advertisements.

Clubs have been deterring theft since the days of the cavemen. Big sticks always have been effective in crime prevention.

The club in this pickup was a big stick also, but made of modern materials. It was meant more for show than for going across somebody's skull.

The club is meant to lock on the steering wheel so thieves can't turn your rig.

Not being able to turn wouldn't be much of a problem for car thieves in North Dakota. If a car thief picked up a vehicle in Grand Forks, he probably could make it as far as Minot before he'd encounter a bend in the road.

In big cities, there are more obstacles, so the club could be a real hindrance.

### Ignorant deterrence

There is another way to deter theft, though — sheer absent-mindedness.

I was about to miss the shuttle bus from my motel to the convention center and was forced to dash from my outside drive-up room door to the street curb to catch the big dog.

Eight hours later, I came back to the motel. There was no need to dig out the key. I'd left the door wide open.

I peeked inside. With a million people running around, one must have found this door and helped himself to the TV, my parka and dirty socks. But everything was there.

It could have been my reverse "club" psychology on crime deterrence that kept my dirty socks safe.

Passing thieves probably walked right by and said, "Nobody's so stupid as to leave their door wide open — they'll probably be right back. We'd better keep on moving."

This psychology could save us piles of money on clubs, locks and car alarms.

Just leave that car unlocked and running. Leave your purse or wallet laying wherever you please.

It works great in the big city — it's bound to work on the barren Plains.

# Where is everybody?
## Press whatever it takes to reach a flesh-and-blood human

Despite all the talk about our growing world population, we still seem to be desperately short of people.

Receptionists and secretaries, in particular, seem to be in real short supply. You can spend the better part of a day calling various businesses and never once talk to a living, breathing person.

We're apparently so short of people we've been forced to rely on recorders and voice mail systems to field our calls.

The people we need to talk to are apparently in short supply as well because they're kept so busy they can't even pick up the phone. Good assistants must be impossible to find, but it'd sure lighten up the load for those who need to ask their computers and machines who called, what they wanted and how could they get back to them.

### Frustrating phoning

If the world had a few more nice people with pleasant voices to answer phones, calling folks would be a lot less frustrating.

I wouldn't call somebody if I didn't have something important to discuss with them, but every time I get someone's voice mail, I envision that person sitting right next to the phone listening to my message and comparing my importance to the other 10 callers on the machine. It's pretty competitive out there.

Voice mail can be as challenging as it is frustrating. You better be pretty handy with your Touch Tone phone when the computer starts running options past you. "Press one for sales, press two for parts and service, press your pants if they're wrinkled and press your head in a vise if you work better under pressure."

Sometimes they test your spelling skills. "If you don't know your party's extension, spell the last name on your numeric keypad." That's great if their name is Smith or Jones, but it gets a little tiring if their last name is Dischimmellpfenning or Jingleheimerschmidt. And you're really sunk if you only know them by their first name

Then after the first 58 choices, they say something really annoying like, "if you'd like to hear more options, press the pound sign." By that time, I'm definitely ready to pound something, but it more closely resembles the person I'm calling than the little # sign on the telephone key.

**Threatening rewards**

If you happen to drift off during the message, the machine gets a little testy and says, "If you do not press a key in five seconds, you'll be transferred to an operator!" Oh no, not that!

Fail to play the numbers game and you'll finally reach a real person.

I'm usually so flustered by the time I get a real person that I forget the reason I even called. "Uh, um, I guess I'll just try back later," I stammer.

So a little later, I dial again to hear, "Hello, you have reached the voice mail system for David Dischimmellpfenning, press one if...."

# Renegade beef
## The days of Dodge City are long gone

People used to know where their food came from. Nobody had any questions about the origin of their barbecue when the cowboys were trailing steers down the streets of Dodge City, Kan.

These days, folks figure milk comes from the carton, bread comes from the bag and beef magically appears in the meat case. It wouldn't hurt any of today's urban folks to spend a little time filling a milk pail squirt by squirt, witness the grinding of wheat into flour or see an occasional cattle drive out their living room window.

A few people in Fargo, N.D., have done at least one of the three.

## Ag college access

One of the great things for people living in Fargo, is the presence of North Dakota's land grant university. North Dakota State University brings football, fine academic discussions and nearly 10,000 vibrant young student citizens to the Fargo community.

Its top-notch agricultural research makes the world a better place to live and better food to eat. And being a land grant university, NDSU makes food production a little more visible to the area's urban food users.

That visibility was clearly evident last week. Part of NDSU's mission is performing livestock research that will make the state's taxpaying cattle producers a little more successful, efficient and consumer focused.

That mission brought a steer to the campus meats lab, but the steer had a mission of its own. His mission was to let the folks in Fargo know where their food came from.

Before becoming beef, the brown-hided bovine decided to take a little stroll around North Dakota's most populous city. After putting a couple of cattle panels in the prone position, he expertly searched out the facility's open doors and took an athletic leap through a plate glass window so he could strut his stuff around town.

His unscheduled food awareness parade brought him to the banks of the Red River before Fargo's finest in uniform caught up with him. He was ready to cross into Minnesota and let the folks in Moorhead entertain him.

But North Dakota wasn't willing to share with its neighbor to the east. The steer was detained, so to speak, and transported back to the college.

The officer in charge of the situation claims the steer charged him. He did what he had to do. He pulled leather and gunned down the beast just in the nick of time. It must have been one of those rare "sideways head-on charges," though, since the bullet hole went through the side of the steer.

## Mission accomplished

I imagine there'll be a little flack in Fargo about the whole deal. I suppose the university's president will catch a little heat from some townsfolk who don't have a healthy Dodge City attitude. At a minimum, some good-natured ribbing will likely occur.

I applaud the steer for his ill-fated stroll down 12th Avenue and I extend a "Cowboy Logic" salute to the fine university that continues to bring food production a little closer to the final food user.

And if the going gets tough, President Plough, come on up to Towner, N.D. Citizens in the cattle capital still appreciate a good, old-fashioned cattle drive, and we understand that good beef comes from good cattle with a zest for publicity.

# Rolling out the welcome wagon
Tour guides are everywhere

You never know when you'll run into a tour guide in your travels.

The other day, I was at a restaurant in Grand Rapids, Mich., with a couple of cronies from Northern Plains Premium Beef, drinking coffee and feeling Western in an Eastern world. Like everywhere else we've been, we got the usual odd looks with our hats, boots and buckles.

All of a sudden, one old boy walked along in a big felt cowboy hat carrying his bacon cheeseburger and coffee cup. "I like those hats, boys. You must not be from around here."

No, we answered, excusing our appearance because we were from North Dakota and Montana. From that point on-it was instant friendship with this fella.

## Michigan hospitality

Dave was his name and he doubted there was much difference between the Northern Plains and heaven. He'd been heading west every year since he was 18, and he couldn't imagine anything nicer than the grass and hills of the Dakotas and Montana.

He started dropping the names of towns and people, and of course we knew what and who he was talking about. Matter of fact, we'd have probably remembered seeing Dave drive through our country.

We started chatting with this telephone man/historian about the old-time ranchers, the Plains Indians, the horses they rode and the trails they rode down.

Our mothers probably told us not to talk to strangers, but in a world where planes fall out of the sky and bombs go off in crowded parks, it was nice to find a friendly stranger in a city the size of Grand Rapids.

We'd been pretty rushed while we were in Michigan. Running hard, stressed out and sticking to the major interstates so we could get to our next meeting on time. Someone must have known we needed to get out of the fast lane and sent Dave to us in that restaurant.

## Back roads and bridges

North Dakota has a lot of nice attractions, but we don't have many covered bridges, maple forests or 150-year-old barns and farmsteads. Our new friend, Dave, offered to show us around the countryside just off the beaten path.

He should have been collecting a paycheck from the state of Michigan for all the good promotion and guiding he was doing with us ranch folks from the prairie. He told us about the history of the area, introduced us to a few of the local farmers and made our visit to Michigan pretty darned enjoyable.

Dave drove us around in his van for a good two hours and taught me something about true hospitality.

So if you see a stranger sitting in your hometown café this week, tell them howdy. And if you can, show them a little bit of our countryside. They sure do a nice job of that in Michigan.

# City horse vs. country horse
## Trading the wide, open for the narrow and closed

You can take a boy out of the country, but you can't take the country out of the boy. The same might be said for horses, as well.

It's been a summer of adaptation for me and Ace, the wonder horse. My work with Northern Plains Premium Beef has got me spending a lot of time in an office in Mandan, N.D., and rolling out my bedroll in Bismarck, an area a whole lot more populated than Smokey Lake Township.

Ace comes into the picture because I knew that I didn't want to be in the big city all by myself. I had two choices for companionship — a girlfriend or a horse.

Like most cowboys, I chose the horse. Horses are loyal and easy to catch. And you don't have to spend a lot of time in the bars buying them expensive drinks and trying to think of something witty to say.

So I loaded up ol' Ace when I headed to Bismarck, and knew I could at least go riding in the evenings and get my daily dose of sunshine, fresh air and the smell of leather and horse sweat.

### New surroundings

Adjusting to the whir of the traffic and the feeling of concrete beneath our hooves was a big change for Ace and me. Riding in the highway ditch is a far cry from riding in the pastures back home. The first couple of trips were pretty hairy.

Excitement used to mean a jack rabbit jumping up from behind a rose bush, or maybe a grouse flying up right in front of you.

But when you're a suburban equestrian, your horse has to get used to fast cars, whizzing pickups with boat trailers, loud motorcycles and kids shooting fireworks. Things get pretty exciting when your horse is making that transition from the noise made by a jack rabbit to the noise made by a Volkswagen Rabbit. Scarier yet, is the whir of some smart alec 10 speeder pedaling by, reminding you why we invented the wheel.

**Smile and wave**

You get a lot of attention from passers by when you ride your horse along the highway. It's kind of nice to have someone wave as you plod on down the road.

I remember riding my pony to the mailbox when I was little. Our mailbox was and still is 3½ miles from home.

You almost wanted to pack a lunch to tide you over until you got home with yesterday's daily news and the latest batch of bills. Most of the time, you could make the seven mile trip and never use your waving hand once.

But if I keep riding the ditch along Highway 1806, it could lead to wrist replacement or at least a the addition of a wrist brace to keep my waver going.

# More cars than cattle
## Old Fort Worth has gone concrete

When you think of the old cattle trail days, Fort Worth, Texas, is probably one of the towns that conjures up images of dusty cowboys and Longhorn steers pointed north.

Recently, I was groomsman for a friend's wedding in Hillsboro, Texas, just south of Fort Worth. My traveling partners and I decided to visit the dusty old cowtown of Fort Worth.

But as we pulled into town, it was plain to see that the dust had settled. Eight lanes of traffic buzzed to and fro at the healthy clip of 80 to 85 miles per hour as we pondered which exit to grab.

We spotted an exit ahead of us labeled "Stockyards" and figured it would be the best exit in town for four North Dakota cattlemen. We hung left after the exit and commenced to looking for some cattle.

We saw some fellas with shaggy, Hereford-like hair and eartags, but no cattle. Fuel was getting short in our van, so we pulled up to a gas station for a little petroleum and some advice.

The gas station had bars on its windows, and I had a sinking feeling that they weren't there to protect the windows from antlered steers. After fueling, we quickly doubled back on the trail we'd come in on.

**Rounding up people**

When we finally found the Stockyards, the streets and corrals were pretty void of cattle. However, the tourism folks had done a good job of converting the Stockyards into a good people-gathering point.

Instead of cattle, the streets had herds of people milling around and grazing on vendor corndogs. They weren't being sorted any particular way, but the entrance gates to the local businesses were doing a good job of peeling off customers from the main herd.

I'm sure the guys handling the $3 cover charge at all the saloon doors were descendants of the old livestock commission men who'd subtract a nice 3 percent fee to market your steers.

We had a fair bit of fun at the new and improved Stockyards. I have to admit that Texas girls out on the dance floor are a lot more fun to watch than the back ends of Longhorn steers heading north.

And I did discover that they still have stampedes in Fort Worth. Leaving the Stockyards, we got back onto the freeway and found ourselves in the middle of a full-fledged car stampede. They were all racing hell-bent for leather and when one of those renegades cut right in front of me, I lost it.

By watching the others, I'd learned that the proper reaction was to lay on the horn, mouth a few cuss words and fly 'em the bird, and I don't mean releasing a white dove of peace out the side window.

I'm not sure what good it did, but it did have a slight calming effect. And as we headed north out of Fort Worth, I had to wonder if the old-time cowboys chasing the big herds north ever cussed and flew the bird at the renegade steer leading the stampede.

# Auction fever
## Cattle or carats, the addiction is the same

I think I know how Tony O'Reilly must have felt after the gavel dropped on the Jacqueline Kennedy Onassis diamond that he'd just bought for $2.59 million.

The H.J. Heinz chairman and chief executive must have snapped out of his bidding daze and thought, "Holy Heinz 57! What did I just do? I'm gonna have to sell a whole lotta ketchup to get out of this mess!"

Buyer's remorse. I've been there. Heck, I once ended up buying a bull for $2,000 and I'd sworn to myself and my banker that I wouldn't bid more than $1,200 for him.

But the chant of the auctioneer had me mesmerized. The nervous twitch of my bidding finger was unstoppable. I was sure that joker bidding against me had another bid left in him.

### Different circumstances

I'm not completely convinced that Tony was in the same kind of auction trance I was, though. The environment at the quaint little Sotheby's

Auction gathering in New York City was a far cry from the scene at Farmer's Livestock Exchange in Bismarck, N.D.

I saw a bit of the Jackie auction on the television. Despite the high dollar figures, the action was pretty low key compared with a good North Dakota bull sale.

The auctioneering talent of Sotheby's was practically sedate. "I've got $2 million bid (dead pause for 10 seconds), does anyone bid $2,100,000? (another painfully long, silent pause) Thank you. We have $2,100,000, now...."

For crying out loud, I've seen half-intoxicated amateurs get behind the microphone at a wedding dance and auction off the bride's garter with a better chant than that!

I don't want to be too hard on the Sotheby's crew, but I bet if they had Neil Effertz or George Bitz at the auctioneer's block, they'd have had ol' Tony so gassed up he would've bid $5 million on that silly rock.

## Some similarities

The Sotheby's crew did have a little in common with our prairie auctioneers.

There's the common commission thread. The Sotheby's take was 15 percent of the $34.5 million extravaganza. Most of the local chanters get a mere 3 percent, but it's enough to motivate and even bring grown men to tears.

I read an AP article that quoted Sotheby's president Diana Brooks sobbing and crying as she said, "It is her (Jackie's) grace and style, her dignity, her courage, that are behind the results of this past week."

I've seen auction blocks turned to wood pulp with the crocodile tears of the auctioneer extolling the virtues of the critter in the ring. "Look at the muscling in his hindquarter, the depth of body, the brute masculinity of his build not to mention the tremendous scrotal circumference... and (sob) his grand dam's maternal half sibling placed first in his pen at the National Western. Now (composure regained) who'll make another bid...."

# Lookin' for the Journal
## Tough to find Wall Street on prairie main streets

Information is power. Power in the financial world definitely requires a lot of information. I'm now realizing that my financial powerlessness may be directly related to my lack of information.

Northern Plains Premium Beef was the subject of a front page full length feature in the *Wall Street Journal* on March 26. Pretty exciting stuff for this rancher/communications director — I hardly could wait to see the story in print under the Dow Jones masthead.

But I would have to wait because there was not a *Wall Street Journal* vendor to be found within an 80-mile radius of the Taylor Ranch.

## Old news

Now, I'm not a complete novice when it comes to the *Wall Street Journal*. In my senior year at college, I won the Wall Street Journal Student Achievement Award.

My prize? A year's subscription to the *Journal*. For a year, our rural mailbox with the broken flag and bullet holes was home to more than just feed bills and junk mail — it was home to the best business and investment information in the free world.

Of course, it came a day late, but we've been getting daily papers a day late for years. It was probably best, for the sake of the markets, that my *Journal* came after the fact. A man with my vast capital resources really could shift the markets if I was given all that investment information before the day's trading at the New York Stock Exchange.

## A prairie pursuit

After the free award issues ran out, I let the subscription lapse. Knowledge can be spendy, you know.

So without a home delivery issue of the *Journal* to look forward to, I was forced to look elsewhere for the Wednesday issue of Wall Street with the front page Premium Beef story. I figured I'd try our closest big city — Minot, N.D.

I tried all the book and magazine stores. No luck. I tried the little cigar shops that sell papers. No dice. I tried the good hotels that cater to the metro area's business travelers. Not a chance.

Last on my list of options was the local bank. Did that trusted, money lending, interest charging, financial bastion get the *Journal*? Nope.

No wonder the rural areas are in such tough shape! No information, no economic power. When you have no idea what's going on in the business world, it's easy to understand why business is slow.

I still had one ace up my sleeve. Even though I'm 12 miles from a paved road, I do have access to the information superhighway.

I quickly logged on the Internet, found the *Wall Street Journal* home page and ordered the free two week trial subscription to the electronic *Journal*. I soon was reading the headline "High Steaks: Hard-Pressed Ranchers Dream of Marketing Own Brand of Beef."

We were right next to the news bites about the U.S. Federal Reserve's interest rate hike and the new $3 million contract awarded to MCI Telecommunications.

Lots of good reading in that *Journal*. Too bad I can only afford the free two-week trial.

# Change of address
## Same ranch, new label

The U.S. Postal Service finally has done what society never could. They made a city boy out of me.

The USPS, in cahoots with the new 911 authority, has made me the not-so-proud resident of 1363 54th St. N.E. That's right, the 1300 block of 54th Street! What a raw deal.

Practically the whole danged country lives on a street or an avenue. Now, I do, too. Personally, I kind of liked being a little different.

I used to take a lot of pride in living on a rural route. I didn't even mind it when I was switched to an HC or "highway contract" route. At least it was still a "route." It still had a definite country flair to it.

### Trying to explain

It's been a tough transition for me. I find myself apologizing for and explaining my new address to people I don't even know. Like the folks who take phone orders from me.

"Where would you like to have that shipped, sir?"

"Well, uh, umm, it's 1363 54th St. N.E. Well, actually, you know, uh, that's the address, but I really live on a cattle ranch out in the boondocks about 17 miles from town. As a matter of fact, I'm 60 miles from the nearest shopping mall. And, actually, I guess that's why I'm getting my jeans from you guys by mail order."

But they're really not that interested. Usually, they just reply with an, "Oh, that's very interesting, sir. Now, what's the ZIP code there."

It's even worse for the phone operators at the companies I've done business with in the past. They'll say something really inviting like, "Are you still at HC 1 Box 71, sir?" and I'll let loose with my whole "don't hold my address against me" story.

You can take the boy out of the rural route, but you can't take the rural route out of the boy.

### Spreading the news

I've actually been living with my new street address for several months now. Since late summer, it's been my responsibility to let everybody in on the switch.

The postcard I got from the USPS said I had to have everybody notified within a year or risk not getting any mail from them. I figure this is my golden opportunity to start being selective about who can send mail to me.

I'm getting the word out in this column so that Cowboy Logic fans

161

can get their kind comments to me. By the way, if you're composing some hate mail, just send it to Ryan Taylor, Western Hemisphere, Earth. I'm sure I'll get it sooner or later.

I'm also letting all my employers, cattle buyers and aluminum can dealers know about my new mailing address. I wouldn't want to risk missing a paycheck.

But, for all the bill collectors out there, I still live at HC 1 Box 71. In a few mere months, I'll be enjoying a tidy little bill-free mailbox.

I know us country boys are supposed to be honest, but us slick city guys living on 54th Street can get away with a few underhanded tricks.

# Riding the cattle cycle

# Timing is everything
## Alternating short grass and good markets

Either my calves are getting smaller or the grass is getting taller. I don't believe my genetics have regressed that much, so I'm pretty sure the good rains and really big Big Blue Stem are creating an optical illusion out in our pastures.

It's a pretty darn nice illusion to see, too. You really have to look to find a calf if it's laying down out on the range. Not too many years ago, pastures had about as much forage as a faded green pool table and the calves stuck out like a town kid at a calf workin' bee.

Now we've got some nice problems to deal with like grass seeds in the pickup radiator, cows with some flesh on their bones and water holes that actually have water in them.

And it all came just in time for the markets to head south. Like a vacuum, our yearly budgets seem to compensate for themselves to make sure the bottom line hovers around zero.

### Cash or carry?

I probably should be thankful that we've been able to dodge the double whammy of both short grass and short markets the last couple years. But what's so selfish about wanting a year with no whammies at all?

Back when we were getting 95 cents for our calves, we ended up spending our profits to buy feed and extra hay to make it through the drought. Now that the rains are coming good, our feed input savings have been mysteriously compensated for with a 70-cent calf market.

The only guy more nervous about this situation than myself is my banker. This roller coaster is running downhill like a bat from below and my banker's about ready to lose his lunch.

Myself, I'm just trying to pull my hat down low so the wind don't take the last thing I own free and clear. A winning sweepstakes number, an oil well or an independently wealthy relative with a bad cough are the only possibilities I see ahead to make both me and the bank feel a little less nervous.

### Just wait

I think there must be an old adage that says if something good happens, just wait, something bad will come along to void it out. But that's a pretty pessimistic view to take.

Being an anti-pessimist at heart, I like to keep on the sunny side of things. If someone gives you a lemon, make lemonade, I say.

And if you're going in the hole $20 a head with your cow herd, make it up in volume. Losing $20 a head on a 500-cow herd would be much better than losing $20 a head on just 100 cows.

If nothing else, making it up in volume will give you more collateral so you can borrow more money and pay more interest. It's enough to make a cowboy want to jump on this cattle cycle they keep talking about and head to the big biker rally down in Sturgis.

I've already got the chaps, so it's just a matter of picking up a black leather jacket and finding someone to tattoo "Cattle markets — born to be wild" across my forehead.

# An autumn attack of FIS
## What we do for sunsets and empty checks

It's done. There's no turning back and no changing our minds. The calves have been sorted, loaded, unloaded, weighed, loaded again, and as I write this, they're probably playing cards and counting out-of-state license plates on trucks headed to Kansas.

We've nurtured the little beefers the best we knew how. We were out at 2 a.m. in April to see if they needed a hand getting here and we monitored their progress throughout the summer while we pumped a bunch of money into them and the local economy.

Now we've got them marketed for $80 a head less than last year and, if we suck in our guts and tighten up our belts, we might be able to breakeven this year. All that's left to do now is beat our heads against the wall, ask ourselves why the heck we're in this business and pitch our annual battle with FIS.

### FIS, an agricultural dilemma

No matter what you raise — cattle, hogs, wheat, corn or yellow-striped pumpkin squash — everyone in agriculture deals with FIS, fall insanity syndrome. Some folks call it the harvest blues or dead leaf depression, but it's still the result of bringing in the crop or weaning the calves and realizing there's no way to get ahead in this game.

There are a lot of factors contributing to FIS. It's partly due to the fact that everything we buy has a price tag on it and everything we sell has a question mark on it. Economists call it price-taking, not price-making.

Wouldn't it be nice to go to the implement dealer, pick up one of their $200 doo-hinkey repairs and say, "Gosh, there's a lot of doo-hinkeys out in the country this year. The bumper supply is really flooding the market. I paid too much for some doo-hinkeys last year and I lost my shirt on them.

I wish I could give you more, but I can't offer you more than $50 for this doo-hinkey."

The dealer could shuffle his feet a little and say, "I can't stay in business with $50 doo-hinkeys, I'll just take them to the doo-hinkey auction and see what I can get." He finds out his doo-hinkey isn't the right color, size or shape and ends up getting $48 at the doo-hinkey auction, minus commission.

Wouldn't it be nice if we could set our own prices, just like the store people? I thought about taking a paint stick and writing "Sale! Only $1 per pound" across the back of my $5^1/_2$ weight steers and run them by the cattle buyers just to see what he'd say. The paint probably would be considered a flaw and would knock them down another nickel, getting them into the 70s.

## Other contributing factors

If you're in the cattle business, fall insanity syndrome can be compounded greatly if you lose a night's sleep listening to your cows beller for their calves after weaning. By 3 a.m., the shotgun in the corner looks pretty tempting, but you don't have enough shells to shoot every one of the bellering buggers.

Other factors of the fall season contribute to the problem. Time is closing in around you as the days get shorter and you scurry to finish the harvest, get your hay in and do all those projects you can't do when there's a foot of snow on the ground.

We all make promises to ourselves about the things we'll do "when the work's all done this fall," but the work's never done, so the promises get shoved under the rug for another year. A more appropriate saying would "when we give up on the work we would have liked to have gotten done this fall."

## Diagnosis and treatment

There's not much to the diagnosis of FIS. You'll know it if you've got it. You'll find yourself in those contemplating moods, staring blankly out the kitchen window at the cows that broke down the fence to look for their calves that are already in Kansas.

You'll probably forget about the work you'd like to have gotten done this fall and instead find yourself on the phone talking to your neighbors about the markets and sharing your disgust with everybody else.

But within a few days, the cows will stop bellering and you'll stop staring. Things could have been a lot worse — you could have been hit with drought and poor market conditions; you could have lost half your calves to some hantavirus; or you could have had to work for somebody else and punch the time clock all year long.

Maybe you'll go for a ride through the hills or take a drive and realize that you are not in this business to get rich. A good horse, a good sunset and a shot of Indian summer will get you back on track and, before you know it, you'll be saying, "Maybe next year."

# Satisfaction in the new year
## Strive for the best — be a rancher

I believe I've discovered the secret of happiness. I stumbled upon this philosophical gem a couple of weeks ago at the sales barn. I'd say sales barns are right up there with Ivy League universities, secluded monasteries and ancient holy places when it comes to unlocking the great mysteries of man.

I had taken some old cull cows to the ring to exchange for some quick cash.

My little bumper trailer was loaded down so heavy the mud flaps were dragging on my pickup. The trailer's sides bulged like a frozen can of pop and my old pickup huffed and puffed its way to a cruising speed of 45 miles per hour.

The cows were classic culls. The few open ones just weren't doing their job. Another one was an udder failure, or maybe she just had a failing udder. The rest were gumming their grass and had been in the herd since the Nixon administration.

### Reachable goals

I looked the cows over as they leaped off the trailer and skidded across the concrete at the sales ring. I set my sights on a 35-cent average for these retirees.

When the check came in the mail, though, I found out they had averaged just under 40 cents. I was ecstatic with the payoff. Only someone in the agriculture business can get excited about selling cows for 40 cents that would have brought better than 45 cents a year ago.

But the point was I didn't go there expecting 45 cents. I was ready to take 35 cents, and that low self-esteem was the secret to my satisfaction.

I've heard the commercials on TV that say "Aim high — Air Force" and I decided maybe mine should be "Aim low — Ranching."

Setting my sights a little lower could be the key to unlocking my happiness. I could virtually eliminate all the disappointment in life. I couldn't believe someone hadn't shared this secret with me earlier.

I could plan on getting 70 cents for my 80-cent calves. If I needed 1,500 bales of hay I could stand in the field and say, "We'd be lucky if we can wrap up a thousand."

**Thanks, but no thanks**

I wondered where our ranch would be if we'd adopted this aim low attitude years ago. Would we really be happy or satisfied, or would we just be bankrupt?

If the cattle buyers knew we were willing to accept a dime less, we all know how much they'd be giving us. If we only hoped to get 80 percent of the cows bred or shot for a 400-pound weaning weight, where would the incentive be to do any better?

The world already has too many people wearing Bart Simpson underachiever T-shirts. Those of us in agriculture ought to have a T-shirt saying "Farmers and ranchers — overachievers and proud of it."

As we roll into the new year, we should take a moment to look back on the new years past. Have we made improvements, changed some things for the better? Remember, not all improvements show up in the checkbook. Some go straight to the heart.

Maybe I didn't discover the secret of happiness at the sales ring. I discovered it a long time ago when I said, "When I get big, I wanna be a rancher."

# Farming with off-farm income
## Working to keep on working

We may be dumb, but we ain't lazy.

That may well be the motto for farmers and ranchers heading into the 21st century.

When I use the term dumb, I don't mean unintelligent. Running a farm or a ranch requires as much, if not more, intelligence than that required by the nation's top business managers.

By dumb, I mean we're out here busting our posteriors in a business that feeds the world yet requires us or our spouses to take a second job just to make ends meet. Dumb, but certainly not lazy.

### The money trap

A USDA report released a couple weeks ago says farmers will have to work a second job just to stay ahead in the next 10 years. It says our household incomes will rise a mere 4 percent by 2005 and most of that whopping increase will come from off-farm income.

The report says farm income will rise $800 by 2005 and off-farm income will increase by $21,200.

Is it just me, or does this sound a little crazy? Should our job titles be changed from farmers and ranchers to off-farmers and off-ranchers?

We're supposed to get up in the morning, slop the hogs, feed the calves, milk the cows and then head to town so we can make enough money to subsidize that glorious lifestyle.

We enjoy feeding the other 98 percent of this country's population so much, we'll do just about anything to keep on doing it. Farmers and ranchers are driving trucks, selling parts, delivering rural mail and even writing columns to keep the homestead from going bust.

## Who else but us?

Is there anyone else who would do what we do just to maintain our way of life?

Picture this. A guy is punching the time clock on a factory assembly line but the wages are so low he can't meet the expenses of the job — work clothes, gas for the commute and tires for the car.

But he loves the assembly line work so much he'll take a second job just so he can afford to keep working at the factory.

Or how about the telemarketer who loves selling Salad Shooters and food dehydrators so much she'll wait tables after work at night just so she can keep her day job of taking orders over the telephone.

Maybe I'm being foolish. Of course these other people wouldn't do what we do just to make ends meet.

Us folks in agriculture have a different mindset than folks who work in factories and offices. Those other people feel like they need to turn a profit at their occupations.

We're just happy to break even. And if we can't break even, we'll do whatever it takes to get the bills paid so we can do it for another year.

But no one's holding a gun to our head. We could quit the farm and go to the cities like everyone else who gives the boss a 40-hour week in return for a monthly paycheck.

But until people get so sick of agriculture's long hours and low profits that they actually leave the land, farming will continue to be a business of long hours and low profits.

I'd love to keep preaching on this theory about people who will work two jobs just so they can watch the sun set, but I've got to go. I need to go cash my off-farm paycheck so I can pay for the feed it takes to put beef in America's supermarkets.

# Going high tech
## Old ways, new names

Technology is slowly but surely making its way out to the North Dakota outback.

Take your basic telephone. Nothing basic about it anymore.

Call waiting, conference calling, voice mail and the Internet can all be added for a small monthly fee. All this originating from the old copper wires strung between the poles planted in the 1950s so we could call the neighbors and see how much rain they got.

### Talk to 'em all

I got in on a conference call the other day. It was kind of neat, but a little confusing and sort of spendy.

I didn't really know when I should jump in and say anything because I couldn't see what everybody else was doing. Usually you can tell if someone's busting at the seams wanting to say something. Not so in a conference call.

You don't know who said what unless you're handy at recognizing voices and you feel kind of silly identifying yourself every time you open your mouth.

"This is Ryan and I'd like to say that's a terrible idea." There's no running backwards from a comment like that because you've just mentioned your name and your complaint in the same sentence.

Putting 10 people on the line makes for a long call, too. After an hour of so, you're wondering if your neck will ever straighten out and it takes a blow dryer to get your ear aired out and feeling normal again.

You gotta hand it to the telephone folks, though. The conference call is a credit to the wonders of marketing. We spent years out in the country with conference calls everyday.

Just change the name from party line to conference calling and start charging extra for it. That's what I call good marketing.

### Call shopping

I put call waiting on the phone here at the ranch a couple weeks ago. I didn't want to chance missing any of those important calls from telemarketers, bill collectors or census takers.

Actually, we've had call waiting for years. We just called it a busy signal. If you called and it was busy, you waited until it wasn't and called later.

That's not good enough anymore though. No more busy signals, just a tone you hear as you wait for the person talking to take a breath so you can put them on hold.

Actually, it's a pretty nice feature. It gives you the power to dump whoever you're talking to and see if there's any better conversation prospects out there.

"Excuse me, I'm really enjoying our chat about why I should pay those 10-year-old parking fines, but I have another call coming in." Hopefully, the other call is something really important like the neighbor calling to see how much rain you got.

This fall, I'm sure I'll be using the call waiting a lot when the cattle buyers start phoning to buy our calves. "You said 70 cents a pound? Excuse me, I've got another call."

"Hello, 67 cents you say? Sorry, I've got to get back to my other caller."

"Yeah, sorry about that. I guess I might pull the pin and let 'em go for 70. Hello? Hello?"

Dang that call waiting.


# Gambling fever
## Casinos don't have anything over on farms and ranches

Move over Vegas, step aside Atlantic City — gamblers may be more at home on the range than they are in the big city.

North Dakotans like to gamble. According to a recent report North Dakotans ranked No. 2, behind Alaska, in per capita spending on charitable gaming. Every man, woman and child (can children gamble?) in our state is plunking down $450 annually in the hope of striking it rich.

Blackjack tables, pulltab jars and bingo barns are shuffling the dollars around, with a cut, of course, for the government that allows it.

Charitable gaming receipts exceeded $284 million in 1994. Excise taxes of $7.9 million and gaming taxes of $3.1 million went to the state. The loudest shout of Bingo! may have come from the Capitol building. Bingo tax amounted to $2.7 million, and they don't even own their own blotter.

No new wealth, just a tidy little voluntary tax coming from the poor folks looking to get rich quick.

**Mere amateurs**

My out-of-pocket gambling budget doesn't even get close to the $450 level, so someone else must be punching out my share of pull tabs. But I wouldn't say I'm not a gambler.

I think blackjack is for wimps. Slot machines are for small-timers, and pull tabs are peanuts. If folks are looking for a real rush, they ought to buy some cows.

A few $900 heifers bought on the top side of the market make the dollar slots look mighty weak. The $3,000 bull that got struck by lightning gives ranch risk-takers the same depressing feeling felt by blackjack betters gone bust.

If that isn't exciting enough for us, we can always take a crack at the futures market and satisfy our gambling lust with some longs and shorts, or a few puts and calls.

We can gamble on the market, we can gamble on the weather. Why on earth would we want to gamble on some puny little cherries or lemons falling in a line or the chances of N-24 closing the gap between I-32 and G-17?

### The better risk

The reason might be in the lining up of the dollar signs. A national study shows that in all forms of legalized gambling, players lose an average of 9 cents for every dollar wagered.

Only 9 cents! Give somebody a dollar and get 91 cents back! Heck, every dollar I put into the cattle business this year will be returning me about 68 cents.

I think I'll just cash in my cattle and start gambling for a living. I could be in business a third longer if I make the switch.

But it's probably too late for me. I've been diagnosed as a compulsive cattleman, and chances are I'll never make the switch to something more lucrative like pull tabs.

The first step is admitting the problem, though, and I am seeking help. Counseling isn't cheap, but my banker's willing to make the investment.

# Chain it down
## Putting agriculture into debtor's prison

Like the dog chasing his tail, farmers and ranchers are getting busier and busier, but we're still going in circles.

Margins are getting tighter and profits are getting slimmer, so we're trying to make it up in volume. Of course, we can't afford to hire anybody to help us handle that extra volume. No room in that slim margin for wages.

It's like the feed salesmen who bought his product for a penny a pound and sold it for $20 a ton. And if he just had a bigger truck, he could really make that system work.

Trouble with us is we can't afford the bigger truck, so we fix up the headlights and make twice as many trips with the little truck. Sleep is optional in the business of agriculture.

## On the chain gang

Back in the old days, debtor's prison was the brain child of the upper class. If someone couldn't pay their debts, you put 'em in prison. That'll teach 'em, by golly.

It was mighty tough getting your debts paid while you're in the brink busting rocks, though. You were pretty much stuck there, unless your wife was able to pay your debts for you.

Despite all the freedom we have out here on the range, ranching really can resemble the old debtor's prison.

Chained down to our tractors, pickups and desks, we work harder and harder for less and less. There's hardly a minute to spare for such frivolous things as meetings, seminars or forums that could enlighten us on ways to add value and profit to our operations.

It seems like the system has got us beat down to the point where we couldn't change things for the better even if we wanted to. Keep the peasants busy enough and they won't be able to organize a revolt.


## Nothing to lose

Only 2 percent of our country's population is involved in production agriculture. But 100 percent is involved in the eating, wearing or using our products.

Would those of us in the 2 percent production category be better off if we started focusing less on production and more on the products being used by the other 98 percent?

If we consider the strides we've made in production in the last century, consider the strides we could make with products in the next century if we put forth the same amount of energy.

New technology and advancements in production have allowed us to add so much volume we've decreased the number of producers in this country to a mere 2 percent, but our profit margin is about the same, if not less.

Take the time away from the production side of your operation to attend a meeting or a seminar on the product side of your operation. The same people who have made American agriculture the most efficient in the world, could make it as profitable as it is efficient if we jump off of the tractor and get off of the ranch long enough to get organized and get out of our debtor's prison.

Us dogs gotta quit chasing our tails and start chasing the fat cats in our industry. And I think we can catch them.

# Living in a state of equilibrium
## A story of stock and livestock

We can all sleep a little easier for another year, now. Forbes magazine's annual billionaire rankings are fresh off the press and it's comforting to know that Bill Gates has $18 billion stashed under his pillow to keep him company tonight.

That's a lot of money, but it didn't really shock me all that much. What did shock me was the fact that Wild Bill's fortune had grown 40 percent from last year's modest $12.9 billion.

No. 2 on the list, Warren Buffett (no relation to the food bar at the all-you-can-eat diner), had a pretty good year as well. Mr. Buffett is worth 43 percent more than he was last year with his bankers tallying up $15.3 billion.

Most of Bill's profits came from the increased value of his Microsoft Corp. stock. And Buffett made money on money, too, playing the stock market and waiting for some poor idiot to get on the wrong side of his little buy-and-sell game.

### Asset equilibrium

This little news article on our billionaires really helped me figure something out. I've been wondering for the longest time where my share of the world's fortune had disappeared.

My $900 cows are selling for $500. My 95-cent calves are bringing 55 cents. A little rough figuring tells me my fortune has decreased 40 percent to 43 percent in the last year or two.

Bill and Buffet got my money! Is it just sheer coincidence that they're both 40 percent and 43 percent richer this year and I'm 40 percent to 43 percent poorer? I think not.

We live in a state of equilibrium. Every push has a pull, every zig has a zag. My zig in cattle apparently popped up as a zag in computers. I was out in the pasture shutting gates when I should have been investing with Gates.

It's plain to me that the stock market is a much better place to be than the livestock market. The heck with creating something of value. We could all just trade a bunch of paper back and forth until someone makes 40 percent and someone loses 40 percent.

### Next time

I won't get on the wrong side of the billionaire's game again. From now on, I'm dedicating myself to a new life of wealth and prosperity.

Like most of my new directions in life, I started by buying a book. If there's something you want to do, someone else probably wrote a book on the subject.

If I'm going to start making 40 percent and quit losing 40 percent, I figured I probably should consult one of the experts. So I picked up a copy of the Bill Gates prophecy, "The Road Ahead."

It should be a positive move. The way I've been operating the last couple years, you'd think I was living by the prophecy of "The Roadkill Ahead."

# Low-cost logic
## Cutting costs can be expensive

The challenge has been put out to ranchers. "You've got to become low-cost producers if you're going to live through the cattle cycle."

I'm always up for a challenge, so I decided to get right to work trimming the fat here on the Taylor Ranch. But before I could even think about my new cost-cutting strategies, my suppliers rolled out their new cost increases.

Petroleum shot up like a gusher, feed costs went through the roof, and everything from lumber to steel fence posts edged higher and higher. These minor setbacks easily would have discouraged the average cost-conscious cattleman.

But not me. I had a few low-cost tricks up my thread-bare sleeve.

### Plan "B"

In the "good times," we used to operate under Plan "A" (almost broke). But now we've switched gears and adopted Plan "B" (broke beyond repair).

We used to get by with just the bare minimum. We've now redefined minimum. It's even barer.

No more cake or fancy feed supplements for the cows. Just hay, water and lots of love.

No more overpriced steel fence posts. Just stretch up the rusty wire, staple it to a couple of telephone poles and hope that the neighbor doesn't have the same strategy.

And mechanical maintenance is a luxury we no longer can afford. I used to change oil in my vehicles every 2,000 miles. They'll be lucky to get a little new lube every 10,000 miles under the new plan.

### System setbacks

But like every new system, there're a few glitches.

The cake-free cows came through the winter looking pretty tough. Milk is a little shy, and it's hard to say if four weeks of grass will get them back into prime breeding shape. Of course, the more thin, open cows I have to sell this fall, the faster we'll pull out of this cattle cycle. It'll be my little contribution to the industry.

Of course, they might fatten up and breed back quicker than I think. My low-cost fencing strategy allows them to leave the pasture whenever they please, helping themselves to the proverbial greener pastures on the other side of the fence.

And my new vehicle maintenance strategy lost a little ground last week. I caved in and dropped the oil in my pick-up after a mere 2,500 miles. After changing the filter, I gave her some brand new 10W-30.

It wasn't long before I saw a pool of fresh, clean oil forming around my feet. If I could offer a little advice on low-cost oil changes, I'd say it's best to put the plug back in before you begin pouring.

But I'm sure I read somewhere that you're supposed to flush the engine with a little clean oil every 120,000 miles or so. I'm just a little better at maintenance than I am at saving money, I guess.

# Getting there on time
## Let the cows in on your appointments

I finally got around to setting up my 1997 operating loan. I've been running on empty for two months and realized that I just can't keep paying that credit card interest to keep the cows fed and the tractor fueled.

Running a ranch with only $42 in the checking account is kind of exciting, though. Kind of like driving into a blizzard at night with an eighth of a tank of gas. It's a real rush, but it's not too smart.

The annual operating loan process does have its highlights. First, it's always fun to try and come up with a budget that'll cash flow in the cattle business. It takes a lot of creativity and confidence, a couple of my strong suits.

It takes confidence to look your banker in the eye and tell him or her that you expect to miraculously hold your expenses to half of your five-year average. And designing a marketing plan that'll allow you to sell cattle for twice the predicted market price requires a fair bit of creativity.

It just makes the annual job of begging and scraping for another year's worth of credit that much more fulfilling.

Anyway, I had planned my work and was ready to begin working my plan. The first step of the plan was to get it approved by my friendly, full-service Farm Service Agency.

### The cow factor

My planned appointment was for 1 o'clock in the afternoon. Of course, all plans are firm until changed, especially during calving time.

Sure enough, I went to check heifers one last time before jumping in the pickup, and one of my schedule-ruining first calfers had decided that her time had come.

I've never used any labor-inducing drugs on the cows here, but I have made quite a few labor-inducing appointments. Speeding up parturition on the Taylor Ranch requires no more than a phone call to set up a meeting time with a banker, doctor or accountant.

If that heifer had only known her selfish birthing process could force me to reschedule my operating loan appointment for the second time, she'd have probably held on a few more hours. That little loan appointment is pretty important to her. It could mean the difference between getting fed or not getting fed.

Luckily, my friendly, full-service Farm Service Agency was able to wait for me and my heifer.

My first appointment was scheduled for January, but I had to cancel and March 4 was the next best available date. Missing my March 4 appointment probably would have put me into July.

Running on empty for two months is bad enough, but six months really would have stretched the ability of my $42 checking account to keep the minimums paid on my newest sources of operating money — Discover Card, Visa and Mastercard.

But I've figured out a way to make sure next year's March appointment goes off without a hitch...summer calving.

# I'd really like to help, but...

## Don't look to ranchers to carry the government through in '96

The year 1995 ended with farm accountants from across cattle country telling their clients, "You can take some more income for '95, you know."

Yeah, we know we could, but, fact is, we can't. IRS Schedule F was bleeding pretty red for most folks in the cattle business this year. There was no rush for guys to make any capital purchases or add any expenses at the end of the year in an effort to reduce their income tax burden.

We won't have a big tax bill to pay by the end of February, but that's a small consolation since "no income taxes" equates to "no income" for those of us who've started keeping cattle for the sheer pleasure of their company.

We usually have pretty lofty goals in agriculture, and it really hurts when we can't meet those goals. Most cattlemen really shoot for the moon, hoping they can pay the bills and maybe take the family out for a steak supper in the fall with the remainders of their calf check.

But just because you sell calves, don't get so big headed as to think you can afford a steak at the local grill. The evening out was spent at home by many in 1995.

## Out of the mix

It'll be hard for the people at the coffee shops to get a cattleman in on the current topics of conversation.

A lot of the local brain trusts will be visiting about the budget battles in Congress, the government's deficit spending and the recent shutdown of parts of the federal government.

Rancher Bill at the end of the coffee shop table will be sitting on his hands since he wasn't able to contribute to the nation's tax coffers. No pay, no say.

We won't be able to cuss the government's spending policies since the government didn't get their greedy little hands on any of our dollars. And since we have less money to spend in our hometowns, chances are that local business people won't have to send nearly as much money out to Washington either.

We'll really be giving them both barrels of a bad livestock economy out here along the cattle trails.

Go ahead, Washington, spend like drunken sailors if you like. You won't get any help from the broke cowboys out on the prairies.

## Short-term glee

We won't be smiling for long, though, about our putting one over on Uncle Sam. Our deficits add to his deficits. Another year or two of budget battles on the farm, and we'll really be contributing to the budget battle on the Hill.

Times really will be tough when the food producers all have to go on food assistance. It's pretty regressive when those of us who can't make enough to pay any tax have to start using everybody else's tax money.

We'd like to have been able to take some more income in 1995, but you can't squeeze blood out of a turnip and you can't squeeze income out of a downhill cattle market.

We might be taking some more income in 1996, but income from food stamps and welfare assistance probably won't make us better taxpayers.

# Charge!
## New fun with old expenses

I finally found a way to make buying overpriced parts, repairs and supplies enjoyable. The secret is credit cards.

But not just any old credit card will bring joy to your daily run for repairs. I'm talking about credit cards with redeemable points, cash back bonuses and free airline tickets. And all you have to do is charge huge amounts of money to earn them.

It's kind of wicked little treadmill, but it gets pretty addictive.

## Change in attitude

It used to be that I just hated breaking down and going to the implement dealer to pay ransom on new parts. It was about as enjoyable as blackmail. "If you want your old worn-out, heirloom of a tractor to live to see another day, it'll cost you dearly," the extortionist parts man would say with an evil grin.

Now I go in there and start pulling stuff off the shelves that I didn't even realize I needed. The parts man and me just stand there and smile at each other. "Will that be Visa or Mastercard?" is the only thing he can say, but the grin is still slightly evil.

The more I spend, the more points and prizes I get. It's got me fixing up tractors I don't even use anymore. I'm replacing bearings before they're shot and doing all kinds of preventative maintenance.

The craziest thing I've done is buy new generators and batteries for the tractors I used to have to pull, jump or park on a hill. But, what the heck, I might get me a trip to Disneyland!

## Paying the price

My new prize-earning scheme does have one serious drawback — whopper credit card bills at the end of the month.

But end-of-the-month bills aren't all bad. When you're living on borrowed money like I am, it's kind of nice to find someone who'll carry you for 30 days interest free. Of course, if you don't pay up, the 18 percent interest rate more than makes up for the graceful grace period.

To reduce my end-of-the-month shock, I've refined my charging to a single credit card. Just one statement to dread and it concentrates my prize-earning efforts.

I gave up on my credit card that merely awarded merchandise "bonus points." I looked through their awards catalog and realized I really didn't need a digital thermometer, Looney Tunes wall clock or a water hammock shaped like a tropical fish. The catalog reminded my of the people on the old "Wheel of Fortune" who only had enough money to buy the ceramic dog.

And I quit using my Discover card when I waited all year for my cash back bonus only to find a check for $7.52 in my mailbox. I just about spent myself broke in pursuit of that windfall.

Now, I'm strictly a Northwest WorldPerks Visa kind of a guy. And when I'm done spending the $25,000 needed for a free airline ticket, I think

I'll need a trip. Especially once my banker finds out how much I overshot my machine repairs budget.

# Life's a ditch
## Then you fill it in

Another big project wrapped up on the Taylor Ranch this week.

I had a couple of stock tank pipelines to run for a new rotational grazing system that'll surely make my pastures productive, my cattle fleshy and my checkbook bulge.

My plans called for a couple miles of fence, some new water tanks and about 9,000 feet of pipeline. I figured 9,000 feet of pipeline would be an easy two day job — if you're young and stupid.

But, being young and stupid, I lined up a rented ditch witch, a slug of plastic pipe and three whole days to try my hand at ditch digging.

### Beg, borrow or charge

The first key to any successful project is lots of borrowed equipment. I started by borrowing (renting) a ditch witch.

The dealer had lots of new machines on the lot, but he took one look at me and realized that I had to have the "old standby" with the faded paint and experienced sprockets.

Of course, my borrowed ditcher was heavier than a trailer full of big crossbred cows. They doubted that Old Gray, the half-ton with a whole lotta heart, could even pull it off the lot.

Borrowed piece of equipment No. 2 took me to a purebred cattle friend who had a one ton dually used to pull their gooseneck stock trailer.

Now that I had a borrowed pickup pulling a borrowed ditcher, I had to borrow a little capital and actually purchase the pipe. I'd have borrowed the pipe, too, but the dealer doubted I'd return it once it was 3 feet in the ground.

So I did the next best thing. I bought it with my credit card.

It was just like the T.V. commercial with the guy whose credit card company calls to check if his card was stolen because he was a "T-shirt and jeans kind of guy" and a tuxedo had been charged against his plastic.

I bought a couple thousand dollars worth of pipe and, sure enough, my credit card company called to see if everything was all right. They apparently knew that I was a "big pastures with water holes kind of guy" and wanted to warn me that some progressive, thieving rancher had gotten a hold of my card.

I told the lady not to worry, my credit card hadn't been stolen. Instead, I had a contract with the soil conservation folks and they were going to cost share this extravagant tuxedo like expense.

Once I got home with my borrowed equipment and my credit card cost-shared pipe, things went pretty well. I buried 9,000 feet in three days and I learned a little about life in the process.

Life is a ditch, especially if you're digging it in the sand. As in life, things usually will go well for a while, but just when you least expect it, the sides will cave in.

And if you feel like you're in a rut, or a ditch, you probably are.

# Tax time here once again

In case you've forgotten, March 1 is the last day for farmers and ranchers to get their income tax returns sent in. No leeway, no extensions, the Internal Revenuers put the "dead" in deadline on this one.

If you've mentally blocked out this little fact, you better get crackin', because there are certain folks you just shouldn't mess with — tired ranchers at calving time, overworked housewives at dinner time and the IRS crew at tax time.

All across farm and ranch country, shoeboxes are splitting at the seams and hair is coming out at the roots as farmers sort through their file piles. Families are subjected to huge amounts of stress as the great missing receipt search is played out once again for fiscal 1994.

All year long, fretting farmers and recordless ranchers dread the day they have to go in to visit the tax man and confess their shortcomings in credits, debits and number crunching.

And each year a resolution is made to do a better job next year. They leave the accountant's office firmly dedicated to making daily entries in their recordkeeping journals and monthly reconciliations of their bank statements.

But before you know it, their minds are dedicated to calving, planting, haying, harvesting, bale hauling and other matters more urgent than some dusty old recordbook on the corner of his desk.

## On the bright side

I happened to be walking by the tax man's office the other day when my hard luck ranching friend, Slim, walked out with a couple beer boxes full of papers and a grin stretching from ear to ear.

"What are you so happy about," I ask my beaming buddy. "I went in the hole last year," he says with a smile. I'm thinking Slim must have just finished off the prior contents in his filing boxes and was on a barley pop buzz and didn't know what he was saying.

But, to be agreeable, I give him a congratulatory slap on the back and say, "That's great, Slim, I'm real happy for ya. How'd you do it?" "Well, I bought some pasture calves real high last spring, put a bunch of money into feed and pasture, then sold them when the market bottomed out in the fall," Slim says.

I'm finally getting worried about my friend, so I put him on the spot and asked him where the silver lining came from in this financial storm cloud. "I just finished doing my 1040 with the tax man and he says I don't owe a single dime in income taxes. The high purchase price, the low selling price and all the deductions in between have put me on easy street. I may even get a refund from my federal fuel taxes," he says.

"Good for you," I say as my friend jumps in his dented up '72 Ford half-ton and heads to the post office to mail his zeroed out return to the bean counters in Ogden, Utah.

## Spreading the national debt

Right after Slim took off, my neighbor, Gus, came walking out of the same office looking as glum as a hound dog. He practically tripped on his lower lip as came down the sidewalk and bumped into me.

"Why the long face," I ask my forlorn friend. "I made too much money last year. I owe Uncle Sam a pile in taxes," he mumbles at me with a tear in his eye. I knew Gus had some income on his place. He worked like a dog on his own farm, did custom work all over the neighborhood, pinched every penny, lived like a pauper and even had his wife working in town to help make ends meet.

"Well, isn't it good that you had such a good year? Even if the IRS gets 28 percent, you still get to keep the other 72 percent, you know," I say in an effort to cheer him up. "But I don't have the money to pay the taxes. I spent all my income on things I can't deduct — principal on my land loan, principal on my livestock and machinery loan, health insurance premiums, groceries for my family and college tuition for junior," he informs me.

"Where are you headed," I inquire as he shuffles off. "Oh, I've got to go to the bank and borrow some money to pay my taxes with," grumbles Gus. "Don't worry, Gus," I say, "things will get better next year. Cattle prices are supposed to get lower and we might even get another drought to help keep our incomes down."

"That's right. Things are looking up," he says with a sheepish smile. "See you, Ryan." "So long, Gus."

# Wrangling the rebates
## A matter of determination

I admit it. I'm addicted to mail-in rebates. It's not that I enjoy the hoops I have to jump through to get them, I don't even get that much satisfaction from cashing the $1 checks at the bank. I'm hooked because of sheer orneriness.

At the stores, they trick me into thinking I'm getting something on sale, but when the cash register makes its final ring, I'm stuck writing a full-price check. "Do you want you're rebate slips?" they ask.

"You bet," I reply, realizing I'd fallen into the rebate trap once again. The big corporate boys can play with my money for 60 or 90 days if they'd like, but they better not get too cozy with my buck and a half because I want it back.

### Go on, send it in

The manufacturers of oil, anti-freeze, air filters, beer, pens and flashlight batteries do all they can to discourage rebate treasure seekers like myself. The harder they make it, the more determined I get. The spoils go to he who perseveres, I say.

Simply fill out the rebate form and mail it in, right? Wrong.

First you need an original, dated, store identified, notarized, immunized and pasteurized store receipt with the price of the product circled, highlighted or marked with blood. And my tax accountant wonders where all my receipts are in case I get audited.

No way can you photo copy that receipt, either. That'd be like an open invitation for the Mafia and organized crime to come right in and work the rebate ring.

Then the real fun stuff begins. Cut out one of five UPC codes on the box, but make sure you get the right one. Soak the labels off of each individual bottle, cut the foil seals from under each cap, or maybe just box everything up after you're done and mail it in.

But don't miss the sacred rebate deadline; a note from your mother won't even get you over that hurdle.

If you do what you've been instructed, stick a 32-cent stamp on a 5-cent envelope and your hour of $5 time will result in a hefty $1 check. Rebates are one of the few activities with returns comparable to ranching and farming.

### The calf rebate

I'm sure the percentage of people who actually mail in their rebates is pretty tiny. But the manufacturer got them to buy their product with the promise of a lower price and it's not their fault if the consumer didn't follow those 38 easy steps to receive it.

I think there're similar opportunities in agriculture. I sold my steers this fall for 66 cents, but I should have sold them for 76 cents and offered the cattle feeder a 10-cent rebate.

Just fill out the form and mail it back along with a dated, original weigh ticket, a signed brand release, the calf's ear tag, the hair from the tail switch, a fecal sample, a hoofprint and a photograph of the calf standing at the feed bunk.

Do that and I'll gladly send the calf rebate. Please allow six to eight weeks for delivery.

# Taxes be gone
## The positive side of negative numbers

Being flat broke and busted does have its advantages.

You don't have to worry about bursting the stress points of your wallet, you don't run the risk of being a high-profile target for muggers, and your lack of income makes the paying of income taxes a non-issue.

I did a little income tax work recently and my Schedule F received a letter grade of F minus. Luckily, I'd scraped together enough 1099, W-2 and Schedule C dollars to raise my grade up to a low D. That's D as in done for another year.

The letter D also could stand for discouraged, depreciated and deducted beyond my deductible income.

### Losing to win

I never quite realized the power of poverty before. I had a little W-2 income this year and let the government hang onto a few dollars in withholding. But now, since I was lucky enough to lose my shirt in the cattle business, they'll give it all back to me so I can go to the pawn shop and buy that shirt back.

Having a refund waiting kind of makes you want to get your taxes sent in a little quicker.

When it comes to income tax deductions, I can see why all the income-laden rich folks like to buy a ranch or two to help keep the tax burden down.

The tax ranches serve a double purpose for those who invest. Not only can they capture a good sized tax write-off, they can wear a cowboy hat, ride horse and talk a little poverty with us common folk.

Of course, it's hard to really connect with a tax break cowboy who's driving a brand new deductible pickup and parks it next to your old, beat-up rig that depreciated out years ago.

Our strategies are just a little too different. They can't spend money fast enough, we can't save money fast enough.

**Ranch for rent**

Personally, I'm beginning to think that owning ranch assets is a lot less glamorous than it used to be.

It's really not fair for me to hog all those good deductions and not have enough income to use them on. I'm sure there's some poor soul out there who's really in a bind, making way too much money and needing a few good deductions.

I know most of the rich folks prefer to buy ranches in Montana where they can look at a few mountains and do a little skiing, but Towner's got a lot to offer, too. A good set of cows to depreciate, lots of ground to build new, deductible improvements on and a couple of old hats for the tax break cowboy to wear so he can mix in with the locals at the local watering hole.

I'd be willing to rent all that and more to help them out of a taxing situation. Just put that rent income on a Form 1099 and I'd gladly add it to my 1997 income.

As a matter of fact, I'm looking forward to maybe paying a little income tax next year.

# What are the odds?
## Drawing the 1 in 100 audit card

It was a rather innocent-looking day in late March. The blue sky and bright sun gave no sign of the ill winds about to blow on the Taylor Ranch.

I drove the 3 1/2 miles to our "curb-front" rural delivery mailbox with nothing but good thoughts on my mind. At the mailbox, I retrieved the usual assortment of free magazines, bills and junk mail.

But mixed in with the usual correspondence was an ominous little manila window envelope with the words "Internal Revenue Service" emblazoned in the upper left hand corner.

"Hmmm," I quipped, "I reckon I'm gonna get audited. Ha, ha." Moments later, my "ha, ha, ha's" had turned to "boo hoo hoo's." It was then that I began my self-inflicted pain ritual, banging my head on the car dash for the "reckon I'm gonna get audited" crack and the jinx it had placed on me as I tore open the envelope.

It was your typical warm-hearted letter from the IRS. "Dear Taxpayer, We selected your federal income tax return for the year shown below to examine the items listed at the end of the letter."

The year they chose was 1994, and they wanted to examine everything from the number of pizzas I bought at the local Cenex to the amount of depreciation I took on my long underwear and thermal socks.

**The search is on**

Now 1994 was a long time ago. That's 21 years ago for my dog — three years ago for you and me. I wasn't too sure that I still had my records from 1994.

But I was in luck. I had them right in the file cabinet labeled "1994 Stuff."

I know cowboys are supposed to keep their receipts in shoeboxes, empty beer cartons and the glove compartments of at least three vehicles, but I guess I'm one of those 90s kind of cowboys. Heck, I don't even chew Copenhagen.

Yes, my receipts were in a file cabinet. My expenses were meticulously recorded on the computer. My bank deposit slips were stapled to the cattle weigh tickets.

Even with all that good bookkeeping, I still had a bugger of a time putting everything together for the audit. Luckily, a horse broke my leg a couple weeks before the scheduled audit and I had a lot of time to spend sitting around, sifting through receipts and running calculations on the computer.

My misery had some company. Several other ranchers I knew got audited this year as well. Looking at myself and those other farm couples, the IRS definitely was fishing for minnows when all kinds of sharks were swimming free.

After all the painstaking audit preparation, the day of reckoning was upon me. I took my file box full of goodies to the accountant, tapped his shoulder with a No. 2 lead pencil and bid him Godspeed on his trip to represent me at the IRS.

The IRS give me a thorough checking over, found less than $100 in discrepancies and said no harm, no foul, no change.

Another minnow swims free.

# Playing the name game
## Bureaucratic alphabet soup getting stirred

If you're like me (in debt up to your ears with the Farmers Home Administration), you can look forward to a joyous event held each December. It's the hallowed FmHA year-end farm analysis.

I just got my 36-page invitation to the FmHA holiday bash. It'd be nice if it was just an invitation to sing Christmas carols and drink hot cider, but from the looks of the forms, it'll be a holiday full of number crunching.

Don't get me wrong. FmHA does a great service — lending money to folks banks wouldn't touch, providing affordable interest rates to beginning farmers and teaching upstart agriculturalists the basics of bookkeeping and financial records.

## An acronymical riddle

I called FmHA a couple weeks ago, knowing that they probably were wondering if I had taken the cattle check and headed to Mexico or if I was going to stick it out another year.

A gal picked up the phone and said, "Hello, Rural Economic and Community Development, may I help you?"

"Yeah," I say, "How about telling me how to get a hold of the FmHA. I must have the wrong number."

I was informed that I had the right number but was being tossed a name they came up with in Washington, D.C.

"Is your office still across the hall from the ASCS office?" I queried. "No, we're across from the Farm Service Agency," she says.

Now I was really lost. She explained that FSA used to be the ASCS and RECD used to be FmHA, that they're still in the same building and they still do the same things.

It made sense now. It smelled like a typical governmental reorganization where names and acronyms are changed, but everything else stays the same.

## Reinventing ranching

Shakespeare once asked, "What's in a name? A rose by any other name would smell as sweet." The old boy hit the nail right on the head, because I still owe just as much money to the RECD as I did to the FmHA, and I probably won't come out of either of the agencies smelling like a rose.

It makes more sense for me because my rural economy certainly could use some community development, whereas our one-story ranch house probably wouldn't really qualify for administration as a farmer's home.

If USDA and the federal government are going to get all efficient on me, I probably should find some new efficiencies myself.

I probably should come up with a new name. Instead of the Taylor Ranch, maybe something like the Taylor Beef Cattle Development Organization.

I'll think about it this morning as I head out to the Beef Cattle Constraining Unit (the corral) to pour some feed in the Nutritional Development Structures (feed troughs). The way those calves have been pushing me around, I probably should bring along a copy of the new TBCDO flow chart and show them just who's in the top administrative position of our new organization.

# Dimensions of debt
## Short checks just don't cut it anymore

Things are getting a little cramped on the ranch this fall.

It's not a lack of elbow room. North Dakota ranches are long on spaciousness. Most of my neighbors and I have at least a couple square miles to ourselves.

Where we're getting cramped is on the "Pay to the order of" line of the checks we receive for our cattle in the fall.

Back in the old days, when lenders and borrowers trusted each other, there was one name on that line. It was the name of the fella selling the livestock, and if he had debts to cover, he'd cover them.

Now, there's so many names on my cattle checks, there's hardly any room for mine!

### In hock

I shouldn't complain. If I didn't want any lender's names penned on my checks, I shouldn't borrow any money. Of course, asking a rancher not to borrow any money is like asking someone to quit breathing or drinking water. No matter how much we wish we could, you just can't run a ranch on hard work and good intentions.

I've heard it said that if you want to be remembered, borrow money. And, if you want to be forgotten, lend money out.

So I guess having a couple other names next to mine on the cattle checks is the banker's way of remembering me and making sure they're not forgotten.

And until someone stocks our pastures with those stationary grazers (oil wells), or until some rich gal takes me to the wedding altar, I'll have to put up with being just one of the three names listed on my paychecks.

### Longer lines

The cattle buyers and sale barns do what they can to humor me. They do give me first billing, but they always follow up with the names of the kind government folks who hold the note on my cows and the benevolent local lender who financed the feed and medicine and every other input that went into those cows.

It's a tight spot to be in, in more ways than one. Not only is it tight being the last one to get any grocery money out of the check, it's darn tight just fitting your name on that short little line.

The check writers do what they can. They print awfully small and they abbreviate wherever possible, but we still end up spilling off the end of the line like a barrel heading over Niagara Falls.

With all the abbreviating going on, I've been thinking of a way to achieve one-stop endorsement at my kitchen table. If I signed the back of the checks with my name and was able to locate someone named Frank S. Anderson and someone else name BobCat C. Underwood, maybe I could get them to sign for the FSA and BCCU.

However, the Farm Service Agency and the Benson County Credit Union might wonder why I haven't been in with my annual payment. But they'll soon realize what happened when Frank, BobCat and I send them a postcard from the sunny Caribbean.


# Bill paying time
## Circulate your money efficiently

I just finished my monthly contribution to the vigor of our nation's economy. The month of November is a wrap, and I did my best to boost the consumer spending index and help our country recover from that little Wall Street incident.

I've heard the saying, "easy come, easy go," when people talk about the monthly exchange of dollars in their checking accounts.

But on this outfit, it's more like, "doggone hard to come by, real easy go." The income either comes in small bite-size chunks, timely medium-sized loan advances or semi-large once-a-year proceeds from the next guy in the food chain.

Expenses, on the other hand, come as a steady stream of larger-than-expected bills due at the end of the month, every month, like clockwork.

### Pinching pennies

Used to be, I'd just pack my checkbook along with me where ever I went, doing the "pay as you go" thing. Then the economist in me began calculating the cost of all those nickel check blanks and I began to look for a better way.

Credit cards and local charge accounts were the way to go, I decided. Not only did you cut down on the number of check blanks, you could postpone taking that advance on your operating loan until the end of the month.

I began to push the pencil. If I wrote 30 fewer checks, I could save a whole buck and a half. I was so excited I went to the bar and had a $1.75 beer to celebrate.

It looked like the real windfall was in the interest savings. If I could save 20 days of 10 percent interest on $3,000-a-month expenses, I could put a hefty $16.44 in my pocket. I felt pretty smart about that deal.

Pretty soon, all the farmers and ranchers were charging their expenses to save that $16.44. Unfortunately, the business owners were on to our new strategy.

They just raised the prices accordingly to cover their cost of interest in carrying us for an extra 20 or 30 days. I think they even put a little cushion in for the delinquent accounts. When all was done, that $16.44 probably cost us $20.

**Getting efficient**

Well, even if the money savings aren't there, I'm saving a lot of time. It takes a lot less time to write a dozen checks versus 50.

Still, paying a dozen bills in one sitting is a lot of work. Those evenings at the desk were getting pretty painful. Eye strain, hand cramps, glue tongue and carpal tunnel syndrome surely would raise my medical expenses in time.

So, I finally got automated. I got some $50 software for my computer and ordered the computer printout check blanks, complete with the little window envelopes. The checks were 15 cents, the envelopes were a dime, and the postman gets 32 pennies every time I take one to the mailbox.

If I get much more efficient, I'll have to borrow some more money. It ain't easy driving this economy.

# Workin' for work shoes
## Going broke or just breaking in?

I said goodbye to a couple of old friends last week. I'd only known them a couple years, but we'd done a lot together.

I hated to see them go, but I guess it was their time. Yes, it was time for me to get a new pair of work shoes.

My old clodhoppers were pretty well wore. The factory traction on the soles was completely gone. Of course, I did inflict a little grip of my own by stepping on some hot welding slag and getting a few pock marks on the otherwise smooth bottoms.

I'd done a little improvisational improvement on the ankle support, too. The original lace hooks at the top of the boots had long since busted off, so I compensated by using some extralong laces that I wrapped around my ankles a couple of times, kind of like hog tying my boot to my leg.

And the boots were extremely well ventilated, but not by original design. At one time, the leather probably was able to "breath" and keep my heels cooled, but a few years of mud, muck and manure had the poor boot's pores clogged worse than an oily-skinned teen-ager.

Luckily, I was able to wear a couple of nice, big holes along the side to keep my old hooves well ventilated. Although it was nice to get a little cross breeze in the boots, it was those holes that finally sent me to the shoe store.

Good ventilation made for bad socks. They'd start out bright white in the morning, be brown by noon and completely black by evening. Hard as you'd try, you just couldn't get that bright white hue back.

### Shoe shopping

So, for the sake of the socks, I went shoe shopping.

I thought about getting another pair of bargain boots like the ones I was retiring, but I figured my feet were worth a little pampering. I decided to go for the genuine leather, form-fitting, super-durable and oh-so-comfortable "Made in the USA" models.

Luckily, I called the bank and borrowed some operating money before I took my checkbook to the shoe store.

The fella at the store measured my flippers and told me I needed a size 11 1/2 B. Then he fitted me with a pair of top-of-the-line work shoes and told me he needed $143 plus tax.

Now I know why they call them work shoes, because I'll have to work a long, long time to get them paid for. Hopefully, the shoes are made well enough to last just as long as it takes to get them paid for.

I was pretty proud of my new treads. I'd never owned such a fine pair of shoes, and the best part was that I'd get to wear and enjoy them every day.

The next morning, I got up, put on my new shoes and went to work. The soles had great grip, the ankle support was divine, and my socks even stayed clean.

Now I just have one problem — sore feet.

# Sure bets
## The safe money is in race horses

After years of experimenting with investments in cattle, land and machinery, I finally found a safe place for my money — the race track.

I spent Sunday afternoon learning the finer points of horse racing at Chippewa Downs in Belcourt, N.D., and, after a day of wagering on the ponies, I was only $14 poorer.

I was ecstatic. The whole day only cost me $14 in losses! I've never lost so little money in my entire life.

## Comparing careers

Just for fun, I checked out the "Schedule F" from my last three income tax returns to see how ranching compares with the high life of a horse bettin' gambler.

The Schedule F form calculates the net profit or loss from farming activities. I assume the "F" stands for farming, but I've heard other "F" words uttered (like "fudge," "for foolish" or something even less polite) by producers as they view the bottom line on that schedule.

The Schedule F does include some non-cash figures like depreciation expense, but I think it's probably proper for a guy to try and cover the cost of rusting machinery and weathering buildings since they will need to be replaced someday.

When I divided the negative numbers on my last three Schedule F's by the 1,095 days they covered, I came up with a loss of $80.43 per day. Every day I got up and put my shoulder to the wheel and my nose to the grindstone cost me about $80. Luckily, I was able to hold down a couple of paying jobs to help me cover my daily ranching losses.

## Off to the races

Now I had the hard data I needed to realize that my day at the horse races cost me $66 less than the average day of ranching. If I'd only realized this sooner.

I could have saved about $70,000 in depreciation and ranching red ink over the last three years by just hangin' around the track and placing my $2 bets on the ponies. No hard labor, lots of excitement—what more could you ask for?

I wouldn't get to be around cattle, but there'd be plenty of horses, so I probably could continue to wear my hat and boots without breaking any cowboy laws. Plus, if I began to go into rancher withdrawal, a short walk to the stables would get me a fragrant snort of fresh hay and even fresher manure.

The thing that really makes me want to change careers from ranching to race track gambling is the concept of pari-mutuel betting that I picked up on at the Chippewa Downs. Pari-mutuel means the winners divide the total amount of money bet, after deducting management expenses, in proportion to the sums they've wagered.

That'd be like having farmers and ranchers divide the total consumer food dollar, after processing and management expense, amongst themselves in proportion to their production investment without having to feed the greed of every corporate shareholder in between.

But, although a few of us are trying, we still don't have pari-mutuel ranching. So, until then, I'll see ya at the race track.

# Not quite Midas
## A magically miserable touch

My apologies go out to the cattle feeding community.

In June, there were about 10 million head of cattle on feed in the U.S. We marketed about 2 million of them and, dangit anyway, we lost about $170 million on the deal.

That's bad news for everybody in the cattle business, but it was really bad news for me since 156 of those cattle and 14,191 of those dollars were mine. And I apologize to the cattle feeding world because I'm sure that the whole reason things went sour in the cattle market was my participation in it.

It's all because I have the Midas touch, only in reverse. I call it the "manure touch" because everything I touch these days turns to crap.

If I'd only stayed out of the cattle feeding business, I'm sure the fed cattle market would have hit $75 a hundredweight and everybody would have made $150 a head. Instead, the market went to $59 a hundred and losses hit $150 per critter. I'm real sorry, guys.

### Double down

Two years ago, I fed out my heifers at a custom yard down in Nebraska and made a couple thousand dollars over their value as weaned calves. I was flush with confidence as I doubled down and decided to feed out both the steers and the heifers last year.

I even bought Dad's share of the steer calves for last fall's going rate of 90 cents a pound. From that point on, you could watch the market take a spiraling free fall.

I'm not sure if any ag economists have charted the phenomena of the Ryan Taylor manure touch, but I think they'd find some statistically significant correlations.

On most any uptrending graph, you can mark the spot (usually with a cowpie) where I enter the market. From the cowpie on, it generally heads south.

Of course, I know there's a better way to do things in the cattle business. It has to do with a cooperative of cattle producers who could control and process their product and take it straight to the niche, premium marketplace.

But a cooperative needs producer equity to get off the ground and there aren't many dollars lying around unclaimed in ranch country. Me and my manure touch probably can take credit for that, too.

If I'd only taken a regular job when I graduated from college in 1992, the cattle market would have probably kept on sailing and ranchers would have had plenty of equity to invest in profitable value-adding ventures.

As it was, I came back to the ranch, bought some $900 heifers and the rest is history. You can check the charts for yourself. The year that I bought those heifers is marked with one of those tell-tale cowpies. My apologies to ranchers as well as cattle feeders.

Now that I realize just how powerful my "manure touch" is, I probably should be more careful.

But, you know, the way this economy is rolling along, I've been thinking that I should draw down my operating loan and buy into some promising stocks on Wall Street. Quick! Someone call the New York Stock Exchange and give them the warning.

And tell them to watch out for fresh cowpies on the trading floor.

# On the road again

# Life in the slow lane
## Rules of the road for rural Dakota

People in a hurry can hurry along a little faster now on North Dakota's major highways and interstates.

If you're cruising on a North Dakota interstate, feel free to kick the cruise up to 70 miles an hour. You can careen along at 65 on our better four-lane state highways. This is good news if you're into speed and blurred scenery, I guess.

But the new rules probably won't affect my traveling habits much. My self-imposed code of travel conduct doesn't put my wheel tracks on the major roadways enough to really take advantage of the new speed limits. I like my little two-lane roads and gravel trails where speed takes a back seat to sightseeing.

When it comes to true enjoyment on the great American highways, just say whoa! Take a little time to enjoy North Dakota.

The way I see it, increased speed limits are just going to get you into Montana or Minnesota a little quicker. Before you know it, you'll have pesky mountains blocking your sunset or have trees and lakes crowding your pathway. You'll wish you'd taken more time traveling across the prairie.

### Rules of the road

When I'm traveling in North Dakota and elsewhere, I have three rules of the road guiding me:
1. Stay off the interstates.
2. Avoid fancy hotels.
3. Never eat in a chain restaurant.

Stick to those three basic principles and your time on the road will become more than windshield time. It will become a study of Americana, a look into the culture you might have whisked by at 1.16 miles per minute.

Now I understand the need for tourists to get from point "A" to point "B" in a reasonable amount of time, but what have they missed in between?

Interstates are fine, but they take the fun out of driving. They lack curves. They don't follow the landscape, they cut right through it with a bulldozer. And they keep you away from small-town North Dakota.

Author William Least Heat Moon calls my kind of roads "Blue Highways." Robert Frost would call them the "ones less traveled by." Me, I simply call them Highway 22, 14 and 46, with the same familiarity and fondness that I use when referring to some of my cows like No. 150, 422 and 80.

The highways I prefer to drive still have a speed limit of 55, but there are times when I'd rather set the cruise at 50.

## Driving, eating and sleeping

The routes I choose are pretty circuitous. That's because they're usually planned around the availability of free lodging with friends and relatives. I agree with rodeo clown Steve Tomac, who measures success by asking himself if he was broke down, how far would he have to go to find a friend who could help him out.

I think a person ought to be able to travel the back roads of North Dakota and, at any given point, be within 50 miles of a friend who could extend a cup of coffee, some conversation and a pillow for the night. Maybe it's just the hobo in me.

If you do have to rent a room in a hotel, make sure it's not one of those four-star models with a bubbling Jacuzzi and French milled soap. If the owner is friendly and the room is clean, I don't even care if they leave the light on for me.

I have nothing against franchised chain restaurants, but when I'm traveling in new territory, I don't want the same super combo meal that I could have gotten in Dickinson, Denver or Detroit.

The best eateries I've found along the roads less traveled generally are called cafe's, and they usually have the owner's name on the sign out front, not some corporate logo designed in New York City. Give me the special of the day at Anne's Family Dining, Alice's Restaurant or Gordy's Cafe anyday.

## Culture you can count on

Some people have the mistaken idea that culture has something to do with the opera, a room at the Ritz and a $100 bottle of wine. Culture on my 55-mile-per-hour road means a Chuck Suchy tape in the deck, a pull out couch at Jeff's place and a cold Old Mil at the Buckskin Bar.

Life in the slow lane will expose you to all kinds of culture. It'll take you past real ranches with barns that lean and machinery that lay resting and rusting on its perimeter. The fences won't be painted and you might even spot a cowboy in the wild, if you can see him from the road.

Summer road construction might slow you down, but the lady with the little stop sign will be glad to visit with you while you're waiting for the pilot car. And if you're traveling during autumm, you might get caught up in a fall cattle drive and be forced to hold your ground till the cows go home.

You can get away from those cell phone towers and free your hands up for more worthwhile endeavors like waving at the people you meet and the farmers out working their fields.

So when you're planning your next trip, remember that getting there is half the fun. And if you take the road less traveled by, you might lose a little time, but ol' Bob Frost would tell you that it could make all the difference.

# Going international
## Beyond the back door of Dakota

I've been pondering the idea of picking up a second language. You know, try and prepare myself for the global marketplace.

I considered Chinese to take advantage of the opportunities in the Far East, or maybe Spanish so I'd feel more at ease in all the Latin American countries. But after some serious thought, I decided to tackle the Canadian language instead.

I had a head start, having watched the Calgary Olympics on television several years back, and I'd been to the Peace Gardens a couple of times, too.

Realizing the challenge ahead of me, I drove to Saskatoon, Saskatchewan, last week to immerse myself in the culture. I figured head first was the only way to tackle my bilingual goals.

### Oh Canada

I picked up a friend of mine from Deloraine, Manitoba, (a "southerner" by Canadian standards) to serve as a translator and keep me out of trouble. I wasn't sure how quick Amnesty International would respond if I called them from the hoosegow with a plea of unjust imprisonment.

You never know, Mounties always get their man, and I have a tendency of driving through yellow lights and jaywalking across streets.

My first observations of Canada were great speed limits and cheap gas. You could drive 100 and buy your gas for 55 cents. Of course, I quickly realized, after passing every car in sight and watching the dollars wrap around the gas pump, that the speed was measured in kilometers per hour and the gas was sold by the liter.

And it only took a couple of brews at the local pub to find out that their silver bullets could darn sure slow you down.

On the positive side, everything in the country was on sale if you bought it with good green American frogskins. Sticker shock wasn't nearly as brutal when you knew you'd get an automatic 25 percent off at the cash register.

### Learning the lingo

It didn't take the Saskatoonians long to figure out I wasn't a native. I'm not sure if it was the long Dakota drawl, or maybe it was just the confused look on my face when they asked if I wanted vinegar with my meal or gravy with my french fries.

"From the states, eh?" they'd say. "Huh," I'd reply intelligently. Once the language barrier had been crossed, I could quickly concentrate on

198

picking up the lingo. Before you knew it, I was saying things like, "ouwwt (out), abouwwt (about), shhedule (schedule), agane (again), rye (whiskey), petro (gas) and eh (huh)."

I was feeling pretty comfortable with my mastery of the Canadian language and my new international image by the time we headed ol' Brownie, the wonder Chrysler, southward.

But sometimes ignorance comes in handy. On the way home, a Mountie whipped around on the highway and turned on the cherries. I knew I was speeding. According to ol' Brownies' kilometers-per-hour gauge, I was going 127 "klicks" in a 100 zone. I also knew a ticket that size would cost me a lot of loonies, with or without the exchange rate.

"I see you're from North Dakota. Did you know you were exceeding the speed limit?"

I quickly replied a thick and hearty, "huh?"

# A milestone of miles
## Charting new ground and wondering where to go

We had an important birthday in my family recently. Ol' Brownie, the wonder Chrysler, turned over 100,000 miles.

I couldn't find a cake that would hold that many candles, so I just bought her a brand new tank of gas and affectionately patted her on the hood. Ol' Brownie isn't the first car I've taken over the centurion threshold, and, as usual, I was distracted by something else when that golden moment of zeros came to the odometer.

I more than likely was doing what I usually do when I'm driving down the road — drinking coffee, eating some fast food, reading over some papers and talking on the cell phone. And, of course, maintaining my course with some careful knee steering.

The next time I looked down to check Ol' Brownie's vital signs, I was working on mile 100,001. What a disappointing feeling.

### Never buy new

I call Ol' Brownie the wonder Chrysler because it's always a wonder if I get where I'm going. That's the great thing about driving old worn-out cars — you fly by the seat of your pants and never know for sure if you'll reach your destination.

I really feel for those poor people who always drive new, dependable automobiles. They never get to feel the surge of adrenaline or sense of adventure that I do behind the wheel of Ol' Brownie, Ol' Gray and Ol' Blue, a few of the high-mileage motor vehicles in the Taylor Ranch fleet.

One thing about our color-coded line of cars, though, is no monthly payments. I've seen some new pickups advertised and have to say there's really something amiss when the word "just" precedes the figure $31,995.

I don't think I'd have the patience to buy a new vehicle and wait all those years to see the odometer make its spin to 100,000. The wait would drive me crazy.

## Tough decisions

I may not have monthly finance payments on the vehicles I drive, but there are monthly expenses. Of course, I get something better than a receipt for the monthly payments I make.

I've got a new transmission, new brake pads, new tires, new axles and a new battery to show for my nonscheduled payments.

The nonscheduled payments are getting to be a bit of a risk, now that Ol' Brownie has gone beyond the 100,000-mile mark.

Do you take the chance on buying a 60-month battery if there's only another 12 months left in the rig? Do you buy the tires with the 40,000-mile warranty when the power train may only take off the first 10,000 miles of tread?

They're tough decisions and can involve a lot of risk. But being in the cattle business, I'm used to taking a gamble.

And I'm gambling that Ol' Brownie will be with me for a few more miles and into the spring rains. She better be. I just gave her a new oil filter and a brand new set of wiper blades.

# Never turn back...
## And never ask directions

Spend any amount of time traveling the open road with a representative sample of the male species and you'll soon realize the two basic rules — never turn around and never stoop so low as to ask for help.

Our female counterparts still are having a tough time understanding these two philosophies as fundamentally male as facial hair and testosterone.

We'd much rather circle a town for an hour than admit geographic defeat. Best to forge ahead with ego and confidence, we say.

## Stubborn since 1492

Christopher Columbus never let anyone convince him to do a 180 with the Nina, Pinta or Santa Maria to find the East Indies.

You can bet Marco Polo, Eric the Red and Ferdinand Magellan didn't ask Mrs. Polo, Red or Magellan to jump out and ask the dimwit at the gas station to tell them where the heck they were.

Lots of new territory was settled by pioneer men too stubborn to admit they were completely lost. The only time covered wagons circled around was to feud off hostile Indians.

Of course, they probably wouldn't have been in Indian country if they'd have listened to their wives.

The discovery of America and the homesteading of the West probably can be accredited to male traveling stubbornness.

But Lewis and Clark probably would tell us that a little female intervention comes in handy.

I'm sure Meriwether and William were convinced that the Pacific Ocean was just over the next knoll until they met Sacajawea.

She definitely kept them on the straight and narrow heading west.

There were no gas station attendants or people on street corners to ask directions from, but she was able to pull aside some roving nomads and find the shortest route to Seattle.

## Still learning

My family could be enjoying good grain prices and be wondering what the heck a cattle cycle was if they'd have listened to my grandmother in Grand Forks, N.D., and stayed where the dirt was black.

From Virginia to Kentucky to Indiana, my ancestors looked at the ground beneath their feet, and if it looked too rich or fertile, they kept on moving.

Our will for humble living was granted when the house movers finally got stuck in the fine yellow sands of McHenry County, N.D.

Cattle figured out this gender disparity in directions and traveling a long time ago. When you chase cattle, you always see a couple good cows out front leading the way and the old bulls bringing up the rear, grumbling something about all the time wasted asking directions to the green grass ahead.

# Wishin' for wind

Wind. Can't live with it, can't live without it.

There's a lot of people who probably could live without the wind, but I contend that wind has its proper place during the summer months.

We spend a lot of time cussing the wind when it's blowin' off our hats and whistling through our coveralls at breakneck speeds in January, but when it's 100 degrees in the shade in August, wind can be a pretty good thing.

## Old-fashioned AC

My car doesn't have much for fancy options. No air, just wind. And wind is better than nothing at all when you're trying to keep from melting into your vinyl seats.

I actually do have an air-conditioning switch in ol' Brownie, the wonder Chrysler, but it's strictly for ornamental purposes. Kind of like fuzzy dice hanging from the rear view mirror. It works a little in the winter, but in the summer, it's about as cool as a glass of warm milk.

Somewhere in my travels to fairs, conventions and farm shows, I picked up a free soil thermometer. I like to keep it in my car just to see how close ol' Brownie gets to the boiling point when it's parked out in the sun.

The mercury only goes up to 120 on my temp-o-matic. Beyond that, you just have to go by touch. Last week, the temperature was limit up. I thought for sure the car was going to spontaneously combust.

My only salvation was to create a little wind. I rolled down all four windows and, sure enough, after 10 minutes of 65 miles an hour, I had the temperature down to 110.

When I jumped out, it looked like I'd driven all the way to Sturgis and back on a Harley without a windshield. My hair, what little there is, was shooting in eight different directions.

A couple of stray grasshoppers flew in and dove down the front of my shirt and a half-dozen mosquitoes were lodged in between my teeth. My gas receipts from the last month had all flown out the window and I'd caught two cassette tapes in midair, saving them from the Chrysler wind tunnel.

It made the movie "Twister" look like child's play. But I had achieved a small measure of coolness in the ol' Saunamobile.

## Econo Air

Wind conditioning isn't quite as good as air conditioning, but it never needs a recharge of Freon and there's no danger of catching pneumonia.

I kind of thought I might be getting better mileage since the engine doesn't have to work so hard to drive the belt and pulley on an AC compressor.

But I think the wind drag from the four open windows probably guzzles more gas than the AC compressor ever did.

Of course, who cares about fuel efficiency? Since all my gas receipts blew out the window, I wouldn't know how inefficient my "wind conditioning" system is anyway.

# Warm pastures, cold roads
## Wantin' and havin' it all

Can you really have your cake and eat it, too? If we could, I know what kind of cake I'd order and just how much I'd enjoy eating it.

Our cake would be warm spring weather, and we'd really enjoy eating it if we could do so while driving down a good frozen road.

Spring is kind of a love/hate season on the Taylor Ranch. I love to see the weather warm up past 40 below, but I hate to see our supposedly gravel roads hit 32 degrees and start turning into mud.

We call some of our trails "gravel roads," just like we call some of our hay meadows "alfalfa fields." If your mower knocks down just one alfalfa plant per round, you can call that piece of land an alfalfa field. Likewise, if you see a couple of pebbles half a mile down the trail, you can label that lane a gravel road.

### Concrete counterpart

Winter gives us folks on the old dirt lane the opportunity to pretend we're parading down pavement. In our winter wonderland of make believe byways, there's no dust, no ruts and no sinking down in mud up to your door handles.

Frozen dirt truly is the next best thing to black top. Our concrete cousins probably don't understand our admiration for frigid weather and firm roads.

Spring strikes this country practically overnight. One day, you're cold and miserable but enjoying pretty good roads. The next day, you're warm and feeling good but driving down some pretty miserable roads.

It's hard to enjoy the sunshine and greening grass when you're fighting the steering wheel, peering through a mud stained windshield and trying to find a little bedrock for your wheels to run on.

It's then that we begin to yearn for the ice-packed season of yesterday.

### Icy infrastructure

In a country that put a man on the moon, you'd think we could come up with a way to affordably improve the avenues of transportation out in the hinterlands.

We now have professional hockey teams in Florida and Texas. These are not states with a lot of knowledge about ice and cold. Still, they've placed enough entertainment value on the game of hockey to foot the bill for artificially refrigerated ice rinks.

Transportation should mean as much to us folks in the sticks, as entertainment does to people in the Southern suburbs. We might want to consider installing a system of pipes underneath our gravel roads, and putting in a few compressors to force some cold air and freon beneath our mud prone routes.

Just imagine it — driving down a rock solid road in the middle of April, watching the grass grow and listening to the meadowlarks sing. And if you feel the need for a cold soda, don't bother with an ice chest, just pull over and lay a six pack on the cold, cool gravel for spell.

# Honest, the dog did it
## One for the insurance convention

There oughta be a law against pets driving pickups in parking lots.

Maybe there already is a law, but nobody told the pets about it.

Last week, my pick-up and horse trailer were sitting in a big parking lot, nice and innocent-like, when an out of control dog came careening down the hill and thumped the back corner of my horse trailer.

Yes, a dog in a pickup. No lie.

The pooch's pickup was in worse shape than my horse trailer, so we filed a police report on the incident. The dog's master came out to survey the situation and I got the feeling that Rover wasn't going to get a Scooby snack when they got home that afternoon.

The police officer raised one eyebrow when we told her the dog did it, but with a little explanation she began to see the amusement in it all. Her report details how the pickup was parked about hundred feet up a slope in the parking lot when the dog knocked the stick shift out of gear and rode the Ford to an impact-induced standstill.

### The other version

Personally, I'd have liked to have heard the dog's version of the incident. Speak, Rover, speak!

Maybe he was a little peeved about being left alone in the vehicle while his master went in to do a little leisurely shopping.

It could have been an act of rebellion to the "no shirt, no shoes, no pets" policy of the store. A rallying act of defiance meant to motivate all dogkind.

Perhaps he was just getting a little hot sitting there with the sun beating down through the windshield. Hopefully, the owner left the windows open a crack so he wouldn't suffocate.

Rover may have realized that without the keys he couldn't run the air conditioning. He may have read last week's Cowboy Logic and decided to try a little wind conditioning by picking up a little speed, creating some momentum and, in the process, a little additional ventilation.

Then again, maybe we're giving the little canine too much credit in his thinking process. It could well be he was just doing what little dogs do best — jumping around and barking like an idiot, when he inadvertently put a paw down on the shifter and knocked it from first down into neutral. He probably still was yapping, panting and smiling that silly doggy smile when the bumper did its best to round out the corners on my trailer.

## Tall but true tales

I can just about imagine the tales that will be told about the delinquent dog of a driver at the conventions of insurance adjusters and gatherings of police officers.

There'll likely be a lot of nonbelievers out there who'll shoot holes in the tale, but any teacher who's let a student by with the story that "the dog ate my homework" should have no problem believing that student grew up and had the dog wreck his pickup.

# Unexpected ventilation
## Exposed to winter once again

Winter travel can be plenty challenging, but little things like car heaters and tight vehicle cabs make it a lot more comfortable.

It's easy to get kind of spoiled when you're traveling and do things as crazy as taking off your jacket or putting up your ear flappers as you head down the road.

I was feeling pretty cozy today in a rental van that was going from Miles City, Mont., to Bowman, N.D., for the seventh of 18 Northern Plains Premium Beef equity drive meetings.

We were doing a little mild complaining about the frost on the windows when a semi passed us and, "Bam!," our big side window shattered into a billion pieces. Our glass was grass. We could quit complaining about the frosty windows anyway.

We still had our heater, but it had a tough time keeping up with the 12-foot-square hole in our side.

The remainder of our trip from Rhame to Bowman was spent trying to stay warm and figure out what hit us.

## Drive by shooting

Highway 12 generally is considered to be a pretty crime-free route, but with the trends in society and violence, we may not be safe anywhere.

When our window exploded, my first thought was a drive-by shootist. That semi driver may not have liked the way we were crowding the center line and pulled out his pistol to move us over a bit.

Or he may have been a hired hit man and had it out for one of us in the van. Dean Meyer and I are both budding young columnists, and it could have been a hit arranged by Dave Barry or Ann Landers.

Luckily, their aim was a little off. Nothing but glass, and not so much as a flesh wound on Dean or myself.

If it was a shooting at all, it was more likely to have been an out-of-season hunter out poaching some game. Our big green van with "Enterprise Rentals" emblazoned on the side easily could have been mistaken for a deer or an antelope.

Next time, I think we'll rent a blaze orange model.

### The road home

Compared with some of the weather we've had this winter, we picked a pretty nice day to be driving down the road with our window knocked out. It was about 10 degrees below zero and relatively still.

A little plastic sheeting and duct tape had us feeling pretty cozy as we cruised into Amidon for supper.

But as we finally headed for Bismarck, we became the victim of every rancher's worst nightmare — duct tape blow out, and once again we were exposed to the North Dakota winter. We really should have used more tape.

This winter's been hard enough, and the one day this month that the wind didn't blow we had to create our own 65-mile-an-hour wind on a minus-10-degree night.

At least we'll be in shape for our next weekly blizzard.

# Passenger car payload
## Ranch cars mean hard luck for hitchhikers

I finally cleaned ol' Brownie, the wonder Chrysler, last week. You'd have thought I was going to the prom or something. After filling a garbage bag with pop cans, fast food wrappers, and Cenex receipts, I took after the interior with a little 80 psi air hose pressure and I topped it all off with one of those fruity scented pine trees.

I found four ice scrapers, the measuring tape I'd lost and a couple of cookies that the mice must have overlooked. I tasted the cookies and realized the mice hadn't overlooked them, they just didn't want to eat them.

I gazed at the floorboards I hadn't seen in ages and admired the roominess in the  back seat. I had more room than I ever could need to start hauling ranch supplies again.

## Heading out

I was supposed to speak at a cattle producer's meeting in West Fargo, so I topped off all the vital fluids and headed out in my freshly cleaned auto.

But first I threw in the tire and wheel from my baler to drop off en route. The wheel had dropped off in the hogwallows when the lug nuts got loose and plowed ol' Yeller, the baler, into the mud.

The holes in the wheel were looking pretty tough, so I figured I'd have the tire put on a replacement rim while I was enjoying the sights in Fargo.

The baler mender looked at the six holes that were ruined, then looked at six other holes that were evenly spaced between the bad ones and asked, "why don't you use these?"

"Oh...yeah...that's what I was going to do. I just wanted to show it to you," I said as I sheepishly threw the tire back into ol' Brownie. "I was just going to haul this wheel to Fargo and back to show it around a little."

## No hitchhikers

While I was in the big city of Fargo, I found some bargains that were too good to pass up. My high flotation tire already took up most of the cargo area, but I was able to pile in a half-dozen cases of oil, a beer cooler full of cattle vaccine and a few other bags of supplies in the remaining cracks and crevices.

Even though ol' Brownie had started out clutter-free, it was filled back up to capacity. I couldn't pick up a hitchhiker if I wanted to. Not that I feel a real urge to pick up grungy, jobless guys who'd kill you for your pocket change.

Of course, good-looking damsels in distress in need of ride could make a fella clean out the passenger side and sacrifice his supplies.

So if you're driving down Highway 2 and you see a big tire, a few boxes of oil and a cooler of vaccine discarded in the ditch, you'll know I ran into a group of Coppertone bikini models with car trouble.

# Lost and found
## The high cost of forgetting

Being absent-minded is an expensive habit.

I can't begin to count the dollars I've spent to replace lost jackknives and misplaced writing utensils. If I could have those dollars back, I probably could afford the finest pocketknife made and the most luxurious Waterman fountain pen in existence.

I've got wrenches that still are lying out in the hay field and fencing pliers that are rusting underneath the fenceline or next to a corner post. I own a half a dozen ear taggers just to make sure I can find at least one during spring calving season.

Winter is a tough time for forgetful folks. We've got gloves, caps and overshoes that are easily left behind. Of course, when it's 40 below, you quickly realize when you don't have your gloves or your wool cap on.

Hats can be lost in the summer, too. Once I thought I'd lost my lid only to realize later that it was still on top of my head. Luckily, I don't have eyeglasses to lose.

## Personal losses

Many of the things I lose hold more sentimental value than monetary worth. The jackknife I lost was only worth $9.95, but it had been riding around in my pocket for four years. It was like losing an old friend.

A good pen is just as treasured as old knives. I get most of my pens for free and I treat them like they didn't cost me a dime. But, once in awhile, I get a nice pen as a gift, and losing those writing sticks with the smooth clicker and the freely flowing ink just breaks my heart.

But there's nothing I hate losing more than my favorite coffee cups. Starting the day with strong coffee in a familiar cup is both comforting and stimulating.

## Trading losses

With that in mind, you can understand my recent anguish when I left my favorite spill-proof coffee cup in a rental van, never to be seen again. It was almost as tearful as my losing a "Sons of the San Joaquin" cassette tape in another rental vehicle last summer.

But what comes around goes around. I got in a different rental van this week for our Northern Plains Premium Beef meetings and got on the found side of the lost-and-found equation.

First thing I found in this new van was a cassette tape to replace my lost "Sons of the San Joaquin." Unfortunately, it was a "rap" tape and the "music" sounded like two tomcats tied by the tail and hanging from the clothes line.

The second find darn near took away my coffee cup grief. In the Velcro-locked headliner, I stumbled across a little artwork. When I folded it out, we just about put the van in the ditch. It's hard to focus on winter roads when Miss August is folded out in complete glory, creases and all.

Admittedly, it was somewhat stimulating, but I still miss my lost coffee cup full of caffeine.

# Car shopping
## An average guy's guide

When Ol' Brownie, the wonder Chrysler, was totaled in my recent car accident, I could hardly imagine driving another car. It just wouldn't be right to sit in the seat of another while Ol' Brownie was sitting all alone in the auto salvage yard. I thought the guilt of being untrue would simply overwhelm me.

Then I realized that I was in dire need of some transportation and that Ol' Gray, the gas-guzzling ranch pickup, probably shouldn't be worn out driving up and down the highway. The last 20,000 miles left in her probably should be saved for hauling cows to town, bouncing around in the pasture and going to the field.

So I had to start looking for a replacement for Ol' Brownie. I began combing the want ads and I started to slow down when I went past the car lots.

### Learning the lingo

The first thing I had to do when I went car shopping was learn the language of automobile marketing. It's like stepping into a foreign country and if you don't learn your way around you might think you're ordering scrambled eggs and actually get deep-fried snails instead.

For instance, if the ad says, "a good work car," this does not mean that it would be a suitable vehicle to get you up and down the road to your job. This means that it is very old and that it would be a "good car to work on." Shine up your wrenches if you buy that one.

Another favorite of the salesmen when they're discussing their deal of the week is that it "really runs out nice." This doesn't mean that the engine sounds good and that it'll motor down the highway purring like a kitten. The meaning behind the phrase is that the car will nicely run out of power, run out of oil and run out of life in no time at all.

If the car jockey tells you that it would make a "great second car," don't be fooled into thinking that he means it'll be a nice vehicle to drive around while you save the miles on your good car. A "great second car" is synonymous with "use it to supply spare parts to your first car."

### Facts and figures

To save space in the want ads, car sellers use the letter K to denote thousands of miles. However, the price has a dollar sign in front of it and the lead number is followed by a few zeros.

The numbers can be interchanged, though, as a rule. A car with 100,000 (100K) miles on it probably will sell for about $4,000. Conversely, a car with 4,000 (4K) miles on it could just as well cost $100,000 because you never could afford it anyway at the price they actually would want.

I finally did wade through the myriad choices and locate a dependable set of wheels. And the truth of the matter is that I'm pretty ashamed of what I bought.

But I'll give the guilt a chance to settle in and tell you about my new rig next week.

# Driving in shame
## Upgrading is a real downfall

I finally did it. I sold out. Gave up. I swallowed my pride and went from one transportation extreme to another.

I bought a replacement for Ol' Brownie, the wonder Chrysler, and I'm afraid I went way overboard with my choice.

I've always taken a lot of pride in driving old, rundown cars with bald tires, weak batteries and loose pistons. I never would think of getting behind the wheel of anything with less than 100,000 miles on it.

Now I've sold out on those principles. I hate to admit it, but I actually bought a car that was made in the 1990s. Worse yet, it's actually a 1996 model and it's only got 39,000 miles worth of experience.

It does have a few redeeming qualities, though. It was relatively cheap, well under my five-digit threshold of pain. Thanks to some former hail damage, it was way under "book price," which meant it fell within the realm of my "checkbook price."

Regardless of the great deal, it's been a tough transition from old to new, wore out to still wearing.

### Community shunning

You don't just drive down the gravel roads of south Towner in a 1996 Buick without attracting some attention.

In my area, pride of ownership is directly correlated to the age of your vehicle. My parents garner a lot of respect with their 1974 Ford Galaxie. Likewise, we get a lot of peer approval when we drive our 1967 Ford pickup out to the hayfields.

People don't take it lightly when you bring a snooty, late model vehicle into the neighborhood. I'm already getting the silent treatment from a few in the area.

I was driving my new rig the other day and nobody would even wave at me when I passed them on the road. Of course, it could be that they didn't recognize me in a car so clean and aerodynamic.

I'm sure once I get a good layer of dirt on it and wrap some bone-jarring, dust-laden miles on the odometer they'll begin to recognize me and soften their attitude toward my new wheels.

But, I admit, it does take some getting used to.

## Attitude adjustment

I'm still getting used to those round, aerodynamic edges. I'm used to those good, square, wind-catching corners that keep your gas gauge and your speedometer pegged close to zero.

That speed difference between the new Buick and Ol' Brownie is darn sure noticeable. Ol' Brownie needed a steep downhill grade and a strong tailwind to reach 60 miles an hour in under an hour.

Now, all I need to do is step on the gas. And if I like the speed I'm going, there's this little knob called cruise control that I can push. It seems like a lot better system than propping a brick against the pedal.

Yeah, Ol' Buck, the blue/green/gray Buick, has some nice qualities. It's just a real shame for me to be driving a car that's only a year old. Maybe I'll feel a little better about it in 1998.

# Happy highways
## The secret to friendly traveling

In this age of drive-by shootings and "road rage," I think I've stumbled across the secret to highway happiness and tranquil traveling. The secret is to drive a pickup and pull a stock trailer.

Everybody waves at you when you're going down the road with a horse trailer. For some reason, it brings out the friendly side of folks.

Maybe it's just pity. They probably just feel sorry for guys like me who go down the road with a gutless, half-ton pickup and an overloaded 16-foot bumper trailer.

It may be that they smile and wave to give me a little encouragement as I struggle to reach 40 miles an hour on a slight incline.

Or, if it's merely a frantic wave and no smile, it could be a sign of anger, frustration or fear. Those kind of waves come about as the cattle commence to fighting and the trailer starts to wagging like a dog's tail, back and forth across the center line and invading their lane.

My trailer has yet to knock anyone off of the highway, but it has gotten within inches of a few side view mirrors on some of the more narrow roads. Some people who go through those close scrapes continue to wave even after we've passed each other. Odd, though, how they're usually waving with just one finger at those times.

## King of the road

Most of the waves, however, are full-handed and enthusiastically positive. I saw a lot of those friendly waves while hauling a few bulls this spring. I had bought the bulls in the winter, and after a couple months of imposing on the breeder's feeding and hospitality, I figured I better retrieve them before they gave up on me and resold them or had them castrated.

I enjoy hitting the open road with my pickup and horse trailer. I get that same "king of the road" feeling that semi drivers must thrive on.

Granted, a high-geared four-speed and a 5,000-pound payload probably doesn't give quite the same feeling of power as a Peterbuilt and 18 wheels humming under the strain of 50,000 pounds, but it's probably as close as I'll ever get.

I think some of the semis I meet understand the way I feel. They generally give me a wave of fellowship from their high-profile seats as they pass.

Of course, the most sincere waves come from other people in similar pickups pulling similar trailers. If they dare ungrip their wobbly steering wheel, they wave vigorously as only road-weary comrades can.

The biggest surprise is when ordinary people in ordinary cars consistently give me a wave. I don't know if they're town folks who enjoy the novelty of seeing cattle and cowboys out on the road or if they're just displaced farmers and ranchers with a soft spot for us low-horsepower haulers.

Either way, a wave is a wave and I'll take every greeting I can. As a matter of fact, I just might start pulling my trailer everywhere I go to capitalize on that extra geniality. But, before I permanently hook up to that wind catching trailer, I better raise the credit limit on my gas card.

# Weather or not

# Good vs. bad
## Wishing for some "bad" weather

I don't know how much more "good" weather I can stand.

Every night, the weather persons and news anchors tell me that we've had another "nice" day. No rain, no clouds, just lots of mild sunshine.

They use words like wonderful, beautiful and gorgeous. I prefer to use words like parched, arid and dry, dry, dry.

Somewhere in our "food comes from the grocery store" mentality, we've concluded that sunny weather is good weather — good for boating, good for golfing, good for camping and recreation of all sorts.

Unfortunately, it's also good for starving to death because the grass, hay and crops in my part of the world really are struggling with all this "good" weather. The sunshine has folks firing up the grills, but the cattle can't find enough grass or feed to beef up their loins and make their contribution to the menu.

There's water sitting in the bottoms, but it's dry as a bone up top. The cows gave up on our pastures, tried the neighbor's pastures, and then came back in disgust. Neither had much to offer.

### Lookin' for a cloud

Maybe we should round 'em up and head to Indianapolis. They've had lots of "bad" weather. So bad, in fact, they had to postpone the Indy 500 twice because of rain.

Or I could head west to Washington or Oregon. They always have a lot of bad weather. They claim it rains so much there that people don't tan, they rust.

I should be careful about wishing for rain when folks around Devils Lake and in the Red River Valley probably have had about all the water they can stand for a long time.

I guess my dissatisfaction with the weather just comes with the job. Nobody can complain more about the weather than farmers and ranchers. We take a lot of pride in never being satisfied — too wet, too dry, too cold, too hot, too windy. We'd probably complain if our ice cream was cold.

Weather's one of those things that everybody talks about but nobody does anything about. That is, except the cloud seeders and the rain dancers.

Newscasters don't realize that their "good" weather is really quite bad for those of us who are trying to feed them, but you can't be too hard on them, they just don't know any better.

# Good sleddin', tough ranchin'
## Season's first snow has lost its magic

I'm not sure when or how, but somewhere between the age of 4 and 24 the season's first snowfall has lost its magic. No longer is my little face smashed up against the school bus window watching the snowflakes fall, bursting at the seams of my noisy nylon parka to get home so I could head to the hills with snowsled in hand.

Those were simpler times. After an hour or so of careening down my backyard sandhills at velocities that had to approach the speed of sound, I'd toss aside my red toboggan and belly up to ma's table for a steamy cup of hot chocolate loaded down with little marshmellers.

Even in my little rancher days, I had the black cloud of disaster hanging over my head. Ranch sledding meant looking out for impending wrecks as you put your life in the hands of gravity.

You had to remember to bail out before you hit the barbed-wire fence at the bottom of the hill and watch out for trees, bare spots and drop-offs that could send you to the house in your little green coveralls with frozen teardrops on your cheeks.

### That was then, this is now

All that has changed now. The green coveralls have been replaced with heavier brown bibs, I drink coffee instead of cocoa and good sledding means tough ranching. The look of wonderment is now a look of disgust as I slosh through the snow carrying feed pails and thinking of the hay left out on the field and the ice in the water tank.

Sledding has kind of taken a back seat to getting the cattle fed and watered. Snow doesn't look as pretty as it used to when you're shoveling it away from the barn door, out of the feedbunks and off of the walkways.

### Getting stuck

Then there's the universal art of getting stuck. Whether you're a farmer, rancher or live in town, chances are you've had the unique pleasure of driving into something you can't drive out of. It crosses all boundaries and ways of life for those of us who live with mud and snow.

You can't upgrade your way out of getting stuck either. Bigger tractors just get you stuck deeper, four-wheel-drive pickups enable you to get stuck in places you never even would have considered before.

The worst part about getting stuck is the lack of a good scapegoat. You really have no one to blame but yourself whether you're trying to combine a muddy field, haul hay off of a wet meadow or just seeing if you can

215

make it to the other side of that 20 foot snowdrift on the road.

The real beauty of getting stuck is the walk home to get someone or something to pull you out. This is where the advance of modern communications has failed us. Because if you can call or radio home for somebody else to come help you, you miss out on the chance to cool down and ponder the situation as you hoof it down the road.

That walk home does you a world of good because it helps you realize that there really is no one else to blame for your troubles. Within a mile or two, you'll be laughing at yourself and the precarious situation you put yourself in.

Be careful, though, when you walk in the house laughing and smiling as you tell the home crew, "I just got stuck tight as a drum, clear up to the axles in that big snowdrift!" People tend to regard cheery people with suspicion and, if you aren't careful, you might get sent out for an analysis by folks with white lab coats and a theory for people who smile when they're in distress.

# Snowdrift archaeologists dig out
## You never miss it till it's gone

Winter definitely has set in. I figured this out when I peeked out our drafty door and realized old man winter had cleaned up the ranch with a thick, fluffy blanket of snow.

Admittedly, the old homestead looked pretty good. The new snow gave the place a fresh, clean look. It had covered up the junk that was laying around, burying our collection of things that were too good to throw away, but not good enough to be taken care of.

I was still able to find most of the important stuff — the pickup, the barn, the cattle. The rest of the equipment and ranch paraphernalia had been converted to rounded, white bumps.

The problem with the tidying efforts of the snowfall is it covers up the good with the bad. It hides the unsightly pile of slightly used and splintered lumber, but it also covers up the fence stretcher we need and the missing spool of wire.

### Ranch archeology

The season's first substantial snowfall always catches us off guard. It could come in October or it could come in February, it'd still catch us completely unaware.

A strange transition takes place when we go out to dig out from under our first big snow. Send a farmer or rancher out in front of the shop to look

216

for that crescent wrench he set there the week before and he's transformed into a snowdrift archaeologist.

Like the fellas you see on PBS brushing dirt away from the leg bone of a prehistoric brontosaurus, you can find us out in front of the shop whisking away snow in a delicate search for the missing wrench. The moments of discovery are equally exciting. An unprecedented prehistoric find or coming up with a rusty wrench — the elation is just as intense.

Some digs are more delicately performed than others. You won't see any power excavation equipment when scientists are on the brink of uncovering an ancient Indian ruin. Likewise, no rough groping is allowed when you drop the cotter key from the hitch pin in the snow.

Cotter keys and ancient Indian pottery require gentle searching. We gently blow the snow away with our frosty breath and peer at the ground while feeling the way with numb fingertips.

The disappointment of a false discovery crosses the boundaries between Ph.D.'s and Ph.F.'s (pretty hysterical farmers). The Ph.D. knows the disgust of thinking he's found King Tut's breakfast bowl only to realize its Corelware. The Ph.F. sees a glint of metal, thinks it's his long lost three-quarter inch socket extension, then has the wind let out of his sails as he uncovers a broken jack handle.

## Keep on diggin'

Our archaeological digs go on long after the initial snowfall. We continue to shovel, brush and feel our way through the snow from November to April. We never quite realize what we're missing until we need it.

We start out looking for our tire chains and progress to jumper cables as our batteries die, fence stretchers as our cows find the best route into the hay yard and calf pullers when the heifers start letting loose in March.

A midwinter thaw can ease the burden of our search. A warm day in February may allow the missing jack to peek out of the snow and catch our eye. A good thaw can uncover items we've searched for futilely for months. Like finding an old birthday card with a $10 bill, we smile appreciatively as we thank the sun for giving us back our pipe wrench.

Some things we can't get along without though. If we can't find them, we're forced to go to town, buy new. That may explain our 500-foot collection of extension cords. If you find your extension cord gobbled up by snow snakes, don't run buy a new one. I may be able to float you through till April when yours miraculously reappears.

217

# Real wonders of the season

## Cool temperatures, frozen cow pies a winter wonder

Winter brings a lot of scientific wonders to farmers and ranchers. Snowflakes (no two alike of course) fall gently and form monstrous drifts for us to push around, pile up and get stuck in.

Cold temperatures do their magic every night, giving us frozen water tanks and fountains, oil the consistency of tar in our tractors and batteries whose cold cranking amps decided it was just too cold to crank.

But one of the real wonders of the winter season has to be the lowly pieces of frozen cow manure that we stumble on, trip over and bounce our tractors across as we feed each morning.

### Space age qualities

Forget what you've heard about the hardness of diamonds and steel, after a night of 20-below-zero temperatures, frozen cow manure has got to be the hardest substance known to man.

If you've ever kicked into a sizable piece with nothing but soft-toed pack boots on your feet, you're sure to agree. If you're unlucky enough to trip and fall on a particularly sharp piece while traveling at a high rate of speed, you'd swear the pain couldn't be any worse if you'd fallen onto jagged rock or broken concrete.

When combined with icy terrain or uphill slopes, it can stop an 80-horsepower loader tractor dead in its tracks and keep the tires on a pickup spinning until the vehicle steers clear of the excretory obtrusion.

Ranchers grimace as they bounce their tractors across the axle-jarring, spindle-breaking material. Cold steel is no match for cold crap. Anyone who's left their tractor in the feeding area while they run to town for a new front spindle can tell you that.

Cows are sometimes victims of their own excretions as the frozen pieces go whizzing by their heads after being cannonballed out from under the edge of tractor tires. The velocity reached by feces in flight may well reach that of a speeding bullet. This is why ranchers consider feeding a solo chore; it's just not safe to be standing around while someone else is firing frozen cow pies every which way.

### The CDI

Something with the supernatural qualities of frozen cow manure really should be put to use at NASA or the Pentagon. Why not scrap the money spent on SDI, strategic defense initiative, and spend a portion of it on the new CDI, cow pie defense initiative.

The Pentagon could enlist cattle ranchers to herd and feed their cattle along the perimeters of potential arctic battle sites a couple days before the enemy is expected to advance. Once frozen, the trail left behind the cows surely would spell disaster for the unwary troops.

Transports would be stuck, lodged up against a hefty frozen cow pie and spinning on the smooth icy ground. Jeeps would be busting axles as they bounce across and the troops would be tripping and falling with every third step. The frozen chips flung out by the tires of the trucks surely would wreak havoc with the foot soldiers left to duck and dodge these Hereford hand grenades.

The CDI has some merit in Northern climates. If relations ever turned sour with Canada, it'd be a dandy way to protect our Northern frontier. I can see some problems to the south though. Using CDI to protect us from a Mexican invasion could leave us with a rather soft defense, so to speak.

# Determination or stupidity
## The essence of youth

Little "I". If the term conjures up images of a lower case vowel in our alphabet, you may be a bit lost on the subject matter of this column. If, however, the term turns your mind to an NDSU tradition of young people, livestock and an event that spans the century, read on, you're apparently familiar with the image.

Little "I" stands for the NDSU Little International Livestock Show, and last weekend I had the pleasure of witnessing its 69th edition in Fargo on Feb. 11.

Undaunted by the fact that I got my four-wheel-drive pickup stuck in the middle of a 100-foot snowdrift the consistency of concrete on the way out of the ranch, I kept my rig pointed east because, storm or no storm, I was bound to revisit my alma mater.

**Braving the elements**

The weather was far from ideal as I struck out for the old college town, but my North Dakota upbringing had me prepared for the worst. I crammed jumper cables, an extension cord, a tow rope, a sleeping bag, overshoes, mittens, caps, coveralls, Heet, oil, anti-freeze, a flashlight and an emergency bag of Gordetto's in ol' gray to prepare for the stormy journey.

I even left room for myself, a non-thermal Stetson and a toothbrush. Not many people would have felt the need to take off in the middle of 60 below windchills, but such is the essence of youth.

A number of college parents found themselves turning back, convinced that the trip was too treacherous to risk life and limb out on the open road. I think that's what you call wisdom.

Many would classify the road trips made by us in the under-age-30 crowd as stupid. I, however, prefer terms like determined or perseverant.

**On the road of life**

Stupidity often is confused with terms like determination when it comes to the acts of the young, depending on your viewpoint.

Visiting with college classmates and friends who made it to the show, I realized that NDSU and functions like Little "I" have done a real service to the future of the state. Capitalizing on one thing our state always has been able to offer, agriculture, the two institutions have trained and retained some of the best people in the state.

I talked to some pretty talented people in their mid-20s who were able to stay in North Dakota because of their love for agriculture and the livestock industry. Pessimists might label talented people who return to family farms and ranches as stupid, I prefer to call them determined and say, "More power to ya."

Still, others have found jobs in ag business, extension and related services. I say, "We're mighty glad to have you here." These are talented folks and they deserve some positive reinforcement if we want to keep them here in North Dakota.

The word "just" seems to have creeped into some of their vocabularies when they tell folks about their careers. They might say something like, "I'm just home farming with my dad."

There's no just about it, but if they want to use the word they could say, "I'm just part of a small, but elite, group of people who feed the world."

If Little "I" was partly responsible for keeping these people in North Dakota, I give the event a Big "A" for a job well done. It's encouraging to know that so many young people have found opportunities in a state like North Dakota or have plans to return as soon as they can.

And if someone calls you stupid for choosing the road you're on, just flash your smile of determination, remember your survival gear and keep heading for the clear skies ahead.

# Lost in a country snow bank
## Not enough country folks to dispatch the snow plows

The last snowstorm left me with road conditions typical for our sparsely populated area. The 17 miles of gravel that separates our ranch from milk, bread and other frivolous items, turned into 17 miles of snowdrifts.

Eventually, a few brave souls busted a path and gave us a pair of well-established ruts. Like a long bobsled run, the two ruts guided our vehicles to and from town.

Our cars began to steer something like bobsleds, too. A pair of skis up front probably would have done a more proficient job of steering the unit than the two tires put up there by some Southern automobile engineer.

The real trick of the Gorman Township bobsled run is to keep your vehicle in the ruts. Like an out-of-control Jamaican bobsled team, if you go too fast, you risk the chance of flying out of the run and having a wreck.

Oncoming traffic is another matter. You can play a game of high stakes "chicken" to see who gives in and swerves out of the way. Or you can come to a standstill, face each other and back up to the nearest intersection, or let the one with the better traction and clearance break a new "passing rut."

Eventually, the snow plow comes out and ruins the ruts.

## A question of service

As taxpaying landowners of the township, my neighbors and I are mildly perturbed with the system of ruts we're left with while other roads get plowed out before the snow even quits falling. The level of irritation is a notch or two higher for my neighbors who work in town and have to navigate the system twice a day.

But we have to realize that roads used by 1,000 people or 100 people will get higher priority than our little thoroughfare traversed by 10 people.

We understand that the workers running the snowplow can only get over so many miles of road in a day's time. They're in the tough position of always having somebody mad at them, so they go down the roads that have the potential for generating the greatest number of angry phone calls.

It's all a numbers game. The louder your collective voice, the better you're heard.

## Great Plains baby boom

Our only hope seems to be a new population explosion. It may go against the zero growth rules for our planet to have more than 2.2 children per family, but if we want to maintain some basic service out here in the sticks, we need some people.

Everything's up for grabs. Snowplows, school buses, rural mail delivery, telephone and electrical service. Repopulating our rural areas will give us new clout and a louder voice.

Get it together, team! With a little focused effort on population growth, we can leave our bobsleds at home and drive the car to town after the next snowstorm.

# A land of extremes
## Expect the unexpected in times of transition

We northerners live in a land of extremes.

The recent temperature swing from 30 below zero to 50 above in less than a week's time serves as a good example of our extremeliness.

The extremes can stretch between weeks, years and miles. But sometimes we see simultaneous extremes. In one spot, at one moment in time, we can see things that just make us wonder.

### Winter or spring

March is a time of transition and extremes as we move from winter into spring.

It doesn't really matter to me whether it's winter or spring because I'm still trying to trying to haul hay and get ready for last fall.

I was heading toward one of my drifted in, froze down prairie hay roll-ups with my grapple teeth bared, ready to rip, mangle and transport some hay.

But before you could say, "where's the bottom half of my left tire?" I was stuck. The funny thing about it was while my left tire was spinning in the thawed-out mud, my right tire was spinning on thick sheet of ice. I had a pair of tires in a real paradox.

It was like having one foot on the ice rink in International Falls, Minn., and the other foot in the Mississippi mud near Waterproof, La. It was as contradictory as fire and ice, heaven and hell, dogs and cats, *Agweek* and that other farm paper.

I've been stuck in the mud before, but it's not usually 10 below zero when I do. At first, I kicked a snowbank, questioned the virtues of that quarter of hayland and cursed the traction of my balding tire lugs. The actions served the dual purpose of both venting my frustration and keeping me warm by circulating my boiling blood.

### A phunny phenomenon

After awhile, I stepped back and found the humor in my strange little predicament. My extremes went from extremely frustrated to extremely perplexed (insert picture of head-scratching cowboy with floating thought cloud that says, "huh?").

I pondered the idea of being simultaneously stuck in both mud and ice as I cinched up my hooded sweatshirt and headed for home.

My choice of routes for the walk home hinged on North Dakota extremes, too. I could have taken the road — a little over a mile of extremely easy walking with the chance of hitching a ride with some passer by. But considering the low level of traffic in Smokey Lake Township, I decided the chances of catching a ride were extremely slim.

Option two was a three-quarter-mile shortcut across the snowbound tundra. I pictured the misery of breaking through the snow with each struggling shortcut step, the sweat running down my body and freezing in the bottom of my shoes.

But I was saved by another North Dakota exteme. The snowdrifts were extremely hard and walking cross country was as easy as a stroll on an asphalt pathway. Of course part of the ease could be credited to my size 12 feet acting like a pair of giant snowshoes supporting my weight on the crusting snow.

The concrete snow was much appreciated. I realized the extreme depth of my prairie pathway as I crossed a hip-high barbed-wire fence that only measured up below my knee caps. Anyway, I made it home and found a pull.

Odd situations sometimes demand odd solutions. I wanted to help add to the momentum as my neighbor tightened the chain between our two tractors. So what did I do? I threw a little mud under the right tire for extra traction and I tossed a little ice under the left tire to help firm up the mud.

# Grab your skates
## Ranching on ice can be competitive and graceful

We had a nice rain here on the ranch last week. Froze up real good, too. In the morning, I took one step out the front door and didn't stop till I hit (literally) the corral gate.

Morning chores were pretty acrobatic, too. Those fellas who perform in the Ice Capades show have nothing over on me.

My skating costume was a little rustic, tattered brown duck coveralls and a wool railroader's cap with the shoelaces half tied, but the sheer grace of my performance made up for the lack of glitter in my outfit.

Sliding to the feed trough with a couple of 5 gallon pails full of feed, I did a couple of quadruple axles, a partial back flip and a triple sow cow.

By the time I got to the feed bunk, I had one of those pails balanced above my head like a female skating partner in the pairs division. I'm not sure if Peggy Fleming would have trusted me to hoist her above my head like that, but I'm confident my replacement heifers would have gathered around and caught her, if by chance I happened to drop her on her head.

### Cows on ice

I have to admit I'm not the only figure skating prospect here on the Taylor Ranch. The cows have some pretty nice moves themselves.

223

Since all the working pens had iced up, I decided it was high time that I get the cows preg checked and the heifers Bangs vaccinated.

I had a Zamboni come out and clean up the corral ice rink and invited the neighbors over for a little cow curling and heifer hockey.

We didn't have any curling brooms or hockey sticks, so we made do with our sorting sticks and paddles.

"Cut out 864 blue!" I'd yell to one of my teammates. He deftly sorted her off and gave her a slap shot through the gate. "Goal!" we'd yell. Spectators were sparse, but we maintained a lot of enthusiasm just the same.

Sometimes, if momentum looked like it was lacking, we'd scurry up in front of ol' Bossy and whisk away at the ice to prolong her slide.

You had to be careful what ol' Bossy you put yourself in front of though. One cow could create quite a bit of momentum of her own. Her idea of making the gate less treacherous included grinding one of us cowhands into the ice for traction. She figured she could get a lot better grip if she had a lumpy pair of tattered brown coveralls to tiptoe across.

**Something missing**

We had some strong teams at the cow workin' on ice that day, but we couldn't help but think that something or someone was missing.

We had cowhands that were tough but lacked finesse. And we had cattle sorters with grace but lacking the mettle to really get in the gritty predicaments.

But I think we've found our new recruit. I'd read that Tonya Harding was ready to call it quits in Portland, Ore. Maybe we could entice her to come to North Dakota and join the ranks of the south Towner sliders.

I bet she'd look good in a pair of tattered brown coveralls.

# Sensible shoes and practical car colors
## Overshoes and color coordination important

This spring's bumper crop of mud and water is adding new worth to two of my major winter purchases — a pair of five-buckler overshoes and a mud brown Chrysler hatchback.

Good overshoes are an integral part of every rancher's spring wardrobe and a practical color scheme in automobiles is never more important than when you've come to the conclusion that you won't be washing your car until June.

My new car and my new overshoes were both in about the same price range and they're both paying big dividends this spring.

## Sensible shoes

It's proving to be a good spring for the five-buckler overshoe.

I'm always a sucker for an affordable upgrade. Why get a large pop for 89 cents when you can buy the 55-gallon drum for a nickel more? Why buy a computer that can boot up in a nanosecond when you can spend another 100 dollars and get one that can do it in a fraction of a nanosecond?

It's the same with overshoes. I could have gotten the four-bucklers but the five-bucklers were only 2 bucks more, so why haggle? The sky is the limit when your budget is backed up by 70-cent calves.

I've patted myself on the back numerous times this spring for having the foresight to buy the five-bucklers. Many is the time I've been able to chase cows through puddles that would have stopped four-buckler men dead in their tracks.

And many is the time I've headed into puddles of muck and realized I'm still a buckle or two short.

You never quite realize you're a buckle short until you've taken on a couple gallons of 33-degree water. There's some definite hang time from when you see the water whirlpooling down into your overshoe to when you get that cold, tingly sensation in your toes.

## Sensible calving cars

The spring season has me really excited about my new ranching car, an '85 Chrysler four-door hatchback.

Most ranchers can't afford to wear out their old pick-ups because the new ones are all made and priced for concrete cowboys who might need to haul a couch or something. Out on the range, ranchers are driving hatch-backs, station wagons and super-long four doors to save wear and tear on pickups that need to outlive the mortgage.

I envision my new hatchback coming in handy for hauling 9 foot mower sickles out to the hay field and the fuel economy will be nice for those repeat trips to town for repairs as I strive to get the right parts.

What I'm most excited about though is its suitable spring color scheme. It's mud brown finish and calf scour yellow interior will be just the ticket this calving season.

No one in town will realize I've just driven 17 miles of mud soup to get there because the car will be ideally camouflaged. When I throw a scouring calf in the hatchback for a trip to the vet, any slip-ups on the calf's part will blend right in with the scour yellow interior.

The smell, however, could be harder to cover up. Thankfully, four doors means four windows for changing the air on the way to the vet clinic.

Mud brown is a workable color for spring, but I'm thinking about a new paint job for the summer months and its transient bird population.

I could park under the high line wires with confidence, slamming the door on my newly painted car of bird crap gray.

# Don't look a gift horse in the mouth...
## It might belch on you

As luck would have it last fall, the first snowstorm coincided with weaning and calf selling.

Grand plans to bring the cattle home early to individually weigh the calves and record a little performance data were quickly forgotten. New "functioning by crisis" plans were made to bust a trail through the section line, hoping the cows would put their tails to the wind and make it home before the semi-trucks pulled up to the loading chute.

The first attempt at breaking the trail was made with a four-wheel-drive pickup. Snowdrifts were as high as where the hood ornament used to be. Four bald tires and sheer determination got me close to the clearing, but close only counts in horseshoes and hand grenades.

With enough snow packed under the hood to keep the engine's belts and pulleys from turning, another management-by-crisis decision was made to clean out the engine and start shoveling a path backwards.

With the horsepower defeated, a real horse was saddled and ridden up the section line. After breaking a one horse path, all the cattle were brought home in orderly single file. At least we thought we had all of them.

### New found fortune

On Nov. 4, the majority of the steers and heifers were shipped out for a tidy 66 and 59 cents. And on Nov. 8, another four calves waltzed home from the hills and showed up at our doorstep.

What a stroke of luck! It was like finding an old birthday card with a $10 bill inside of it. The lost had been found, and plans quickly were made as to what we'd do with this bovine bonanza.

Well, last week we took them to market — vaccinated, weaned, back-grounded and in good health. Run through the ring as singles on a day when the corn climbed and the hogs dropped, our boon went bust and brought a whopping 50-cents per pound.

It really knocked the wind out of our lucky windfall.

It almost made me wish that their mothers had come in open last winter. The cull market was pretty good last year, and I'd have saved the 70 cents a pound it takes to produce a 50 cent calf.

The least we could of done is gotten a hold of some tainted, recalled delouser and had them keel over from a toxic reaction. Insurance claims usually have the best calf market.

**Zucchini calves**

But times are tough all over. I heard about one guy who was taking a calf to the market in his horse trailer and got a flat tire. He pulled off to the side of the road and caught a ride into town to get his tire patched.

By the time he got back to his rig, some dirty trickster had slipped another five calves in the trailer!

I guess calves are getting more and more like zucchini every day. During zucchini harvest in this area, you've gotta lock your car doors when you go to town for fear someone might load your back seat with the pesky produce.

And if you have to leave your stock trailer along the road this winter, you better chain and padlock the gate.

# Blizzard camaraderie
## Look both ways and travel together

Every city in North Dakota is synonymous with something. Bismarck — state capital, Minot — state fair, Jamestown — big buffalo, and Grand Forks — consistently terrible winter weather.

I have yet to be surprised by sunshine and a calm breeze when I go to Grand Forks anytime between October and June. But everyone deserves the benefit of the doubt, so I gave them another chance last weekend.

### A new dawn

I'm almost afraid to ever fall asleep again in Grand Forks. One minute, you're hittin' the hay and planning your next day, the next morning, you're rollin' out of the sack to find your car buried, the streets blocked and your day ruined.

A foot of snow, 50-mile-per-hour wind gusts, and sub-zero windchills kept the Grand Forks weather hex intact for another day.

After digging ol' Brownie, the wonder Chrysler, out of its form-fitting snowbank, I began my "get stuck then shovel out" rotation. When I got tired of digging myself out, I began helping the others since I hadn't had a chance to donate blood or give to the poor recently.

### Blizzard byways

After listening to the "no travel advised" warnings and the "venture out only for emergencies" radio reports, I decided to not take the advice and I classified feeding cows as an emergency worth venturing out for.

Of course, like any good North Dakotan, I had all my winter survival gear along, just in case I had to camp in my car for a couple of snowed-in days. As a matter of fact, I had everything in ol' Brownie but a dog sled and a couple of Husky mushers.

Visibility was minimal. I began to panic when the snow blew and I couldn't even see the hood ornament on my car. That is until I realized my car didn't have a hood ornament.

I soon discovered that I wasn't the only hardy soul heading west into the winter frontier that day. Magnetically, we began to travel together like pioneers in a string of wagons bound for the promised land (somewhere on the other side of Devils Lake).

Somewhere east of Lakota, the wagon train ground to a halt and we all pulled to the side of the road. No one was too sure why. Those of us with hood ornaments were able to see them, those of us without were able to spot the frozen sparrow crap that served the same purpose.

I decided to investigate and pulled ol' Brownie forward to the wagon master's lead vehicle. I soon found the wagon boss standing next to his car with his back to the wind and his hands in his pockets.

Pulling closer, I saw that the rather embarrassed-looking wagon boss's hands weren't exactly in his pockets. I quickly realized that it wasn't the weather, but rather a thermos full of coffee and a brimming bladder that brought our wagon train to a halt. Before long though, it was "fill that cup back up" and wagons ho!

# Cold enough for ya?
## Whatever doesn't kill you only makes you stronger

Ask a stupid question, get a stupid answer.

Last week, stupid questions flowed like spring runoff. All over the north country, you could hear those gut-splitting cold weather comedians. "Cold enough for ya?" they ask. Hardy har har har! That's where I usually come back with an equally stupid answer. "Well, actually, no. I'm never really comfortable until the thermometer reads at least 51 below zero."

Towner had the coldest North Dakota temperature on the front page weather map of Saturday's *Grand Forks Herald*. A cool 45 below zero edged out Cando's competitive minus 44 and kicked the stuffing out of Jamestown's paltry minus 26.

We did have to concede the regional championship to Fosston, Minn., though. Those overachievers recorded a temperature of 50 below zero just to show us folks on the other side of the Red that the weather wasn't "cold enough for them yet."

**Too cold**

It's good to act tough and shrug off windchills of 80 below zero, but you do reach a point where it's just too dang cold.

If this kind of weather keeps the riffraff out, I'm seriously considering becoming one of those riffs and heading my raff south.

I do have to admit, though, that is kind of fun talking to folks from Texas, California and other weather-weak states when we get a shot of weather like this.

"How do you ever survive up there?" my sunshine-addicted friends ask. "Aw shucks, it's really not that bad. The mercury's only showing about 40 below right now — it's a little brisk out there."

Brisk is a code word I use on my Southern friends that really means I'd rather watch a really bad episode of Ricki Lake than go out and do chores. Even the "I married my teen-age mutant transvestite cousin and now we're divorced but I still love him/her" episode would be better than freezing your fanny out in the corral.

**Flowless fluids**

No matter how "brisk" or "fresh" the weather was, I still had to mosey out and do the chores.

Of course, the tractor was low on engine oil, so I sliced off a couple chunks of 10W-30 and stuffed them down the spout.

Checking the hydraulics, I discovered it was time to contribute some universal fluid as well. I'm not sure what universe that stuff is fluid in, but it certainly wasn't our universe that day. I cut off a couple chunks of that, too, simmered it lightly over low heat and fed it to the transmission.

It was all systems go. Except for the batteries. They had turned their last cold-weather crank shaft and they were going on strike. I checked the date. The dang things were only 6 or 8 years old; they should have lasted longer than that.

In desperation, I began to talking to the tractor. "Is it cold enough for ya?" And I swear that tractor groaned a "yuuuup" when the starter made its final spin.

# Slowing down
## A New Year's resolution

It just doesn't pay to be in a hurry all the time. The more you hurry, the less you get done. That point was driven home so hard last week that I've decided to make a New Year's resolution to quit hurrying.

## Hurry up and wait

There's nothing like a little 60-below windchill weather to hurry you up. The colder it is, the less time you want to spend outside, so you hurry along with thoughts of a warm fire running through your head.

I'd loaded up a couple of bales, hurried out to the feed ring, and at just the point where I was as far away from the buildings as possible, the front wheel fell off.

It was almost like that wheel knew I wanted to get done feeding a little quicker so I could get back to a hot cup of coffee. I'm certain the steel in that wheel was waiting for just the right moment to give out and plop the spindle down on an unsuspecting frozen cow pie.

Of course, driving the tractor back to the shop where the tools were handy and the wind was blocked was out of the question. A three-legged tractor just doesn't roll like it should. Something about those round, circle-shaped deals bolted on to the front make tractors travel a whole lot easier.

After a brisk walk to the shop, I was back at the tractor spinning the world's coldest wheel nuts off with my bare hands. Before you could say frostbite, I had the wheel off and was ready to head into town for new one.

## Rush hour traffic

I was still in a hurry of course, so I rushed right down the road in the four-wheel-drive pickup. But snow drifts 4 feet deep and  hard enough to walk across are difficult to hurry through.

So I did the shovel-and-drive rotation till the snow plow came. I waved at the plow driver in appreciation and continued to hurry along my way.

When I got to our mailbox 3$^1$/$_2$ miles down the road I decided to quickly pull aside and grab the three-day collection of mail that had built up during the recent blizzard.

But being in a hurry, I decided to keep going and read the mail while I drove. It seemed like the efficient thing to do until I looked up from the Christmas card I was reading and realized I'd just put the pickup into a ditch full of snow.

That was the last straw. I called the neighbor on the cell phone for a pull, looked to the sky and asked for two things — the will power to slow down my pace in the new year and a little wind to cover up my tracks in the ditch before the school bus, the snow plow and all the neighbors would drive by and say, "who in the heck would go in the ditch here?"

# Short gates and long arms
## Ground level snow

Looks like another good winter for the snowmobile crowd this year.

I hate to wish a poor recreation year on anybody who has that much money invested in a snow sled and matching clothes, but I wish their embroidered ski cap was still in the closet and that their machines were out depreciating in the sun.

Maybe if everyone invested in recreational gear that didn't require snow and cold, we'd collectively will ourselves a milder winter.

I believe that the amount of snow we have on the ground this fall is highly correlated with the number of new snowmobiles sitting in the front yards around the area. If we all had surf boards in our yards, we probably could wish a tropical winter on ourselves.

That's probably very unlikely, but I have seen an awful lot of gals running around in two-piecers lately. Unfortunately, they were North Dakota bikinis — insulated bib bottoms with a parka top.

If I really want to experience a beach bum's winter, I may just have to borrow one of those snowmobiles and drive south until somebody asks me what the heck kind of machine it is I'm riding on.

### Slip slidin' workin'

It looks like I'll either have to start pushing snow or else hang a set of upper level winter hinges on all my gateposts. As it is, we're dragging our gates as much as we're dragging our behinds in these early-season snowdrifts.

I've seen some high-tech ranchers put wheels on the end of their gates to keep them rolling easy when they start to sag. Of course, you have to wean, sort and work cattle while there's still dirt on the ground to make that work. I think I'll just put a ski on the end of my gates.

The truckers and vets are sure glad I waited until there was 2 feet of snow on the ground to start shipping calves and preg checking cows.

The veterinarian was really glad that I put my cow alley under the eaves of the barn where we could best get the snow to drift off the roof and run down our backs. And the trucker really was pleased with the icy, uphill angle running under the lowline highline leading to my cockeyed load out chute.

At least when you wait to truck the cattle until there's snow on top of the ice you don't have to worry about standing by the chute to direct the driver as he backs up.

This year, the crew and I just stayed at the kitchen table, drank coffee and let the trucker direct himself. By cocking an ear to the chute, we knew exactly what was going on. "Vroom, vroom, vrooooooooom....snap, crack!

Pssssss." Once the posts were completely broke off and the brakes were set, we knew it was time to put on our two piece and head out to the dock.

I think next year we'll just truck the calves by snowmobile.

# Winter wins
## Blizzard ranching not all its cracked up to be

All right, I give in. I'm tired of winter.

I'm tired of 10 foot snow drifts, polar wind chills and weather that would send the toughest Eskimo into his igloo. I'm tired of pushing snow, pushing snow, pushing snow.

But most of all, I'm tired of being tired.

### Blizzard calving

A foot and a half of snow, 60-mile-an-hour winds and 30-below-wind chills made things pretty interesting here on the Taylor Ranch last week, especially since we were calving at the rate of about a dozen calves a day when it hit.

I'm not ashamed to admit that it was a pretty fair struggle for this rancher and his 220 cows. The sandhills offer pretty good protection, but 60-mile-an-hour wind and horizontal snow pretty much does what it pleases.

I honestly can say we didn't lose a single calf in the storm. Several died, but I know where every one of them is at. Let's see, there's two in the loader bucket, one by the back door of the barn, one out in a snow bank...

We did save the majority of the calves, though, thanks to a little bay horse, the hood off a 1969 Chevy pick-up, a rope, a piggin' string and three good rubber tarp straps. We wore a lot of Chevy bluegreen paint off that deluxe calf sled as the horse and I drug cold and comatose calves into our old drafty barn and our not-so-drafty calf warming box.

At times, I wasn't sure if that hood was an ambulance or a hearse, but the barn did turn out to be more of a hospital than a morgue.

### Career change

While I was out bucking the wind, I got to thinking about some of the mail I've gotten from readers. About 99 percent of it is good, kind comments from people who appreciate Cowboy Logic and my telling it like it is.

However, I did get one e-mail from a small-town, northern Minnesota reader who had read a few of my articles about "how tough farmers have it." He figured agriculture was a pretty easy row to hoe because of all the interest buy-downs, CRP payments and bailouts that he assumed all farmers and ranchers got. "Welcome to the real world in 6.5 years," he said, referring to the impending end of farm programs.

He said I ought to try running a radio shop like him or maybe dealing the motor homes and boats that he sees in all the farmyards. I won't go into a major essay on how few farm program benefits ever have found their way to the Taylor Ranch or how few motor homes and boats he'll find in my yard.

But I do believe he had one good point — that I should try running a radio shop. And it seemed like a damn good career move when I was out in the "unreal" world bucking a blizzard wind, punching through hip-deep snowdrifts and dragging dead $400 bills out of the barn.

# Move over Jane Fonda
## A new workout with real resistance

There's nothing like a little good physical activity to get you feeling in tiptop shape. After battling flus and colds this winter, I've found that the best treatment is to just get outside and pump a little cold air through your lungs.

Last weekend, my cows decided to help me get that much needed exercise. Helpful critters they are. I had a bale in the grapple and one on the three point, and I commenced to calling the sweethearts to get them locked into the northernmost of my two pen feeding area.

### Resistance herding

Rather than go through the gate and join the feast, about 30 old bossies who really should have known better decided to stay back. They just stood and drooled at their counterparts who were knee deep in forage on the other side of the fence.

No amount of coaxing could get them to follow the tractor and hay through the gate, the most logical point of entry.

Seeing the lack of logic and the new level of stubbornness amongst my animals, I realized I'd have to get down on foot and start chasing them toward the hole they couldn't seem to find.

When I started chasing after the bovines, I weighed 180. When I got done, I'd swear I dropped to about 160. Most of it I lost in sweat, but a good percentage of it was shear calorie burning and fat shedding from an already fat-free frame.

There were a couple paths of least resistance and the cows did everything they could to avoid them all. If there was a crotch-deep snowbank they could make me flounder in, they found it.

Resistance was the motto for the chase. The resistance came from the snow, the 40 pounds worth of coveralls and the 20 pounds worth of overshoes I wore, not to mention the resistance of the belligerent bovines themselves.

**Make it burn**

I think I might have discovered what could be the latest exercise craze. I can just see folks trading in their leotards for insulated bibs, their cross-training tenny runners for five-buckle rubbers.

Rather than strap on ankle weights, people could get all the workout they'd want by just heading into the deep snow for a little running in place.

It'd be a lot like going to aerobics class. I can just hear the session leaders. "Now everybody, get in that snowbank and run! Run harder, the cows are getting away you cellulose laden porkers! Oh yeah, feel it burn now! One, two, three — cuss at 'em now! I can't hear you! And toss those frozen cow turds! Throw 'em hard, really launch 'em! Okay, they're almost to the gate, let's take it down, breath deep, now work it out ... alright, great session people. We'll see you next week when the sheep get out."

I think I'll get right on the phone and invite Jane Fonda to come out and do the filming for the video next week.

# Induced vacationing
## Relax, you're going nowhere

Have you had a nice, relaxing, sit-around-the-hotel-pool vacation lately?

I sure haven't. That is, until last week when Mother Nature grabbed me by the shoulder and slammed me down in a poolside chair at the Holiday Inn in Mitchell, S.D. The Northern Plains Premium Beef crew was in a dead sprint, and we were looking forward to our fifth equity drive meeting when the blizzard of 1997 took us down to a dead stop.

At first, it was pretty frustrating to be snowed in and stuck in Mitchell, S.D., but after awhile, it kind of grew on me. We had a pool, hot tub, bar, restaurant and cable television. It beat the heck out of being stuck out on the highway with a couple of F-14s flying over head looking for you.

We were really pretty lucky.

**Blizzard basketball**

One positive outcome of the blizzard was my long-awaited re-entry to the world of basketball. If the sports commentators weren't so busy with football and the Super Bowl, I'm sure they'd be discussing the return of the South Towner Stretch.

I retired my jersey about eight years ago and I have to admit it's been pretty hard on the fans of barn wall basketball. I never played basketball back in high school. Instead, I went straight to the big leagues, drafted as the tall guy under the hoop for a local franchise called the Smokey Lake Lakers.

We were a scrappy team — a lot like the Harlem Globetrotters. Our specialties were dribbling the ball around mud puddles and bounce-passing on gravel. We struck fear in the hearts of our arch rivals, the Sandhill Cranes of Denbigh, N.D.

But that was a long time ago. The only posting up I've done lately has been out on the fenceline. My hook shot has been replaced with a calf hook and the last time I "drove the lane," I was in a pickup chasing bulls down a pasture lane.

But last week at the college gymnasium in Mitchell, S.D., I strapped on a pair of freshly bought $14 tennis shoes and got back in action. Luckily, my Premium Beef teammates were ranch tough and able to take the abuse of my angular elbows, knees, hips and shoulders.

**Pure misery**

Basketball was just one of the recreational activities used to help us during our storm tenure. There were cards to be played, laps to be swum and waitresses to be harassed.

There was time to sleep late, grab an afternoon nap and watch John Wayne movies till the sun went down. The toughest part of the trip, actually, was explaining our dire situation to the folks back on our ranches, feeding cattle and fighting snow.

With a little effort, we could make our voice quiver with sincere sorrow. "You wouldn't believe how tough we've got it here," we'd sob into the mouthpiece of the telephone. "I can't wait to get home to give you a hand with the chores, see ya," clink!

"Hey guys, don't forget to deal me in. And, ma'am, could we get another round?"

# Destructive improvements
## Getting ready for the next Ice Age

Sometimes I get a little behind on ranch improvements.

The corrals are getting weaker, the barn's got holes in it you can throw a dog through, and the barbed-wire fences have more rusty splices than a Fargo phone book has Larsons.

But just when I begin running the risk of whole ranch meltdown, something motivates me to rebuild and renew a little something every year.

I've got one corral made of rapidly rotting poplar poles that I know needs some serious updating, but I never can find the time to tear it down and build it back new and improved.

Then I put a few amorous bulls in it who were battling spring fever and they got right after the tearing-down part of the project. Now I had the motivation, and the need, to rebuild a couple sections of that old corral.

The bull's lack of impotence became the impetus for me to make some incremental ranch improvements.

That's the way most of the improvements get started here on the Taylor Ranch. Completely unplanned, and uncalled for, destruction.

## Snow fence is no fence

Looks like I'll get the opportunity to update, improve and rebuild a lot of barbed-wire fence this year, too.

Fence improvement has been prompted by the winter of 1996/1997. I knew the heavy snow was going to take down a lot of fence, but I was kind of hoping the neighbor's fences would catch the brunt of the drifts and spare my spindly oak posts and rusty wire.

No such luck. The blasting blizzards of last winter took down my fence, the neighbor's fence, the trees, the grass, the anthills and a few small boulders.

And the snow's not even gone yet! I really want to get out there and start fixing some fence, but there's still snow in the dips where the fence is down. Of course, it's only the middle of May. Much longer, though, and I might have to get out there with a blow torch and melt a swath through the snowbank so I can get to fencing.

I really think the geologists ought to come out and take a look at my summer snowbanks. I believe they could qualify as our continent's newest glaciers. We might need to declare my pasture a national park and let the public in to witness the coming of the next Ice Age.

National park status would bring in a lot of sweaty tourists in shorts and T-shirts. I could prey on them with a little sno-cone stand by the road-side and get rid of my glacier one scoop at a time. If the sno-cones don't sell, I know I could move a lot of sodas poured over genuine glacial ice.

Dangit, anyway. I just heard the weather forecast and they say there's a warming trend ahead.

Guess I better scrap the idea of a second Glacier National Park and just concentrate on fixing another section of fence. I'll be turning the bulls in there pretty soon, and they hate the sight of a shabby fence.

# Blowin' in the wind

## Receiving from the west, giving to the east

I'm not sure if it was Hurricane Nora who brought the gale force winds to North Dakota last week, but something sure had us shutting our shop doors and hanging on to our hats.

Shingles hung on for dear life and windows rattled for all they were worth. The 50-mile-per-hour prairie winds were great for about half the people traveling on U.S. Highway 52. The other half had it pretty tough.

I was one of the lucky ones who happened to be going southeast on that road last week. Heading down to Jamestown to do some live Cowboy Logic for a banquet, I got unbelievably good mileage in Ol' Brownie, the wonder Chrysler.

I contemplated winging open a couple of doors to get the full benefit of the strong tail winds. Like the sails on a ship, the open doors really would have cut down on the gas consumption. I decided against it, though, for fear of getting picked up for speeding.

I had the best of both worlds that night. I had a good tail wind on the way down, and, by the time the banquet was over, the winds had subsided. I got normal mileage on the return trip and I didn't have to worry about high-velocity tumbleweeds crashing through my windshield.

### Scattered around

Things weren't going so good back on the ranch, however. The hay bales took a real beating and our fertile one-half inch of topsoil was last seen heading east.

My cows seemed to handle it all right, but one fella told me that the wind had wrecked his fence and all his cows had gotten out.

"You mean the wind actually blew the barbed wires down on the ground?" I asked. "No," he said, "that wind blew so hard all the barbs slid down to the corners and the cows just walked right through those smooth, barbless wires!" Sure, uh-huh.

Honestly, though, the worst part of the wind that swept through the Taylor Ranch was my loss of stockpiled building supplies. Before the breezes came, I had some materials for a pump house stacked out in the pasture next to a well that I wanted to winterize.

They're no longer stacked and no longer next to the well. The two-by-six boards didn't move too far, but the plywood took a little trip and the rolls of fiberglass insulation did a fair bit of rolling.

The real loss was the five big sheets of 2-inch styrofoam that used to lay beneath the plywood. I now have $40 worth of bite-size Styrofoam chunks scattered from here to Minnesota.

It's pretty much a total loss, but I did learn something. Everyone always talks about how cheap that "blown-in" insulation is for building projects, and now I know why. If it blows in your yard from the northwest, it can't get any cheaper.

And if you live southeast of me and had some insulation blown in for your latest building project, you're welcome.

# Autumn rush
## The heat is on when the heat turns off

It's that time of year again when we all wonder what we wasted our summers doing.

Whatever we did this summer, it sure wasn't pouring concrete, digging in water lines or doing anything else to get ready for winter.

All of a sudden, we're faced with the impending possibility of permafrost. Phone lines are buzzing as we all get on the horn to beg our friends in the building, concrete and bulldozing business to do a "couple little jobs" for us before things freeze up for another six months.

A lot of us had hoped that the manure in our corrals would just naturally compost and melt down before we had to use the corrals again this fall. It's an easy, affordable theory, but I'm quickly learning that it takes more than three warm months to naturally dissolve 3 feet of manure.

I've got neighbors who've put off concrete pours for so long that they're installing hot water heaters near the sites so they can mix up cement that's as warm as hot chocolate. Plus, they're laying in a lot of straw nearby so they quickly can cover up the pours before being blinded by the rising steam. They're hoping they can pour well into January with this strategy.

Personally, I've had 500 feet of black plastic water line laying on top of the ground since last spring when water troubles forced me to push a little water from a different well. All summer, I've been hoping for an earthquake that would open up a 7 foot deep crack in the ground, swallowing up the pipe and spitting out a frost-free hydrant at the other end.

But North Dakota just doesn't have enough seismic activity, so I had to break down and weasel my way into a contractor's busy fall schedule to get that water line buried and ready for winter.

### Malfunctioning calendars

Since so many people I know are getting caught unprepared for winter freeze up, I'm beginning to think that there has to be a common, underlying reason.

We know winter comes every year. Why is it we're just now hustling to get the hay hauled, the post holes dug and the contractor work completed?

The only reason I can come up with is that we all had a serious calendar breakdown. Maybe the pages got gummed up and somehow the months of August, September and October got stuck together.

One day, it's July, and you flip the page to find out it's already November. No wonder we're all behind!

Luckily, I have a solution — reliable electronic calendars that sit by our beds right next to our alarm clocks. Every day when we get up, we're quickly and accurately reminded of the days ticking by.

And when the electronic calendar lands on, say, Sept. 1, a loud and extremely obnoxious alarm goes off, telling us to start getting ready for winter. If it works, we all should be caught up on fall's work by Oct. 15.

I just have to make sure that the electronic calendar doesn't come with a snooze button.

# Sweatacizing
## Lettin' it pour at the old dance hall

In Finland, the community sauna is the place where locals go to sweat out their pores, cleanse their souls and rejuvenate their spirits.

Across the prairies, where folks are a mixed batch of Scandinavians and German Russians, we accomplish the same sweating, cleansing and rejuvenation in airtight dance halls.

Community dance halls are built by all kinds of civic-minded groups and have even found themselves the subject of songs. Chris LeDoux sings about the Grange Hall dances in Wyoming. Chuck Suchy's tune, "Saturday Night at the Hall," pays tribute to the Bohemian Hall and the good times there in southwestern North Dakota.

Towner's offering to the lore of prairie dance halls is this column and the Veterans of Foreign Wars hall, Vernon T. Starks Post No. 7067.

### Sweat swap

I've been to a lot of hot summer wedding dances at the old VFW Hall, and I'm always amazed by how much heat a human can take in that hall. I was especially amazed at the dance last Saturday when the temperature was only exceeded by the humidity.

The place was packed. Two 32-inch doors and a couple of 12-inch fans did their best to provide a little ventilation. We'd have all liked a little air conditioning, but we were just glad to have electric lights and indoor plumbing.

The people inside were so drawn up from water loss, I hardly recognized some of them. Without so much as a pill, a diet plan or a rowing machine, they'd each lost at least 10 pounds.

And although the perspiration had everyone looking like wet muskrats, it didn't much matter. The people there had a common bond.

Like the blood brother relationship between the Lone Ranger and Tonto, the people at the dance were sworn sweat siblings. No need to slit their palms and transfer red blood cells, just put your arm around someone and swap a little salty sweat.

There was no need to slick the dance floor with sawdust. It was plenty slippery from sweat, spilled drinks and humidity dripping from the ceiling.

Despite the slippery surfaces, mental faintness and impending heat stroke, nobody was seriously injured. I thought a couple of gals risked losing an arm in a jerky jitterbug dance, but everyone survived nicely, limbs and all.

## Ironic signs

Although the hall never got any cooler, the night finally did wind down and folks stepped outside in hope of a cool breeze.

The old VFW hall had done its job again. It cleaned out our pores and rejuvenated our souls like an oversized sauna. And, for at least one writer in the crowd, it offered a classic piece of literary irony worth repeating.

It seems like everybody has something that needs to be hung up on the hall's walls from wedding well wishes to the banner of the band. And it's only natural for those panel hangers to reach for some gray duct tape when push pins and poster putty fail them.

But you need only look at a warning sign on the north wall to learn that management frowns on the use of good gray tape. "DO NOT USE DUCT TAPE TO HANG SIGNS!" it said.

Of course, you know what held that sign up? Yup, duct tape.

# On the serious side

# Were you born in a barn?
## Finding the real meaning of Christmas

Ever had anyone ask you, "Geez, were you born in a barn?"

I'd get that question from time to time when I was growing up if I forgot to shut the door behind me, failed to wipe my feet on the doormat or didn't take my hat off at the table.

It was a question meant to embarrass me into remembering my manners, a tool used to housebreak little boys who spent most of their time outside. Eventually, I learned to mind my manners, becoming the courteous young man my parents and teachers wanted me to be.

But the question about being born in a barn never did make much sense to me. I always thought barns were pretty neat places, and I didn't think being born in one would make me any less cultured.

### Barn-born babies

I was out in the hay mow of our barn the other day, forking down a little hay into the manger for my horses to graze on. The sight of hay in a manger got me to thinking about a little baby born a long time ago in a barn far, far away.

For me, Christmas is a time to celebrate the birth of a baby born in a barn. As a rancher's son and a die-hard believer in the country lifestyle, I've always felt a certain amount of pride in the birthplace of the king of kings.

The baby Jesus could have been born in a great palace surrounded by royalty and high priests, but instead, he entered the world in a stable, lying in a manger and surrounded by farm animals.

Even His first visitors were simple country folk. Shepherds out watching their flocks got the scoop on the good news from angels. There's not a lot of excitement in a job herding sheep or cattle. It's about as thrilling as watching grass grow, or grass being grazed as the case may be.

Shepherds don't get many visitors of any kind, much less winged messengers from God. Simple graziers, not haughty aristocrats, heard the message, "Glory to God in the highest, and on Earth peace among men with whom He is pleased!"

Cowboys can even relate to the three wise men who came riding into camp camelback to present the newborn saviour with gifts. These fellas had ridden a far piece and definitely had wore a lot of leather off the tree by the time they reined in their mounts in at Bethlehem.

### A real farm boy

So here's the picture. The Son of God lying in some hay, surrounded by cattle, donkeys, sheep herders and saddle-sore wise men. Something tells me Jesus was an aggie.

Us folks out in the country can take pride in knowing the first Christmas took place in a barn with herders schooled in range management, cud-chewing ruminants and guys with bowed legs. Farmers and ranchers from the Great Plains would have fit right in with that crowd.

This year, I invite you to trade the warmth of your house for the chill of a barn on Christmas Eve. Trade the sight of a plastic-needled artificial tree for the aroma of alfalfa hay in a manger, leave the sound of hi-fi jingle bell rock and go listen to the cows munching their hay and a horse stamping his feet.

Instead of staring at the glow of multicolored blinking electric lights, take a look out the barn door at the starry sky that once led folks to Bethlehem. And, as you stand there, pondering the commercialization of an all-important birthday, feel safe in the realization that you have found the real meaning of Christmas — right there in the barn.

*Author's note: Judging by the mail I got, this "born in a barn" column was probably the most popular I've written. It actually was inspired by a priest who told me to take my thumbs out of my pockets when I was standing in the front of the church for a wedding rehearsal. He said, "we're not out in the corral you know," with a tone of voice that made corrals sound like awful places. I didn't have the nerve to tell him that the fella hanging on the cross behind him spent a lot of time in corrals and probably wouldn't have used that term so derogatorily.*

# Across the miles
## Two Westerners in a big Eastern city

It was Aug. 10, 1992. I had flown out to Pittsburgh to attend the annual meeting of the American Society of Animal Science and pick up a second-place outstanding senior award in the National Block and Bridle Club.

It was quite a deal for this country boy. I wore my customary hat and boots as I walked amongst the high-rise buildings, homeless folks and hurried-looking city people.

The hurried-looking people did break their stride for just a second as they passed this cowboy. They paused just long enough to look at me like I was from outer space and make some crack about me looking like John Wayne.

The walk from the hotel to the convention center in downtown Pittsburgh had me yearning for the company of someone who wouldn't ask me where I'd left my horse.

I found just what I was looking for when I met the first-place winner in the outstanding senior scholarship contest. Her name was Rene' and she made her home on a cattle and sheep ranch in the big country of west-central Texas.

243

We got to visiting and soon realized that folks who live a thousand miles apart still can have a lot in common.

Smack dab in the middle of a million urbanites, a gal from Texas and a fella from North Dakota were talking about livestock, wide horizons and what it was like to drive 60 miles to go see a movie.

Rene' had a lot going for her. She was bright, outgoing and ambitious. She was also very pretty and very nice to visit with on that August day so long ago.

We parted ways after the awards ceremony. She headed back to Texas, where she planned on doing graduate work in agricultural communications. She wanted to do public relations work in the beef industry and maintain her partnership in the family ranch.

Me, I went back to my family's ranch in North Dakota, where I wanted to raise cattle, write stories and contribute to my industry.

A couple months ago, I was paging through a trade magazine called *Agri-Marketing*. I saw a picture of this girl I'd met in Pittsburgh in an ad for the "Voice of Texas Agriculture," a successful southwestern radio broadcasting company.

I looked up her phone number and gave her a call. We had a nice visit, talking about the things we were doing and the things we were looking forward to doing.

It didn't surprise me that she was accomplishing her goals. I knew she had all the ability in the world.

Last night, I got a call from Rene's mother. The 25-year-old girl who had everything going for her had lost her life in a head-on car collision.

And this soon-to-be 25-year-old rancher who makes part of his living with words didn't know what words to use or how to arrange them to express his sorrow or his feelings for what the family was going through.

I went out to pitch some hay to the horses, trying to find some answers in the cool night air. I'm not sure if I found many answers, but I did realize that a friend is still a friend whether they're in Pittsburgh, Texas or heaven.

And this voice of "Cowboy Logic" is going to miss the friendly voice of Texas agriculture. Happy heavenly trails, my friend.

# Dear Santa, all I want is...
## A rancher's wish list

Dear Santa,

How's the weather up north on the arctic range? Is your reindeer remuda wintering well and in good flesh?

We've had a spell of tough weather down here. Thirty below zero one night and the wind chill didn't much matter — it was just cold.

You're probably enjoying the same cold blast of arctic air. I reckon your reindeer had a hump in their back just like my cows did the other morning, and I'm sure you're huddling next to the fire like we are when you get done with your feeding chores.

I'm probably a little older than your average letter writer, but I've been minding my P's and Q's pretty well this year and thought I'd run a couple of requests past you.

There's a lot of other folks down here like myself who have the same kind of wish list. We've been working pretty hard trying to raise some beef, take care of the land and support our communities.

But times have gotten pretty tough. Our cattle aren't worth much. Supply's high, demand's dropping, feed's gone up, and so has everything else we buy. We just don't seem to have much control over things.

We're working a few full-time jobs to try and pay the bills, and we're borrowing more money than we really ought to.

So I was wondering if you could find an extra dime for us in the cattle market, maybe put a lid on the input costs, and tell the hog farmers and chicken ranchers to ease up a bit on those other affordable proteins?

Or maybe you could have the folks out in Washington, D.C., leave us a nice, big, green check under the tree to ease our pain. And tell all the ranchers to sell more cows and keep fewer heifers, and maybe convince the feeders, packers and retailers to hand all their profits down to us cow/calf producers. And ask everybody around the world to eat more beef and pay more for it, even if it isn't consistent.

Maybe I'm being a little demanding. I'm probably asking for a lot of things you can't bring my neighbors and me. It could be that I'm asking the wrong man.

I probably should go over your head, past the North Pole and up into the stars.

And if I was talking to Him during this season that celebrates His gift to us, I'd probably just say thanks for everything we already have.

And if He wanted to grant us anything more this Christmas, I'd just ask for the strength to persevere, the courage to go forward and the resourcefulness to figure out our own answers. You know, take the reindeer by the antlers and fix our own problems out here in cattle country.

Thanks for your time, Santa. You really don't need to come down our chimney, just wave as you go by and take something nice to the people who really could use your Christmas generosity.

But if the reindeer need a bite of hay and a drink of water, feel free to touch down in my feed ring and help yourself.

# N.D. teachers, saaalute!

## Ag class, the land of Milken and honey

It's good to see our teachers getting the recognition and the rewards they truly deserve.

Another North Dakota ag teacher just received the $25,000 National Educator Award from the Milken Family Foundation in Santa Monica, Calif. His name is Curtis Leslie and he teaches ag in Kindred, N.D., population 569. Saaalute!

I'm fairly familiar with the Milken award because I received a little instruction in my formative years from another Milken winner, Steve Zimmerman, or Big "Z", from Towner, N.D., population 669. A double saaalute!

We should consider ourselves lucky to have these world-class teachers in towns whose entire K-12 population is smaller than the graduating class of most other schools.

### Learning to do

Vo ag was the class where I learned how to weld, hammer, saw, wire and build.

It was the class where I learned not to wear tennis shoes when using the cutting torch. One lump of hot molten slag on the top of my foot quickly taught me that lesson. I reviewed the lesson as I hopped over to a bucket of water and quenched my sizzling size 12.

It was the class where I attempted to learn the secret art of drill bit sharpening. I'm still buying new bits whenever the old ones get so dull they couldn't cut through Silly Putty.

It was the class where my electrical wiring project smoked, fizzled and threw the breaker. I've since learned to keep my grounds ground and my lives alive. My insurance agent is especially glad that I figured that out.

Big "Z" and the FFA took me to Albuquerque, N.M., for a national horse judging contest, introducing me to jet planes, airports and infrared toilets. I still find myself looking for the handle to flush, and I'm still a little surprised when I back away and it flushes without prompting.

And it was in vo ag where I learned how to carry lumber. "If it's longer than you, it takes two." But it was Ross Perot who taught me my other catchy carpenter's slogan: "Measure twice, cut once."

### Doing to learn

But Big "Z" taught me a lot of big lessons about life and he had a big influence on some big decisions that I've made.

Big "Z" introduced me to computers and technology. Today, I use a computer everyday and have even begun surfing the Net. He taught me a ton of practical math, made science fun and showed me the finer points of business management.

And Big "Z" taught me things that no other class offered. Things like leadership, teamwork, problem solving and effective public speaking. These lessons came through many school bus miles to FFA meetings, contests and conventions.

He inspired me to pursue a college degree in agriculture and convinced me to stay involved in agriculture. I've been meaning to have a little chat with him about that since I bought those $900 cows and sold those 59-cent heifer calves this fall.

But, to Big "Z" and Curtis Leslie, a "Cowboy Logic" salute. Small-town North Dakota, hundreds of students and a couple of school boards already know what the Milken Foundation just recently recognized.

# Merry Christmas
## All year long, around the globe

When this column reaches you, it'll be the day after Christmas. The presents no longer will be under the tree, the wrapping paper will be thrown in the garbage, and shopping malls will be shifting gears, running clearance sales and taking back the returns.

Most of us will return to our regular work schedules, somewhat relieved that the hustle and bustle is over. We'll make some plans for New Years and go into 1996 with renewed energy for all our goals.

Maybe, though, we should take the time between Christmas and New Year's to reflect a little on how we felt before Christmas. We probably smiled a little quicker, gave a little easier and showed some extra appreciation for those around us.

We probably put some money in the can for the bell-ringing Salvation Army, donated some canned goods to the food pantry for the homeless and felt some sincere sorrow for the less fortunate.

In the days before Christmas, we spend a little less time fretting over our own little problems and focus in on the big picture and our place in it. Farmers and ranchers put aside their unpaid bills, weather problems and market worries and begin to think of the role they play as food producers who supply Christmas feasts around the globe.

### Christmas all year

They say there're 12 days of Christmas. I don't think that's nearly enough. The world really could use 365 days of the Christmas spirit. Charities need donations throughout the year, people need to eat every day, and our hearts can't afford to harden up just because we turn the page on the calendar.

If the government retreats from its programs that care for the elderly, the poor and their little children, will we be there to do what the Child born on Christmas would want us to do? Our churches pass the plate every week and their good work goes on every week as well.

We wouldn't consider not feeding our cattle every day. We leave the house every morning, dedicated to the duty of carrying feed pails and rolling out hay bales for the livestock that depend on us.

And the people who eat at soup kitchens and homeless shelters depend on us, too. We could argue about why they're there and how we could change their plight, but the fact remains that they need to eat.

### Ring the bell

Some shopping malls have banned the Salvation Army and their red kettles from those tiled walkways and neon storefronts that symbolize the commercialization of Christmas. Don't bother people with things like the art of unselfish generosity, they have shopping to do.

The kettles and the bell ringers will be out of sight after the holidays anyway, but they shouldn't be out of mind. Helping others has no season and those of us in rural areas maybe know that better than others.

Neighbors help neighbors all year long. Our livestock are cared for each day and the fruits of our labor can do good things way beyond the harvest. Let's not forget to help and care for the neighbors we do not see every day.

Have a Merry Christmas — all year long.


# Walkin' the walk
## Where are the animal rights folks at 2 a.m.?

It's certainly a comforting feeling for us ranchers to know that the animal rights movement is alive and strong, especially at calving time. In places like Washington, D.C., and Los Angeles, Calif., there's all kinds of well-meaning folks who say "I just want to help the animals."

Out on the coasts and in the big cities, these people are talking the talk. Meanwhile, back on the ranch, America's truest advocates of animal welfare are walkin' the walk.

### The walk

Last week, I was walkin' that walk at 2 a.m.

It was during my evening rounds in the heifer pen. The windchill was about 100 below zero or something equally crazy and No. 317 surprised me by dropping a bouncing baby bull right in the middle of it all.

She wasn't exhibiting much of a maternal bond and little 317 Jr. was beginning to feel the effects of the cold on his slime-covered body. So here was an animal in dire need of help. I looked everywhere for an animal rights activist to take this calf under his or her wing and give him some of the help they're so willing to give.

I couldn't find one anywhere. They must have been cozy in their climate-controlled bungalows resting up for a "ranchers are cruel, abusive barbarians" speech they were scheduled to give the next day.

So I took it upon myself to walk the walk. The walk was more of a jog and it covered about 300 yards through three gates, two barn doors and one kitchen door with a 100-pound calf in my arms and a flashlight in my hand.

By the time I hit the house, that calf felt like he weighed a ton. The calf found himself on some newspapers in a warm kitchen. The "barbarian" went back out in the 15 below zero (not counting windchill) cold to get the needy animal his first meal.

**Big softies**

I milked the colostrum out of the calf's mother, so the calf could have a warm, nutritious meal. I could of used a synthetic colostrum with a fraction of the disease protecting antibodies, but I wanted the calf to have the best and not have his life threatened by scours and dehydration in the future.

I have to admit that there were financial considerations in my taking care of this calf, but like most ranchers, I also had emotional ties to this helpless thing that lay on the kitchen floor struggling to stay alive.

It wasn't financial considerations that had my 73-year-old father out of bed holding a warm hair dryer on the calf at 2:30 in the morning. It was a mother's concern, not money, that had my mother opening her home and her floor to this slimy, newborn calf.

Ranchers and ranchwives are big softies when it comes to baby calves. When we're talkin' the talk with a needy calf, it usually sounds something like, "easy there wittle calfy, ohhh boy, you'll be all better when we get some milk in your tummy."

There's nothing financial about the smiles on our faces when we realize we've saved a life or brought comfort to a creature born in an uncomfortable world.

All across rural America, farmers and ranchers quietly go about the business of helping animals. We do it with little praise and little fanfare. We are humble witnesses to the miracles of life, and we do all in our power to save those lives without a lot of hype or publicity.

# Earth Day, Earth Year
## Official days unofficially celebrated
## all year long on the ranch

Earth Day came and went without a lot of fanfare here on the Taylor Ranch.

I guess those of us closest to the Earth don't feel the need to parade around and pontificate about saving the planet. Actions speak louder than words, I reckon.

There are those who treat poor people nice during Christmas, go to church on Easter, wave the flag on Independence Day, call their mother on Mother's Day and briefly think of Mother Earth on Earth Day.

Then there are those who don't need an official holiday to do things that ought to be done the whole year through. Farmers and ranchers are those kind of people when it comes to Earth Day.

### Another day, yawn

Earth Day was like most spring days here. Up at the crack of dawn checking cows and going about my daily doin's.

Of course my mode of transportation for cow checking fit right in with the Earth Day theme. Completely organically fueled, Ace, the renewable resource-fired Quarter Horse, took me around the pasture with minimal disturbance to the environment.

The cows we were checking were sure celebrating Earth Day. Converting grass and water into milk and muscle, they were giving birth to calves that would grow up converting that grass into tasty and nutritious beef to help sustain mankind.

With grains being in such high demand, it's getting more and more important to have ruminant cattle converting the wasteland and byproducts of America into usable protein for us pesky humans. Cattle make use of 800 million acres of grazing land in the U.S. that isn't suitable for farming.

Some of that miserably poor land is right here on the Taylor Ranch. Luckily, Mother Earth has been at work for hundreds of years designing native grasses that thrive on grazing. I'm glad my cows can lend a hand.

And cattle can be found in feedlots making good use of rejected french fries and tater tots; wheat mids from pasta plants and flour mills; beet pulp from sugar refineries; corn gluten; distillers' mash; outdated bakery goods; frozen melons; and oil seed meal.

**Seeing the sights**

The more I rode, the earthier I felt on Earth Day.

I rode along the cross fence we'd built for a rotational grazing system to help improve the health of the range. We passed the sand dunes I'd been feeding hay on to reduce erosion and boost plant growth, and I admired the evergreens my family had planted 20 years ago to slow down the endless prairie winds.

Ducks were enjoying life in the water hole we dug, bluebirds were checking out the houses our friends from town had nailed on the fence-posts, and my flea beetles were going to work to reduce leafy spurge without the use of chemicals.

Yup, just another everyday, ordinary Earth Day. I just can't see what all the fuss is about.

# Dedication
## The backbone of American agriculture

"It's not the size of the man in the fight, it's the size of the fight in the man."

I don't know who deserves the credit for that quote, but, in the farming and ranching business, I know many people full of "fight" who lend a lot of credibility to the quote's message. I call a couple of those fighters "Mom" and "Dad."

**Call to duty**

Last Friday, I took off at 4 a.m. to go to Mandan, N.D., and help coordinate the press conference for Northern Plains Premium Beef. I put a half a dozen heifers in the barn and told the folks, "Don't worry, I doubt if any of them will calve before I get back home."

That was a little optimistic. We had three new calves by 6 p.m. They all came easy, came in the barn and were relatively comfortable, despite the temperature of 20 below zero.

I was pretty proud of the job I did sorting the heifers, assuring the newborns a chance to enter the world indoors, out of the wind and on some straw. I decided to catch a few hours of sleep before driving back to the ranch. Then Mom called me at 3 a.m. and told me I had one heifer calve outside and the little guy was pretty shocked at going from a 101-degree womb to a -20-degree slab of frozen ground.

A few details about my folks. Dad is 75 years old. He's been ranching since he was 18. For the last 10 years, he's been battling Parkinson's disease. This past brutal winter has made it seem like a losing battle, with the days being passed by sitting and looking out the window.

Mom is a mere 64 years old. The pressures of caring for Dad and worrying about everything that could possibly be worried about make for a lot of physical and mental fatigue as well.

There's no retirement account, no 401(k) plan in ranching. Everything's tied up in the cows and the land. The best any rancher can do is talk a son or daughter into buying the place, transferring one generation's lifelong debt load onto another.

But no one ranches to get rich. You ranch because of the lifestyle, because you like to care for the land and the animals. That night, Mom and Dad were called upon once again to care for an animal.

Mom took the flashlight, Dad took his cane. Together, they pulled the freezing newborn into the barn. Dad fell down, but he got back up. He summoned all his strength to lift the calf and carry him to the warming box where the calf could lay in 65-degree comfort and come back to life.

It's nothing that would make the headlines, but it saved an animal's life. And it proved something about the size of the fight in the man.

# Fence post lotto
## The fate of casting lots for free fence posts

I knew North Dakota would join its neighbors in the world of state-sponsored lotteries sooner or later.

Until now, residents who were feeling lucky had to jump across state lines to exotic places like South Dakota and Minnesota to buy winning, and losing, lottery numbers.

I've only played the lottery once and that was down in South Dakota. I was hoping my donation of $10 to the state fund would allow South Dakota legislators to lower the speeding fines on their roads where the wrath of the state patrol is well known for its ability to impoverish hurried motorists.

If I had won I would have pocketed something like a zillion dollars. But, as it went, I just unpocketed $10 and dragged my losing butt back up to lottery-free North Dakota.

Personally, I'm not much of a gambler. That is, unless you count my daily dealings in the rancher's cow casino.

I'm one of those guys who'd rather "invest" $1,000 in a bred heifer than waste $2 in a slot machine. Incidentally, slot machines pay out about 92 cents for every dollar put in them. Ranching pays about 93 cents on the dollar, so it's more or less a wash.

But now there's a state lottery in North Dakota that I really can get excited about. No longer will I be driving to South Dakota to feel the thrill of losing in a lottery. I can stay at home, dial a toll-free number and get entered in fence post lotto.

Fence Post Lotto is a real rancher's game of chance. Thanks to the benevolence of Robert Julian at the Julian Lumber Co. in Antlers, Okla., the North Dakota Department of Agriculture has two semi-loads of treated fence posts to deal out among weather-beaten Dakota ranchers.

Julian's pine posts will help 75 lucky ranchers and farmers fix their water-swept and blizzard-wrecked fences. Mr. Julian must have driven across North Dakota at some point in his past and realized that fence posts are a hot commodity out here on the treeless plains.

Fence posts may be the best raffle prize I've seen yet. I've bought raffle tickets from just anybody who's ever asked me to buy one to support their church, youth group, wildlife club or community cause. They've given me chances at grills, guns, gas, quilts and an all-expense-paid weekend getaway for two in Minot, N.D.

But none of the raffle prizes have given me the same level of excitement as Fence Post Lotto. Sure, a handmade quilt is a nice prize, but can you build a solidly braced, three-post corner with a quilt and expect it to hold eight strands of barbed wire taut?

I hope they draw the names soon, though. Not only is the suspense getting to me, the cows are getting out.

But win or lose there's something that needs saying. Thanks Mr. Julian. You're a good person.

# Taking care of animal friends
## When the right thing is the toughest choice

There aren't many things that can get through the hard outer shell surrounding a rancher's heart. A few spouse's have accomplished this feat, but there's probably a larger population of horses and dogs who successfully have gotten to a cowman's soft and tender side.

Most rancher's have a natural fondness for their animals, but we do have our favorites. Cows and cats come and go, but horses and dogs tend to become our friends.

Cattle and cats are pretty aloof. As long as they get fed, they really don't care if you show up the next day or not. But horses and dogs, they're companions. They've got a look in their eyes that says they care about what kind of day you're having.

I've lost track of most of the cows I've known, but I can recite with accuracy every horse I've rode (Geronimo, Queen Elizabeth, Adam Pete, Sharky, Buck, Red, May, Dude, Dolly, Lena and Ace) and every dog I've owned (Waldo, Tommy, Maid and Babe).

Most horses get sold before they become too old to survive the winters, but we have to watch nearly all of our dogs die.

### A tough job

The drive to the sales ring with an old horse is a tough drive. We unload them, say goodbye, and know that the stranger who buys them will be bidding on a per-pound basis. But the only other option is to let them grow decrepit and watch them become more and more prone to sickness, predators and the starvation that can result when they no longer can chew or digest their food.

We once had a Welsh/Quarter Horse pony named Adam Pete who taught my brother, sister and I how to ride. We never sold Adam. He stayed around the ranch until he was 26 — pretty old for a horse. By that last winter, his teeth had gotten bad and he began losing a lot of weight. We began to grain him, but knew he wouldn't see another spring.

One day, I led Adam out behind the hills and put him out of his misery. I was 16 years old and it was the hardest, most responsible thing I had done as a young man.

### Babe, the cow dog

Adam's ordeal was painful, but dogs are even harder to deal with. It had been a tough year for Babe, our borderline border collie. The vet said she had diabetes. She was getting terribly thin and she had become totally blind this winter after a bout with a skunk.

She was running into fences and getting lost for days at a time. Her condition was getting worse with each passing day. I finally did the most responsible and humane thing possible. It certainly wasn't an easy thing to do, but oftentimes, the right choice is the hardest choice.

I buried her on a green hillside overlooking a small pond and I thanked her for the companionship she'd provided. I hope she understood why I did what I did.

# The rancher's disaster
## Before the flood, there were the blizzards

Blowing snow had just caused me to miss my third turn of the evening. It was Friday night, April 4, and I was trying to get back to the ranch after speaking at a co-op grain elevator banquet in Maddock, N.D.

Even though calving season was just beginning in earnest, I had agreed to speak at the banquet because of my motto, "never turn down a job." I'd told a few stories, did a few Will Rogers-style rope tricks and relayed a little rural optimism and Cowboy Logic-like motivation. But, out on the road, following the banquet, I was trying hard to just motivate my pickup home and optimistically keep it between the ditches.

The weather forecasters were exactly right — for a change. They had told us a severe blizzard was coming into the area, carrying with it a lot of snow, wind and cold. It began as freezing rain and a ferocious wind. I wasn't far from Maddock when I was forced to lock in the four-wheel drive just to stay on the slick pavement.

I had to get back home. There was a lot at stake. The cows were out in a 120-acre spring calving pasture and Friday was the fourth official day of calving. In fact, 11 newborn calves had arrived that very day before I even left for the banquet.

There was good cover in the pasture, though. I figured the sandhills and poplar trees would protect the cattle until the squall passed. Besides, I didn't have many other options. There were no large, luxurious calving barns to house all the cows on the Taylor Ranch. I couldn't afford them, and I didn't need them to house calves that were born so late in the spring. Or so I thought.

As I turned the last snowy corner home, I swung into the pasture to check a calf that was born just before I'd left earlier in the evening. His mother had him about a half-mile from the rest of the herd in a small thicket of trees. They were wet and surrounded by snow but seemed relatively comfortable, holed up out of the wind.

There wasn't much more I could do. The main herd of cows had plenty of feed and bedding. All I could do was grab a few hours of sleep and check them with the horse in the morning.

### Bad day dawning

I awoke to a full-fledged North Dakota blizzard. Uncharacteristic, but not unheard of, for April. The winds were gusting at 60 miles per hour, and the windchill was sinking to 30 below zero. Snow was falling by inches and feet.

It's not the kind of weather a cattle rancher likes to wake up to when he's calving out cows. I had a bad feeling about what I was going to find out

255

in the cow herd. I saddled my most ambitious horse, dallied my rope to the '69 Chevy car hood that served as a calf sled and began busting through the half-mile of snow drifts out to the cows.

One dead. Three dying. Another new one poking his front feet out from under a cow's tail. Calving in a blizzard forces one to prioritize. Like battlefield hospital triage. Who can be saved? Who's too far gone. Who can wait?

I could hog tie and haul two calves on the car hood with the aid of a few rubber tarp straps. The hood slid nicely on top of the deepening snowdrifts, and, if I was lucky, I could get the corresponding cows to follow behind and fulfill their duties of motherhood in the barn.

## Life and death

I knew I could save the calves if I could just get them to our old barn. I had a "calf warmer," a homemade plywood box with an electric heater and a heat lamp, inside the barn. The box could warm the calves to 70 degrees and dry them off in as little as an hour.

The drifts were getting deeper by the minute. The trail broke by the horse practically filled in right behind us. I was riding out every hour or two to check cows and drag in calves.

I discovered one cow out in the herd whose water bag was out — she was about to give birth. I tried to chase her into the barn to no avail. Try as I might, I could not force her to go through the same drifts the horse had just gone through. Going to the barn meant traveling into the wind, and she wouldn't subject herself to the hard, pelting snow crystals that the horse and I already had faced a dozen times that day.

Fine, then, I told the cow. I'll just come out in an hour and drag your calf to the barn after you've had it. An hour proved to be too long. By the time I got back, the calf had been born from his mothers 101 degree womb and now lay in the subzero windchill, already froze down to the ground.

## Too late

The cow hadn't even gotten up to lick him off. But he was still breathing. I poked a finger in his eye. He blinked. To capitalize on the slim chance that he might live, I put him on the sled and drug him toward the house instead of the barn.

I got the sled within 200 feet of the house and came to a fence. I decided to get off and carry him the rest of the way on foot. It was a harder task than I had thought. The snow was hip-deep, and my hips are 4 feet from the ground. The 95-pound calf on my shoulder didn't make the walk any easier.

But I made it. Out of breath and out of patience, I barged through the door and dropped the calf in the bathtub. Collapsing at the edge of the tub, I began running warm water on the comatose newborn.

Nothing. No reaction. He'd quit breathing. But his heart still was beating. Without any inhibition, I tried to resuscitate him by putting my mouth to his slimy nose and breathing into his nostrils. It was too late. He was gone.

Like any caregiver, I blamed myself for the death. I should have gone out sooner. I shouldn't have ever left that cow. I could have done this, I should have done that....

By Monday night, the blizzard began to subside after dropping 17 inches of snow and creating snow drifts as high as 10 feet. It took three days and nine of my calves. But my losses were small compared to many in the cattle business in the Northern Plains.

A weekend that had started with this rancher/writer spinning rope and speaking to a banquet of farmers and ranchers about perseverance and ambition ended as an exercise in those very ideals for thousands of stockmen across the state. But, like the bumper sticker I saw at a stock show says, "...and to protect and care for all His creations, God made ranchers."

*Author's note: The harsh winter of 1997 with its many blizzards claimed the lives of 123,000 cattle in North Dakota, an estimated loss of $59 million. In South Dakota, an estimated 250,000 cattle perished.*

# Time to reflect
## If you're not buckling up, start

It began as a pretty average day. I had to be in Carrington, N.D., for a meeting, so I jumped in Ol' Brownie, the wonder Chrysler, and headed southeast.

By 9:45 a.m., I was driving south on Highway 3 just enjoying the morning and the freedom of the road. In a fraction of a minute, the enjoyment ended.

A pickup driving west on a gravel road failed to see me going south on the highway. All of a sudden, there was a pickup in front of me and my car hit it at highway speed.

There wasn't much time to react. My only memory is of breaking glass, crunching metal and the swirl of grass, sky and asphalt as Ol' Brownie pushed the pickup, went end over end, then rolled and landed on its roof in the ditch.

I couldn't hang on to anything. But my seat belt hung on to me. I remember the tightness of the shoulder harness and the eerie comfort it brought to an uncomfortable situation.

When the car quit rolling, I hung there upside down, held by the seat belt that had, without a doubt, saved my life.

I reached down, but it was really up, and unbuckled the belt. I dropped on my head and crawled out the broken driver's side window.

On shaky legs, I walked to the pickup that was still on the highway. A little boy and his father sat tight against the passenger door.

A conscious 6-year-old boy in little green coveralls looked back at me. He had a big cut, really a hole, on the side of his jaw. It was bleeding badly. His father sat next to him, slumped and motionless. Cuts and bruises from the impact covered his face. I didn't know if he was even alive.

I hobbled back to my car, crawled in and retrieved my cellular phone. Standing in the middle of the highway and holding it above my head to get a signal, I called 911. Amazingly, the phone worked and the signal held. Ambulances were on their way.

The little boy pulled himself out of the pickup while I was calling 911. He came over to me. We sat in the ditch together and I got some Kleenex from the car to try and stop the bleeding.

It began to hit me then that I should've been dead. The only thing that kept me alive was a seat belt and, I think, a guardian angel who wanted me to stick around for awhile.

People began to show up, but there wasn't a lot we could do until the paramedics got there. Eventually, we all got a ride to the hospital in Rugby, N.D.

I was checked over and released with some scrapes and a banged up knee. Last reports I had were that the little boy was doing okay, but that the father was still dealing with some pretty major injuries. I haven't quit thinking about them since that morning, and if the readers of this column could send some good thoughts and prayers their way, I'd appreciate it.

And, if you're driving anywhere, please fasten your seat belt.

*Author's note: I'm glad to report that the father and son in this story are doing relatively well. The boy is fully recovered from his injuries. The father, remarkably, lived through a very rough time in the intensive care unit, and, although, he is paralyzed and in a wheel chair, he is able to use his arms somewhat. Most importantly, he has the kind of perseverance and positive attitude that North Dakota farmers are famous for.*

# Dogged determination
## Setting the challenge for 1998

The past year was a tough one for the dog herd at the Taylor Ranch. Both of my old dogs, a blind, diabetic border collie and an English setter struck with mammary cancer, had to be put down.

But we're not dogless yet. Last summer, we brought a new border collie pup into the herd. He's supposed to be a purebred short-haired border collie, but my neighbors are all certain that it's a beagle/collie composite crossbred. That's just fine with me; he should be able to both herd cows and hunt rabbits.

We call him Smokey, the cowdog, and although he's just a pup, I've already taught him the two most important skills a cowdog can have — how to jump in the pickup and ride in the tractor cab. A good cowdog not only has to herd cattle, he also has to keep the ranch boss company. In the spring, I'll work on getting him to ride with me behind the saddle.

He's just a little guy, but Smokey has a neck on him as strong as a Rottweiler. I know, because he's been exercising it by dragging everything he can into the front yard. He used the stair step conditioning method to build up his neck muscles — starting out with plastic jugs but quickly working up to hefty chunks of frozen manure and tyrannosaurus-size cow bones. Next week, I expect he'll be able to drag a couple of small haying implements up to the step.

The only thing my new cowdog hasn't quite mastered is how to chase cows in the right direction. He's real good at those random chases, but it's still a struggle for him to move cattle in a predetermined direction.

As for the cows, some of them still think that they're the chaser and not the chasee. This is when brave Smokey hides under the tractor, and his nervous master starts riding the clutch to make sure he doesn't hide right under the back tires.

## A dog-driven mission

Don't get me wrong, Smokey may well be the smartest dog south of Towner, N.D., but he's still a pup so it's hard to tell.

He does have a lot of those good qualities that are inherent to the canine species.

Like most border collies, he's always smiling. I like to be around people, and dogs, who appear to be in a good mood. Smokey's always pretty happy.

He's ambitious and eager to please. He's as loyal as a day is long. And he really likes me — that's always a plus. When he's riding in the tractor cab with me, he gives me that look that says, "Hey boss, you're the best person in the whole world." It's a real boost on mornings when I don't quite feel that way.

So, in this world of "mission statements" and in this season of New Year's resolutions, I've come up with one to take me into 1998 — to be the kind of person my dog thinks I am.

# Free advice
## Take your pick of opinions

Sometimes it's hard to know just what to do in this business of feeding the world. When I'm at a loss and needing a little guidance, I try to get out and seek some advice.

259

Last November, I was a bit confused about the cattle market, so I headed true north for some straight information on the future of ranching. After several hours on the road, me and a few of my cattlemen cronies found ourselves at the Canadian Western Agribition in Regina, Sask.

My buddies were intent on looking at cattle, but I somehow talked them into going to a quaint little beer joint called "the swamp." Right there in the cattle barns, the Swamp would be a prime spot to find some words of wisdom.

It was early in the evening, but there was already a lot of wisdom flowing in the Swamp.

One Alberta cattle feeder that I ran into pulled me aside to give me some tips on the stock (cattle) market. He told me that stock cows were way underpriced. For our current point in the cattle cycle, they were a real bargain. "Buy all you can," he said.

It was good advice, but I was already a half step ahead of him. I'd already bred more heifers and culled fewer cows in my herd. I appreciated his optimism, though. By the time we left, I was feeling pretty positive about my future in the cattle business.

We did finally leave, and went looking for some more fresh advice. Me and the boys decided to expand our horizons. We migrated to one of Regina's trendy downtown bars where cowboys stick out like a Charolais bull in a registered Angus cowherd.

We did our best to blend in — we even got out on the dance floor and exhibited rhythm as smooth as a two-cylinder John Deere with a bad spark plug. We'd forgot all about our quest for philosophical fodder on the future of the cattle business. But even though we weren't looking for any advice, we did get some.

One of my traveling partners ran into a gal who didn't quite agree with the fella at the Swamp who'd advised us to buy all the cows we could. She was a not-so-polite vegetarian nature lover and she didn't think much of cattle ranching or commercial agriculture in general.

"Why don't you guys just hang up your hats and do something else for a living," she advised. She flushed our plans for ranch expansion right down the drain.

My level-headed friend began to think about his choice of careers and he asked her just how she planned to eat without any farmers or ranchers in the world. She said, quite matter of fact, "We'll just grow our own gardens."

My friend didn't push the issue. We just went back to the ranch and I suppose she went back to her bountiful Saskatchewan winter garden. However, we couldn't help but think that a little famine would do a lot of good for at least a few people in our ungrateful world.

# I'm crazy, too
## Moving quickly and imperfectly seizing opportunities

I've been doing some pretty dangerous things this week. No, I wasn't flirting with a PTO shaft, breaking a rank colt, or pulling a tractor with a frayed nylon rope and chain.

I was exposing myself to new ideas.

Now the danger really isn't in the ideas, it's in implementing the ideas and then taking the subsequent verbal beating at the local pub or coffee shop for daring to do something different.

My idea quest began on Monday with the Tom Peters seminar in Bismarck, N.D., about "embracing the challenge of change." Then, to embrace a little challenge and change, I went to Aberdeen, S.D., to help with a Northern Plains Premium Beef meeting.

Finally, the next morning, I stopped at a grazing tour in central North Dakota to get some new ideas on managing grass. The design of the rotational grazing systems reminded me of Tom Peter's book, "The Circle of Innovation."

### Take your beating

Unfortunately, I made one more stop before I headed home. While gassing up the Buick at a local filling station, I ran into my old acquaintance, Dire N. Pessimistic (the "n" stands for negative).

"Hey Dire, how's the world treatin' ya today?" I asked. He grumbled something about the world going to pot.

Dire caught me smiling, and asked me where I'd been and what I possibly could have to smile about. First, I told him about the Tom Peters seminar.

"What a waste of time! You wouldn't catch me at no seminar with some smartypants guru flapping his gums about innovation and success and all that other baloney," Dire said.

"I bet I wouldn't," I said. At times like these, an invisible thought bubble begins to float just above my cowboy hat. The bubbles usually contain quotes and thoughts in mental parentheses. Like (Winston Churchill: The most important thing about education is appetite. RT: Hmmm, I can see Dire's appetite is a little lacking).

Just to get Dire's reaction, I told him a little about Northern Plains Premium Beef and the meeting I'd attended. I tried to express my excitement for a cooperative that finally would give me direct access to customers and the high-value, niche marketplace. I told him the business plan looked really profitable and I told him about all the good people who had designed the plan and spent countless hours reworking and refining the idea.

After about 10 seconds of fleeting thought, Dire simply concluded, "That'll never work. The big meat companies will crush it."

"Whatever you say, Dire. I can see you've really studied it," I said, too tired to argue. Thought cloud (Tom Peters: We're going from a world where the big eat the small to one where the fast eat the slow. RT: I'd much rather stake my future on a fast-moving niche-focused cooperative than ride along with the super-slow commodity system's mega corporations, hoping that things will get better if I only stand back and do nothing).

"I know I ain't going to buy any shares," Dire continued. "That's too bad," I returned, "but I think you're missing the boat." Thought cloud (Kevin Kelly: Wealth is not gained by perfecting the known, but by imperfectly seizing the unknown. RT: Go ahead and try and produce your way out of this sorry cattle situation, I'm going to go with some unknown innovation and marketing).

I didn't even bother telling Dire about the grazing tour and the rotational grazing systems. I already knew what he'd probably say, "Building all that fence and moving those cows around is plumb crazy!" Thought cloud (Hajime Mitari, Canon: We are crazy...we should do something when people say it is crazy. If people say something is 'good,' it means someone else is already doing it. RT: I'm crazy, too).


# Reunion time
## Ten year reunion a good time to take stock of your contributions

The Fourth of July is the big day of the year for Towner. It means going to the rodeo, heading in to the street dance, taking a bath and changing your long johns for the year ahead.

It's also reunion time for us graduates of Towner High School. By using some of the math skills I picked up at THS, I quickly realized that 1998 meant 10 years had lapsed since graduation.

A letter in the mail confirmed my calculations. It invited all 19 graduates of the class of 1988 to Towner's not-so-exclusive country club for a little reminiscing.

### Unprepared

This reunion kind of caught me off guard. Ten whole years had passed and I didn't have a whole lot to show for it. No wife. No kids. No divorces. No child support.

I hadn't even made my first million. I'd probably circulated and traded at least a million dollars in this money-in/money-out business we call cattle ranching, but that's not quite like having it in an account earning interest.

I thought about doing what most people do at reunions — lying — to make up for my shortfalls in life. I toyed with the idea of renting a wife for the event, but someone told me that might be considered prostitution, so I scrapped that plan.

I checked my 3-year-old nephew's schedule to see if he'd like to come along and pretend to be my son, but his calendar already was booked.

And, try as I might, I could not locate a million dollars to dangle out of my wallet for the day's reunion. So I jumped in the car and went as I was.

### Contributing citizens

We didn't get all 19 to show up, but the turnout was pretty decent.

We'd done a lot of things since we'd voted on our corny class motto, "We have no path to follow, but behind us we will leave a trail." I'm not sure if we were quite that trail blazing and pioneer like, but we were doing everything from teaching school to working for Bill Gates. Some were busy raising kids, some of us were busy raising cattle and crops.

I realized my own contributions to society at the bar uptown after our reunion activities. I was sitting there visiting with some friends and drinking a Coke when one of the town's most inebriated came stumbling over to annoy us.

He looked at me kind of cross-eyed and asked me who I was. I told him my name and he said, "Yoooou know (hiccup), yurrrrr one kid that Iiiii never (gurgle) figgggerrrrred would turn out (slurp) to beeeee worth a damn!" (belch)

And the way he said it kind of led me to believe that he figured he was right and that I hadn't turned out to be worth a damn.

So, I looked at him, and then kind of inspected myself, sitting there kind of clean cut, drinking a Coke and contemplating going home so I could get up the next day to work a couple of extra jobs to help support my global food production habit. The self-inspection was a good way to cap my 10 year reunion experience.

"Yup, buddy," I said, before walking away, "you sure know how to call 'em."

# The big picture
## The view of things from several miles up

It's tough to put things in focus when you're too close to your subject matter. Like my aging friends with failing eyesight, you sometimes need to hold the newspaper out at arm's length to read the words.

I actually can read a newspaper without doing the arm stretch, but it is tough to "read" the ranch when I'm hunkered down and working right on location. It's easy to get caught up in the little things that rule our lives and lose sight of the big panoramic picture.

As they say, it's like "not seeing the forest for the trees."

Last week, I had the chance to get out of the trees and see the forest.

## Identifiable dots

I was on my way home from a banquet speaking job in Alberta and flying from Minneapolis to Minot, N.D. Actually, the plane was doing the flying, I was doing the riding.

Looking at a map, it's hard to figure out why someone going from Edmonton, Alberta, to Minot, N.D., would be in Minneapolis, but if you live in North Dakota and fly Northwest, you soon realize that you couldn't go to hell without going through Minneapolis first.

It was a beautiful, clear day of flying. The pilot actually could see the Minot airport from 100 miles out. It was a good day for a rancher to peer out the window and look for landmarks from a few miles up.

## Real assets

I was amazed to actually recognize and see our place, but I was more struck by what I didn't see through the window of that jet plane.

I didn't see the buildings, cattle, tractors or the junk pile on the east side of the hill. I didn't see the corral in need of repair, the barn that needed painting or the bull that should have been culled.

You couldn't tell that one farm or ranch might have had a neater yard, a nicer house or a newer tractor. You couldn't see who was out feeding cows and who was sleeping in.

What I did see was the things that truly matter in the business of agriculture. I saw the land and the water. I saw land that was healthy enough to be quite diverse. Hills, trees, brush and the different plants that thrive best under grazing and haying — a true polyculture. I saw a healthy water table, evident in the full, stable levels of the lakes and sloughs around the ranch.

It was a pretty new perspective for a fella who spends most of his time "sweating the small stuff."

We're by no means a big operation, but I could look down from the sky and say to my seat mates, "You see those hills and that lake and that strip of hay meadow, that's my family's place." There are a lot of millionaires who couldn't spot their 10,000-square-foot mansion or their 40-foot yacht from that elevation.

I landed in Minot convinced that healthy land and good water may be the best assets a human could hold. And, although my bank account wouldn't show it, this rancher felt truly wealthy for once.